Ring-tailed cat   *Mallette Dean*

SIERRA NORTH

100 BACK-COUNTRY TRIPS

Thomas Winnett, Jason Winnett, Lyn Haber, and Kathy Morey

WILDERNESS PRESS

BERKELEY

FIRST EDITION May 1967
Second printing July 1967
Third printing July 1969
SECOND EDITION May 1971
Second printing April 1972
Third printing September 1974
THIRD EDITION January 1976
Second printing February 1978
FOURTH EDITION May 1982
Second printing July 1983

FIFTH EDITION June 1985
Revised second printing May 1987
Third printing November 1988
SIXTH EDITION May 1991
Second printing September 1992
Third printing September 1994
SEVENTH EDITION May 1997
Second printing August 1999

Photos by the authors except as noted
Drawings by Lucille Winnett
Design by Thomas Winnett and Kathy Morey
Cover design by Larry B. Van Dyke

Library of Congress card number 97-18964
ISBN 0-89997-212-8
Manufactured in the United States of America

Published by   **Wilderness Press**
1200 5th Street, Berkeley, CA 94710
(800) 443-7227; FAX (510) 558-1696
mail@wildernesspress.com
www.wildernesspress.com

Contact us for a free catalog

Front cover photo: **Banner Peak and Mt. Ritter from Island Pass,**
Ansel Adams Wilderness —© 1997 Larry Ulrich
Back cover photos: **Peak above Foerster Lake** *(top)*, **Rainbow Falls** *(below)*
—© 1997 Thomas Winnett

 Printed on recycled paper, 20% post-consumer waste

Library of Congress Cataloging-in-Publication Data

Sierra North : 100 back-country trips in the High Sierra / Thomas
    Winnett . . . [et al.]. -- 7th ed.
        p. cm.
    Includes bibliographical references (p.) and index.
    ISBN 0-89997-212-8
    1. Hiking--Sierra Nevada (Calif. and Nev.)--Guidebooks.
    2. Backpacking--Sierra Nevada (Calif. and Nev.)--Guidebooks.
    3. Sierra Nevada (Calif. and Nev.)--Guidebooks. I. Winnett,
    Thomas.
    GV199.42.S55S54 1997
    917.94'404929--dc21   97-18964
                                                        CIP

Read This

Hiking in the backcountry entails unavoidable risk that every hiker assumes and must be aware of and respect. The fact that a trail is described in this book is not a representation that it will be safe for you. Trails vary greatly in difficulty and in the degree of conditioning and agility one needs to enjoy them safely. On some hikes routes may have changed or conditions may have deteriorated since the descriptions were written. Also, trail conditions can change even from day to day, owing to weather and other factors. A trail that is safe on a dry day or for a highly conditioned, agile, properly equipped hiker may be completely unsafe for someone else or unsafe under adverse weather conditions.

You can minimize your risks on the trail by being knowledgeable, prepared, and alert. There is not space in this book for a general treatise on safety in the mountains, but there are a number of good books and public courses on the subject, and you should take advantage of them to increase your knowledge. Just as important, you should always be aware of your own limitations and of conditions existing when and where you are hiking. If conditions are dangerous, or if you are not prepared to deal with them safely, choose a different hike! It's better to have wasted a drive than to be the subject of a mountain rescue.

These warnings are not intended to scare you off the trails. Millions of people have safe and enjoyable hikes every year. However, one element of the beauty, freedom, and excitement of the wilderness is the presence of risks that do not confront us at home. When you hike you assume those risks. They can be met safely, but only if you exercise your own independent judgment and common sense.

Contents

Introduction

This book's purpose

The Sierra Nevada is the longest and most extensively trailed mountain range in the United States. With its complex valley-ridge makeup, its lofty eastern escarpment, and its mild weather, it is a backpacker's paradise unequaled in intrinsic beauty and scenic grandeur. Much of the finest scenery and best fishing lie in the backcountry, accessible only by trail. There has been, therefore, a growing trend toward wilderness trips, and with the trend has come a demand for reliable backcountry trip suggestions. This book is a selective effort to meet that demand.

Galen Clark, Yosemite's beloved "Old Man of the Valley," was once asked how he "got about" the park. Clark scratched his beard, and then replied, "Slowly!" And that is the philosophy the authors have adopted in this book. Hiking descriptions, with the exception of a few "Moderate" ratings and an occasional "Strenuous" trip, are based on a leisurely pace, in order that hikers can absorb more of the sights, smells and "feel" of the country they have come to see. Pace may not be everything, but Old Man Clark lived to a ripe old age of 96 and it behooves us to follow in his footsteps.

This book's terms

Sierra North encompasses the region from the volcanic battlements of Carson Pass to the aspen-lined banks of Mono Creek, where the companion volume, *Sierra South*, takes over. The individual trips were selected on the basis of (1) scenic attraction, (2) wilderness character (remoteness, primitive condition) and (3) recreational potential (fishing, swimming, etc.) After walking the trip, the author decided how long it should take if done at a leisurely pace, how long at a moderate pace, and how long at a strenuous pace. In deciding, he or she considered not only distance but also elevation change, heat

1

exposure, terrain, availability of water, appropriate campsites and finally, his or her subjective feeling about the trip. For each trip, then, we suggest how many days you should take to do it at the pace (*Leisurely, Moderate* or *Strenuous*) you prefer. Some trips simply don't lend themselves to a leisurely pace, maybe not even a moderate pace. Such trips have a blank in the number-of-days spot for the corresponding pace at the beginning of the trip. Some trips are never strenuous unless you do the whole thing in one day; they are labeled "Day" after "Strenuous."

The last decision about pace was the decision of which pace to use in describing the trip, day by day. Since this book is written for the average backpacker, we chose to describe most trips on either a leisurely or a moderate basis, depending on where the best overnight camping places were along the route.

Subjective considerations also carry over to the evaluation of campsites. Campsites are labeled *poor, fair, good* or *excellent*. The criteria for assigning these labels were amount of use, immediate surroundings, general scenery, presence of vandalization, availability of water, kind of ground cover, and recreational potential—angling, side trips, swimming, etc.

Angling, for many, is a prime consideration when planning a trip. The recommendations in this book are based on (1) on-site samplings and feeding evaluations, (2) word of mouth, (3) *Sierra Trout*, by Dean Cutter, (4) literature of the California Department of Fish and Game, and (5) interviews with commercial packers. When a conflict arose between paper research and trail sampling, the later was given precedence. Like the campsites, fishing was labeled *poor, fair, good* or *excellent*. It should be noted that these labels refer only to the size, quantity, and general catchability of the fish, not the fishes' inclination to take the hook at any moment. Experienced anglers know that the size of their catch relates not only to quantity, type and general size of the fishery, which are given, but also to water temperature, feed, angling skill, and that indefinable something known as "fisherman's luck." Generally speaking, the old "early and late" adage holds: fishing is better early and late in the day, and early and late in the season.

Deciding when in the year is the best time for a particular trip is a difficult task because of yearly variations. Low early-season temperatures and mountain shadows often keep some of the higher passes closed until well into August. Early snows have been known to whiten alpine country in late July and August. Some of the trips described here are low-country ones, offered specifically for the itchy hiker who, stiff from a winter's inactivity, is searching for a "warm-up" excursion. These trips are labeled *early season*, a period that extends roughly from late May to early July. *Mid season* is here considered to be from early July to the end of August, and *late season* from then to early October.

Stream crossings vary greatly depending on snow-melt conditions. Often, the same small creek you saw in September will be a raging torrent the next June. We have indicated the problems of fording some creeks as "wet in early season," meaning that in times of high water you will probably have to wade, perhaps in water over your waist, but that the crossing is fairly easy and not dangerous. If a ford is described as "difficult in early season" fording that creek may be difficult because it is hard to walk through deep or fast water, and getting caught in the current would be dangerous. Whether you attempt such a crossing depends on the presence or absence of logs or other bridges and of downstream rapids, your ability and equipment, and your judgment.

Most of the trails described here are well maintained (the exceptions are noted), and are properly signed. If the trail becomes indistinct, look for *blazes* (peeled bark at eye level on trees) or *ducks* (two or more rocks piled one atop the other). Two other significant trail conditions have also been described in the text: (1) degree of openness (type and degree of forest cover, if any, or else "meadow," "brush" or whatever); and (2) underfooting (talus, scree, pumice, sand, "duff"—deep humus ground cover of rotting vegetation—or other material).

Three other terms used in the descriptive text warrant definition. *Packer campsite* is used to indicate a semipermanent camp (usually constructed by packers for the "comfort of their clients") characterized by a nailed-plank table and/or a large, stand-up rock fireplace. *Improved campsite* is a U.S. Forest Service designation for a place where a simple toilet has been installed. A *use trail* is an unmaintained, unofficial trail that is more or less easy to follow because it is well worn by use.

The text contains occasional references to points, peaks and other landmarks. These places will be found on the appropriate topographic maps cited at the beginning of the trip. ("Point 9426" in the text would refer to a point designated simply "9426" on the map itself.)

In recent years the Forest Service and the Park Service have had a policy of letting fires in the backcountry burn so long as they were not a threat to people or structures. One result has been some pretty poor looking scenery on some trips in this book. However, most of the fire-damaged areas have begun to recover soon enough that the authors have chosen not to delete the affected trips from the book.

The Care and Enjoyment of the Mountains

Be a good guest. The Sierra is home—their only home—to a spectacular array of plants and animals. We humans are merely guests—uninvited ones at that. Be a careful, considerate guest in this grandest of Nature's homes.

The mountains are in danger, particularly the High Sierra, because about a million people camp in the Sierra wilderness each year. The vast majority of us care about the wilderness and try to protect it, but it is still threatened with destruction.

Litter isn't the only issue. Increasingly, wilderness campsites, even when free of litter, have that "beat out" look of over-crowded roadside campgrounds. Fragile sod is being ground down under the pressure of too many feet. Lovely trees and snags are being stripped, scarred, and removed altogether for firewood. Dust, charcoal, blackened stones and dirty fireplaces are accumulating. These conditions are spreading rapidly, and in a few years *every* High Sierra lakeshore and streamside may be severely damaged.

The national park service and the forest service are faced with the necessity for reservation systems, designated campsites, restrictions on fire building, increased ranger patrols, quotas, and even a fee for wilderness permits. Not only the terrain but the wilderness experience is being eroded. Soon conditions may be little different from those we wanted to leave behind at the roadend.

The solution depends on each of us. We can minimize our impact. It's a fine art that develops as we deepen our relationship with the wilderness. The saying, "Take only memories (or photos), leave only footprints," sums up the minimum-impact attitude. To leave no trace of one's passing is a skill that Native Americans practiced and that we can learn through conscious intent and experience.

Learn to go light. This is largely a matter of acquiring wilderness skills, of learning to be at home in the wilderness rather than in an elaborate camp. The "free spirits" of the mountains are those experts

4

who appear to go anywhere under any conditions with neither encumbrances nor effort but always with complete enjoyment. John Muir, traveling along the crest of the Sierra in the 1870s with little more that his overcoat and his pockets full of biscuits, was the archetype.

Modern lightweight equipment and food are a convenience and a joy. The ever-practical Muir would have taken them had they been available in his day. But a lot of the stuff that goes into the mountains is burdensome, harmful to the wilderness, or just plain annoying to other people seeking peace and solitude. Anything that is obtrusive or that can be used to modify the terrain should be left at the roadend: gas lanterns, radios, saws, hatchets, firearms (except in the hunting season), gigantic tents, etc.

Carry *all* your trash out. You packed that foil and those cans and bags in when full; you can pack them out empty. Never litter or bury your trash.

Sanitation. Eliminate feces at least 100 feet from lakes, streams, trails, and campsites. Bury feces at least 6 inches deep wherever possible. Intestinal pathogens can survive for years in feces when they're buried, but burial reduces the chances that critters will come in contact with them and carry pathogens into the water. Your object is to keep them from getting into the water, where they could infect others. Where burial is not possible due to lack of enough soil or gravel, as at some places above timberline, leave feces where they will receive maximum exposure to heat, sunlight, etc., to hasten the destruction of pathogens. Help reduce the waste problem in the backcountry by packing out your used toilet paper, facial tissues, tampons, sanitary napkins, diapers, etc. Even if buried, these items may last long enough that they can be unearthed by animals or runoff and be washed into the water. It's easy to carry them out in a heavy-duty, self-sealing plastic bag.

Protect the water from soap and other pollution. In many areas the water is unsafe to drink, even apart from the *Giardia* it may contain.

Pick "hard" campsites, sandy places that can stand the use. Camp at least 100 feet from any stream, lake, or pond. The fragile sod of meadows, lakeshores and streamsides is rapidly disappearing from the High Sierra. It simply cannot take the wear and tear of campers. Its development depends on very special conditions. Once destroyed, it does not ordinarily re-form. Camp at least 100 feet from water unless that's absolutely impossible; in no case camp closer that 25 feet. Don't make campsite "improvements" like rock walls, bough beds, new firerings and tent ditches.

Spare the trees. Throughout popular places in the Sierra, thoughtless campers are burning up wood faster that it is being produced. Wood is a precious resource; use it sparingly or, better still, not at all.

Trees, both live and dead, are not only part of the scenery but are also food and shelter to many creatures, and when they fall, they return essential nutrients to the soil. Standing trees, live or dead, should never be cut or broken. The exquisite, golden trunks left standing after lightning strikes should be left completely alone. Sadly, in some popular areas they have already been destroyed for firewood, and you would never know they had been there.

Use a modern, lightweight backpacking stove. It frees you of campfire chores. With a stove, you won't have to waste time gathering wood, wondering why your fire won't get going, and finally dousing the coals till they're dead out. Food spilled on the coals while cooking over a campfire is a fragrant invitation to bears. Using a stove means your eyes won't be so blinded by campfire flames that you can't enjoy the stars. And your and your gear won't stink from campfire smoke. You greatly increase your choices of campsites with a stove, because you won't be limited to sites with wood. A stove works just fine in the rain—no more problems with wet wood.

At the same time, the use of stoves leaves precious downed wood to replenish fragile soils, to shelter small animals, and to provide that essential stick for bearbagging as well as that fine log to sit on for stargazing or to lean against for a worthwhile afternoon of critter-watching.

Always use a stove when you are above 10,000 feet or in a place where wood is scarce. If you use a stove that requires fuel cartridges, be sure to pack out all the cartridges you bring in.

Or don't cook at all. If you don't want to use a stove, let your next choice be to take food that doesn't need cooking. What a great way to reduce camp chores and weight in your pack!

If you must have a campfire, try to camp in established, regularly used campsites where a single, small, substantial fireplace can serve each group of campers for both cooking and warming. If kept scrupulously clean it should last for many years. Unfortunately, fireplaces (and campsites) tend to become increasingly dirty and to multiply. There are now a hundred times as many fireplaces as are needed in the High Sierra. The countless dirty fireplaces should be eradicated. It is a noble service to use and clean up established campsites where they are present and legal, and to restore them to nature where illegal.

Elsewhere build a small fireplace, if one is legal. A fireplace 6 inches wide internally is enough for 1–2 people to cook on. Please eradicate your fireplace and restore your campsite to a natural condition before you leave. This is facilitated if you build with restoration in mind: two to four medium-sized rocks along the sides of a shallow trench in a sandy place. When the camp is broken the rocks are returned to their places. Never build a fire against a boulder; it disfigures the boulder and thus the scenery with ugly black scars.

Extinguish fires half an hour before you leave by adding water and stirring the ashes until the entire bed of coals and the ground beneath it are thoroughly saturated and cold. It is the only way to be sure that a fire and the organic matter in the soil beneath it are dead out. Do not add dirt, as this fills in the fireplace and will lead to its becoming needlessly enlarged.

Never leave fires unattended, even for a second. Many disastrous forest fires have begun from unattended campfires and campfires that weren't adequately put out. Fire is part of the natural course of events, but only when it's caused by Nature.

Respect the wildlife. Avoid trampling on nests, burrows, or other homes of animals. Observe all fishing limits. If you come across an animal, just quietly observe it. Above all, don't go near any nesting animals or their young.

Safety and Well Being

Hiking in the high country is far safer than driving to the mountains, and a few precautions can shield you from most of the discomforts and dangers that could threaten you.

Health Hazards

1. Altitude sickness. If you normally live at sea level and come to the Sierra to hike, it may take your body several days to acclimate. Starved of your accustomed oxygen, for a few days you may experience shortness of breath even with minimal activity, severe headaches, or nausea. The best solution is to spend time at altitude before you begin your hike, and to plan a very easy first day.

2. Giardia. Giardiasis is a serious gastrointestinal disease caused by a waterborne protozoan, *Giardia lamblia.* Any mammal (which includes humans) can become infected. It will then excrete live *Giardia* in its feces, from which the protozoan can get into even the most remote sources of water, such as a stream issuing from a glacier. *Giardia* can survive in snow through the winter and in cold water as a cyst resistant to the usual chemical treatments. Giardiasis can be contracted by drinking untreated water. Symptoms appear 2–3 weeks after exposure.

Since giardiasis can be very debilitating and difficult to treat, prevention is best. And prevention is easy. First, assume that all open sources of water are contaminated. Second, treat all water you take from open sources, like lakes and streams. Bringing the water to a rolling boil and keeping it there for 1–3 minutes will suffice and is easy to do when cooking. Or use filters. To be effective, the filter must be sturdy and reliable and must filter at least down to 2 microns to catch both protozoans and cysts. Before you run out to buy a filter, see *Cryptosporidium,* below.

Chemicals like the popular iodine tables are hard to use properly against *Giardia*—but better than no treatment at all. Consider chemicals a back-up system to be used only when boiling or filtering isn't possible. To kill with chemicals, first bring the water temperature to about 70° F so that the cysts will open and the protozoans will be vulnerable to the poison. Then use the chemicals as directed.

Cryptosporidium. A new pest, *Cryptosporidium,* lurks in the wings: It's several times smaller than *Giardia lamblia* and causes a similar disease. It's been found in the streams of the San Gabriel Mountains of Los Angeles, and is spreading throughout Southern California. Probably it will eventually infest Sierran waters. It's resistant to any known chemical treatment. Boiling and filtering are the only known defenses at this time (spring 1997). To be effective, the filter needs to filter at least down to 0.4 micron.

3. Hypothermia. Hypothermia refers to subnormal body temperature. More hikers die from hypothermia than from any other single cause: it represents the greatest threat to your survival in the wilderness. Caused by exposure to cold, often intensified by wet, wind, and weariness, the first symptoms of hypothermia are uncontrollable shivering and imperfect motor coordination. These are rapidly followed by loss of judgment, so that you yourself cannot make the decisions to protect your own life. To prevent hypothermia, stay warm: carry wind-and-rain-protective clothing, and put it on as soon as you feel chilly. Stay dry; carry or wear wool or a suitable synthetic (not cotton) against your skin; bring raingear even for a short hike on an apparently sunny day. If weather conditions threaten and you are inadequately prepared, flee or hunker down. Protect yourself so you remain as warm and dry as possible.

Treat shivering at once—remember, hypothermia acts quickly and destroys judgment. Get the victim out of the wind and wet, replace all wet clothes with dry ones, put him or her in a sleeping bag, and give him or her warm drinks. If the shivering is severe and accompanied by other symptoms, strip him or her and yourself (and a third party if possible), and warm him or her with your own bodies, tightly wrapped in a dry sleeping bag.

4. Lightning. Although the odds of being struck are very small, almost everyone who goes to the mountains thinks about it.

An afternoon thunderstorm may come upon you rather quickly, but not so fast that you can't get to a safer place if you are exposed. All exposed places are dangerous: a mountain peak, a mountain ridge, an open field, a boat on a lake. But so are a small cave and an overhang.

Then where should you shelter if a thunderstorm catches you? The safest place is an opening or a clump of small trees in a forest. But one is not always handy. If you are above timberline, and can get next to any pinnacle, do so, taking a position no farther from the pinnacle than its height. Lacking any pinnacles, position yourself atop a small boulder that is detached from bedrock. If caught in an open area, get to the lowest place that is not wet.

Wherever you position yourself, the best body stance is one that minimizes the area your body covers. You should drop to your knees and put your hands on your knees. This is because the more area your body covers, the more chance that ground currents will pass through it.

Most people believe that metal as such attracts lightning, but the actual danger from your packframe, tent poles, etc. is due to induced currents. We won't explain them here, but just be sure to get all your metal away from you as fast as you can.

And what if lightning strikes you anyway? There isn't much you can do except pray that someone in your party is adept at CPR—or at least adept at artificial respiration if your breathing has stopped but not your heart. It may take hours for a victim to resume breathing on his or her own. If it's your companions who are victims, attend first to those who are not moving. Those who are rolling around and moaning are at least breathing. Finally, a victim who lives should be evacuated to a hospital, because other problems often develop in lightning victims.

Wildlife Hazards

1. Rattlesnakes. They occur at lower elevations (they are rarely seen above 7000 feet) in a range of habitats, but most commonly near riverbeds and streams. Their bite is rarely fatal to an adult. If you plan a trip below 6000 feet along a watercourse, you may want to carry a snakebite kit of the "Sawyer's extractor" type, which is somewhat effective if used properly within 30 minutes after the bite. Better yet, don't get bitten: watch where you place your hands and feet; listen for the rattle. If you hear a snake rattle, stand still long enough to determine where it is, then leave in the opposite direction.

2. Marmots. They live from about 6000 feet to 11,500 feet. Because they are curious and always hungry, and like to sun themselves on rocks in full view, you are likely to see them. Marmots enjoy many foods you do, including cereal and candy (especially chocolate). They may eat through a pack or tent when other entry is difficult. Marmots cannot climb trees or ropes, so you can protect your food by hanging it.

3. Mosquitoes. If you have no protection against mosquitoes, they can ruin your trip. However, protection is easy. Any insect repellent containing *N, N diethylmeta-toluamide* ("DEET") will keep them off. Don't buy one without it. Clothing is also a bar to mosquitoes—a good reason for wearing long pants and a long-sleeved shirt. If you are a favorite target for mosquitoes (they have their preferences) you might take a head net—a hat with netting suspended all around the brim and a snug neckband. Planning your trip to avoid the height of the mosquito season is also a good preventive.

4. Bears. We've devoted a separate section to bears; please see "The Bear Problem" below.

Terrain Hazards

1. Snow bridges and snow cornices. Stay off them.

2. Stream crossings. In early season, when the snow is melting, crossing a river can be the most dangerous part of a backpack trip. Later, ordinary caution will see you across safely. If a river is running high, you should cross it only if 1) the alternatives to crossing are more dangerous than crossing, 2) you have found a suitable place to ford, and 3) you use a rope.

As for #1, obviously it's better to turn back than to risk accident. As for #2, it may take considerable looking around to find a suitable place to ford. If you can find a viewpoint high above the river, you can better check out the river's width, speed and turbulence, any obstructions in it, and the nature of its bottom.

Whichever method you use to cross a stream, you should:

- If the water is at all high, wait till morning to cross, when the level will be at its daily low.
- Unfasten the hip belt of your pack, in case you have to jettison it.
- Keep your boots on. They will protect your feet from injury and give your feet more secure placement.
- Never face downstream. The water pushing against the back of your knees could cause them to buckle.
- Move one foot only when the other is firmly placed.
- Never allow your legs to cross; keep them apart.
- Use a stick as a support on the upstream side.

The Bear Problem

What bears? The bears of the Sierra are American black bears; their coats range from black to light brown. They're relatively unaggressive unless provoked, and their normal diet consists largely of plants. The suggestions in this section apply only to American black bears. These suggestions *don't* apply to dealing with the more-aggressive grizzly bear, which is extinct in California.

American black bears run and climb faster than you ever will, they are immensely stronger, and they are very intelligent. Long ago they learned to associate humans with easy sources of food. Now, keeping your food away from the local bears is a problem. Remember, though, that all they want is your *food*. They aren't interested in inedible *you*. They will try to avoid you whenever possible. So don't let the possibility of meeting a bear keep you out of the Sierra. Respect these magnificent creatures—sighting one is a rare privilege. Learn what you can do to keep yourself and your food safe. Some suggestions follow.

Bears: any time, anywhere. Bears are normally daytime creatures. But they've learned that our supplies are easier to raid when we're asleep, so they're working the night shift, too. *Bears are active at all times of day and night.* Also, it used to be that you rarely saw bears above 8,000–9,000 feet. As campers moved into the higher elevations, the bears followed. *You can't rely on altitude to help protect your food against bears.*

To avoid bears while hiking, make noise as you go. Some hikers tie cowbells or clanking hardware—pots, pans, Sierra cups—to their packs; others sing, talk or just hike noisily. American black bears are shy and will scramble off to avoid meeting you if they hear you coming.

In camp, store your food properly and always scare bears away immediately—see the suggestions under **Food storage**, below.

You **are responsible for protecting your food.** Backcountry management policies now hold campers responsible for keeping their food away from bears. *If a bear gets your food, it is* your *fault.*

The bear is just being a bear. You, however, can be fined. You're also responsible for cleaning up the mess once you're sure the bear has had its fill and won't be back for seconds. You also have an ethical responsibility for your part in the process that leads to that bear becoming a repeat-problem bear, maybe a bear that has to be killed.

Plan ahead. Think and plan to avoid problems. Avoid taking smelly foods and fragrant toiletries; they attract bears—bears have a superb sense of smell. Check the hypoallergenic section of the drugstore for fragrance-free toiletries; use baking powder or baking soda instead of toothpaste. Ask rangers where there are bear problems, and avoid those areas. Ask rangers and other backpackers what measures they take to safeguard food and chase bears away; maybe some of their ideas will work for you. Consider camping where you can use a bear box (below). If you need to counterbalance your food bags (also below), practice the skill before you need it. Cook and clean up afterward in a way that doesn't leave food residues to attract bears. Clean any food out of your gear and store it with the rest of your chow; otherwise, you could lose a pack to a bear who went for the granola bar you forgot in a side pocket. Don't take food into your tent or sleeping bag unless you want ursine company. Store your garbage just as carefully as you store your food.

Food storage. Here are some food-storage suggestions:

1. Bear-resistant food canisters are lengths of sturdy plastic pipe fitted with a bottom and a lid only a human can open. You'll see them advertised in various outdoor publications; they are also available for rental and purchase in outdoor stores. There are two sizes available; they weigh 3–5 pounds empty; the smaller size holds 3–5 days' worth of food for one person. You carry the filled canister in your pack. It's heavy, rigid, and bulky. Our experience is that it's suitable only for a short trip on a route that lacks bear boxes. Using a canister is far easier than bearbagging. In areas with severe bear problems and no bear boxes (see 3, below), like most of Yosemite National Park, canisters are considered the only way to save food from raiding bears. Canisters aren't perfect, but they work very well—so far.

2. Counterbalance bearbagging. If you don't have a bear-resistant food canister (above) and bear boxes (see 3, below) aren't available where you camp, counterbalance your food. Note that in areas with severe bear problems, like Yosemite National Park, counterbalance bearbagging is regarded as ineffective. Assuming you're traveling in an area where bears aren't yet a severe problem, counterbalance bearbagging may protect your food not only from bears but from ground squirrels, marmots, etc. It's best to get to camp early enough to get your food hung while there's light to do it by. Counterbalancing is not secure all by itself, but it slows the bear down. It gives you time to hear the bear going after your food and time to scare it away. When you get a permit, you typically get a sheet on counterbalance bear-bagging. Here's the technique as we use it; practice it at home before you go:

- Find a tree with a live, down-sloping branch that's well off the ground but that you can throw a rock over. Make sure there are no objects below the branch—like another branch—that could support a bear.
- Divide your food and anything else with an odor, like toiletries and garbage, into two bagged, approximately equal loads of not more than 8–10 lbs. each—they'll counterbalance each other. Or, if you have only one bag, counterbalance it with a rock. The bags should be heavy-duty nylon stuff sacks.
- Use enough rope to go over the branch and back to the ground. Use *strong, thin* ($\frac{1}{8}''$–$\frac{1}{4}''$) rope, like parachute cord.
- Tie a rock to the rope's end and toss it over the branch as far out as will support the weight of your food but not a bear cub.
- Tie things like pots or Sierra cups to one or both bags—things that will make a lot of noise to alert you if a raiding bear disturbs the bags.
- Tie the first sack onto the rope and hoist it up to the branch.
- Tie the second sack (or the counterbalancing rock) as high as you can on the other end of the rope. Put the excess rope in the sack, or wrap it around the counterbalancing rock, leaving a loop out for retrieval.
- With a stick, push the second sack up until the sacks are about at the same height and they balance each other. Both bags should rest far enough off the ground that you can't touch them even when you're on tiptoe—even higher if you're short.
- To retrieve your food, use a stick to push up one bag until the other descends to where you can reach it or at least the loop of rope. When you untie the first bag, remember to keep hold of the rope so the other doesn't come crashing down.
- Sleep a couple of dozen feet or so away from your properly hung food—close enough that you can hear a raiding bear and scare it away as soon as possible.
- If a bear goes after your food, jump up and down, make a lot of noise, wave your arms—anything to make yourself seem huge, noisy and scary to a bear. Have a stash of throwing rocks at hand and throw them at trees, boulders, etc., to make more noise. Bang pots together. Blow whistles. The object is to scare the bear away. *Never directly attack the bear itself.*

3. Bear boxes. Two extremely popular backcountry camping areas in Yosemite National Park, Little Yosemite Valley and Merced Lake, offer food storage lockers, popularly called bear boxes. These are large steel lockers intended for storage of food only, and they will hold the food bags of several backpackers. Everyone shares the bear box; you may not put your own locks on one. It's designed so that its latches, simple for humans, are inoperable by bears. Food in a properly fastened bear box is safe from bears; however, some boxes have holes in the bottom through which, if the holes aren't plugged, mice will squeeze in to nibble on your goodies.

An open bear box is a fragrant temptation for any bears in the vicinity, so don't leave the box open even when there are people around. Open it, use it, close it and latch it promptly. The presence of a bear box attracts campers as well as bears, and the area can become overused. However, it isn't necessary for *everyone* to cluster right around the box. A campsite a few hundred yards away may be more secluded and pristine; the stroll to and from the bear box is a pleasant way to start and end a meal.

Bear-box "don'ts." Never use a bear box as a garbage can! Rotting food is smelly and very attractive to bears; it takes up room and fouls the box for other users. Never use a bear box as a food drop; its capacity is needed for people actually camping in its vicinity. Never leave a bear box unlatched; it's literally an open invitation to raiding bears and other critters.

4. Cables are lengths of steel cable strung high between two trees. You counterbalance your food over a cable as you would over a branch. Once found at a number of locations in Yosemite National Park, cables are being phased out because ineffective.

5. Above timberline, there are no trees to hang your food bags from. But there are still bears—as well as mice, marmots, and ground squirrels—anxious to share your chow. Look for a tall rock with an overhanging edge from which you can dangle your food bags high off the ground and well away from the face of the rock. (Unlike bears, marmots, etc., have not learned to get your food by eating through the rope suspending it.) Or try the stash-in-a-crack technique below.

6. Stash-in-a-crack. One of us has had good luck with this technique; use it only above timberline. Bag your food and push it deep into a crack in the rocks too small and too deep for a bear to reach into—but be sure *you* can still retrieve it. You may lose a little food to mice or ground squirrels, but it won't be much.

7. When dayhiking from a base camp where you can't bearbox your food or leave it in a canister, it's safer to take it with you instead of leaving it hanging or stashed in a crack.

Once a bear gets your food, never try to get it back. It's the bear's food now, and the bear will defend it aggressively against puny you. You may hear that there are no recorded fatalities in bear-human encounters in recent Sierra history. Of course, this isn't true: plenty of *bears* have been killed as a result of repeated encounters. And there have been very serious, though not fatal, injuries to humans in these encounters.

If, despite your best efforts, you lose your food to a bear, it may be the end of your trip but not of the world. You won't starve to death in the maximum 3–4 days it will take you to walk out from even the most remote Sierra spot. Your pack is now much lighter. And you can probably beg the occasional stick of jerky or handful of gorp from your fellow backpackers along the way. So cheer up, clean up the mess, get going, and plan how you can do it better on your next trip.

A Word About Cars, Theft and Car Bears

Stealing from and vandalizing cars are becoming all too common at popular trailheads. You can't ensure that your car and its contents will be safe, but you can increase the odds. Make your car unattractive to thieves and vandals by disabling your engine (your mechanic can show you how), hiding everything you leave in the car, closing all windows and locking all doors and compartments. Get and use a locking gas-tank cap. If you have more than one car, use the most modest one for driving to the trailhead.

Bearproof your car by not leaving any food in it and by hiding anything that looks like a picnic cooler or other food carrier—bears know what to look for. To a bear, a car with food in it is just an oversized can waiting to be opened.

Maps and Profiles

Today's Sierra traveler is confronted by a bewildering array of maps, and it doesn't take much experience to learn that no single map fulfills all needs. There are topographic maps, base maps (U.S. Forest Service), shaded relief maps (National Park Service), artistically drawn representational maps (California Department of Fish and Game), aerial-photograph maps, geologic maps, three-dimensional relief maps, soil-vegetation maps, etc. Each map has different information to impart, and the outdoorsman contemplating a backcountry trip is wise to utilize several of these maps in his planning.

For trip-planning purposes, the reader will find a plan map in the back of this book. Trails and trailheads used in the trip descriptions are shown on this map in red, the access roads in black, and water in blue.

The profile of each trip in this book gives a quick picture of the ups and downs. All profiles are drawn with the same ratio of horizontal miles to feet of elevation; the vertical scale is about 1000 feet/0.3 inch, and the horizontal scale is about 10 miles/inch. The vertical scale in all is exaggerated.

On the trail most backpackers prefer to use a topographic (topo) map, because it affords a good deal of accurate information about terrain and forest cover. Topo maps come in a variety of sizes and scales. In the past, the United States Geological Survey (USGS) 15' series was popular because it covered the whole Sierra in one useful scale. Each covered 15' of latitude and longitude, or 14 x 17 miles, at a scale of 1:62,500 (about 1" = 1 mile), with an elevation-contour interval of 80'. The USGS is letting this series go out of print in favor of the newer 7½' series.

Fortunately, Wilderness Press now publishes regularly-updated 15' topos for many areas covered by *Sierra North*. These Wilderness Press 15' topos include indexes of the place names on them and are printed on waterproof, tear-resistant plastic. If any one or more of these maps covers all or part of a given trip, their titles appear in

boldface at the beginning of the trip. So far, Wilderness Press publishes the following 15' quads that apply to *Sierra North*: **Devils Postpile, Mt. Abbott, Fallen Leaf Lake, Hetch Hetchy Reservoir, Tuolumne Meadows, Merced Peak, Yosemite**. These are by far the best maps for backcountry travel.

The newer, more-detailed USGS topo series, the 7½' series, covers about 7 x 8 miles at a scale of 1:24,000 (2⅝" = 1 mile), almost all with a contour interval of 40'. A few are metric. It takes 4 of the 7½' topos to cover the area a single 15' topo covers. Each trip in *Sierra North* is completely covered by 7½' topos, and their titles are also listed at the beginning of each trip.

Another useful map series is the USDA Forest Service topographic series for each individual wilderness area. The scale of most maps of this series is 1:63,360 (1" = 1 mile), which is very close to that of the USGS 15' series (1:62,500) but conveniently covers the entire wilderness area on one map. This series is also more nearly up to date.

How to Acquire Your Maps

All pertinent maps and books are available in person or by phone from:

The Map Center
2440 Bancroft Way
Berkeley, CA 94704
(510) 841-MAPS (-6277)

The Map Center
63 Washington Street
Santa Clara, CA 95050
(408) 296-MAPS (-6277)

US Geological Survey topographic maps and US Forest Service maps are available locally at many Yosemite and National Forest ranger stations and other wilderness-permit sources.

Additional Map Sources

USGS offices:
345 Middlefield Road, MS 532
Menlo Park, CA 94025
(415) 329-4390

USDA Forest Service:
Pacific Southwest Region
630 Sansome St., Room 807
San Francisco, CA 94111
(415) 705-2874.

Wilderness Permits

Everyone who travels overnight into a national park or national forest is required to carry a wilderness permit from the agency which administers the entrance trailhead. If your trip extends through more than one national forest or through both a national forest and a national park, obtain your permit from the forest or park where your trip begins. The permit system has several functions: the agencies responsible for the backcountry learn how many people and stock are using each trailhead, so they can make better decisions to prevent overuse of these areas; and by giving out information with the permit on how to camp safely, avoid impact on the wilderness, and properly deal with bears, the agencies educate wilderness users.

During the summer months forest rangers patrol many backcountry trails. One part of their responsibilities is to ask you to show your wilderness permit. If you do not have one, you may be fined and expelled from the backcountry. The purpose of this section is to inform you how to obtain your wilderness permit.

There are two ways to get a permit. You can go in person for a permit to an agency location near your entry point the day before or the day you plan to begin your trip. The national forests and the national parks maintain a number of conveniently located facilities to serve you. Because of the severe cutbacks in funding, however, the agencies don't know from year to year which locations will be open during the summer season. Use the list below to call and discover the visitor center, ranger station, or satellite most convenient for you. You can also reserve a permit by mail up to six months in advance of your trip.

For very popular trailheads, the agencies have set limits on the number of people who can enter a trailhead per day. These limits are called **quotas**. Quotas are in effect mainly in the summer months, and only for some trailheads. Where quotas apply, only a limited number of advance reservations are accepted by mail. The remainder of the allotted quota is set aside for in-person applications, up to 24 hours in advance of your entry, on a first-come, first served basis.

(Inyo National Forest is unusual in this respect: the entire trailhead quotas may be filled by advance reservation.) If you plan to begin your trip from one of these high-use trailheads, especially on the weekend, and particularly if your trip begins in Inyo National Forest, you would be wise to reserve your permit in advance. A reservation for a permit is **not** the same as the permit itself. Only a few agencies mail you the actual permit. Most require that you pick up the permit near the trailhead entry. The purpose of the reservation is to guarantee you permission to use that trailhead on the day you wish. Where no quotas apply, the only reason to reserve your permit by mail is to allow you to pick it up off-hours.

A wilderness permit is issued for a single trip with a specific start date, specific entry and exit points, and for a specified amount of time. **Your permit is inflexible as to the trailhead entry point and start date.** A separate permit is required for each trip. As a general rule, groups are limited to a maximum of 15 people, and stock to 25 head. Some agencies charge a fee for each reservation (usually $3/ person); others do not. For some, it depends on which wilderness you plan to visit.

If you apply for a permit reservation in advance by mail:

(1) Call to inquire whether a fee applies; if so, include a money order or check for that amount made payable to the U.S. Department of Agriculture—Forest Service (except Yosemite, where it is payable to the Yosemite Association), or include a credit card number and expiration date. Applications lacking this fee will not be processed.

(2) Enclose a completed wilderness permit application form, one for each trip, like the one at the end of this chapter, or write a letter containing the same information.

(3) Be sure to provide a second choice of trailhead and/or entry date, in case the one you request is not available.

(4) If the agency will not mail your permit, find out where you should pick it up.

Whether you plan to apply for your wilderness permit in advance by mail, or at the time of your trip in person, we strongly suggest you telephone the administering agency first. Rules, regulations, and procedures for issuing permits are changing rapidly. Further, weather, runoff conditions, and forest fires sometimes close trails in the backcountry. Call ahead!

In the next chapter, starting on page 25, we list the endpoints to which you drive to begin your trip. These roadends and parking areas are numbered, and are the entry and exit points for the trips in this book. Each endpoint location has been numbered (Oyster Creek is #1; Plasse's Resort is #2; etc.) These numbers also appear with the endpoint name, just before the Highlights section of each trip description. **The name on your permit refers to the specific trail you will use.** When several trails originate from the same parking area, you need to identify which trail and your intended destination when you request your permit.

The section that follows contains the agencies you should call, and then write to, to reserve a wilderness permit by mail. Under each agency, we have listed the entry points (for the trips in this book) governed by that agency.

West side

El Dorado National Forest, Amador Ranger District

Phone: 209-295-4251

FAX: 209-295-5994

Address: El Dorado National Forest, Amador Ranger District
   26820 Silver Drive
   Pioneer, CA 95666

Fee: Depends on destination, $3/person where applicable

Advance reservations: Yes, you may apply up to 6 months ahead

Quotas: None

Entry points: (1) Oyster Creek; (2) Plasse's Resort; (3) Echo Summit; (4) Carson Pass; (5) Upper Blue Lake

Stanislaus National Forest, Summit Ranger District

Phone: 209-532-3671

Address: Stanislaus National Forest, Summit Ranger District
   #1 Pinecrest Lake Road
   Pinecrest, CA 95364

Fee: None as yet

Advance reservations: Yes, you may apply up to two weeks in advance

Quotas: None

Entry points: (8) Ebbetts Pass; (9) Mosquito Lake; (10) Bull Run Lake; (11) Lake Alpine; (13) Kennedy Meadow; (14) Gianelli Cabin; (15) Crabtree Camp; (16) Sonora Pass

Sierra National Forest, Pine Ridge Ranger District

Phone: 209-855-5360

Address: Sierra National Forest, Pine Ridge Ranger District
   P.O. Box 559
   Prather, CA 93651

Fee: $3/person
Advance reservations: Yes, you may apply starting March 1
for upcoming season
Quotas: Yes, in effect from last Friday in June through
September 15
Entry point: (43) Vermilion Campground

Sierra National Forest, Minarets Ranger District

Phone: 209-877-2218
FAX: 209-877-3108
Address: Sierra National Forest, Minarets Ranger District
P.O. Box 10
North Fork, CA 93643
Fee: $3/person
Advance reservations: Yes, you may apply starting March 1
for upcoming season
Quotas: Yes, in effect from last Friday of June through
September 15
Entry points: (34) Chiquito Pass; (35) Granite Creek Camp-
ground; (36) Fernandez Trailhead

Yosemite National Park

Phone: 209-372-0740
Address: Yosemite National Park, Wilderness Center
P.O. Box 545
Yosemite, CA 95389
Fee: $3/person, payable to Yosemite Association
Advance reservations: Yes, you may apply up to 6 months in
advance
Quotas: Yes, on all trailheads
Entry points: (17) O'Shaughnessy Dam; (24) Lembert Dome
Trailhead; (26) Tuolumne Meadows Campground; (27)
Tuolumne Lodge; (28) Cathedral Lakes Trailhead; (29)
Tenaya Lake; (30) White Wolf; (31) Happy Isles; (32)
Glacier Point; (33) Bridalveil Creek

East side

Toiyabe National Forest, Carson Ranger District

Phone: 702-822-2766
Address: Toiyabe National Forest, Carson Ranger District
1536 South Carson Street
Carson City, NV 89701

Fee: None

Advance reservations: None required; no advance permits issued; sign yourself in at the registration box at the trailhead

Quotas: None

Entry points: (6) Upper Wolf Creek Meadows; (7) Wolf Creek Meadows; (12) Rodriguez Flat

Toiyabe National Forest, Bridgeport Ranger District

Phone: 760-932-7070

Address: Toiyabe National Forest, Bridgeport Ranger District
        P.O. Box 595
        Bridgeport, CA 93517

Fee: Depends on destination; $3/person where applicable

Advance reservations: None required. No advance permits issued

Quotas: Yes, on some trailheads

Entry points: (18) Leavitt Meadow; (19) Buckeye Roadend; (20) Twin Lakes; (21) Green Creek Roadend; (22) Virginia Lakes Roadend

Inyo National Forest

Phone: 888-374-3773 (toll-free)

FAX: 760-938-1137

Address: Wilderness Reservations
        P.O. Box 430
        Big Pine, CA 93513

Fee: $3/person

Advance reservations: Yes; apply up to 6 months ahead

Quotas: Yes, on some trailheads, from last Friday in June through September 15

Entry points: (23) Saddlebag Lake; (25) Gibbs Lake; (37) Rush Creek; (38) Agnew Meadows; (39) Devils Postpile; (40) Rainbow Falls Trailhead; (41) Lake George; (42) Coldwater Campground; (44) Horseshoe Lake; (45) McGee Creek Roadend; (46) Hilton Lakes Trailhead; (47) Mosquito Flat

On the next page, there's a Wilderness Permit Application form for your use.

Wilderness Permit Application

To: [name of agency] _____
Areas to be visited: [names of wildernesses, park backcountry]
_____

Number of people in party: _____
Number of stock in party: _____
Method of travel (foot, horse, ski, snowshoe) _____

Itinerary

Entry date: _____   Exit date: _____
Entry trailhead: _____   Exit trailhead: _____
Overnight camp areas (list):   Nights in each camp:
1. _____   _____
2. _____   _____
3. _____   _____

(Etc., for every night you plan to be in the backcountry)

Alternate Itinerary

[Same format as above. It's recommended that you propose at
least two alternate itineraries, even if they differ only by having different start/end dates.]

Organization/Group Name: _____
Applicant's name: _____
Address: _____
City: _____State: _____Zip: _____
Phone (include area code): (_____)_____

I will insure that my party and I follow all wilderness rules and
regulations while on this trip.
                    Applicant's signature: _____
                                       Date: _____

If paying the fee by credit card:

Credit card type (e.g., Visa) _____
Credit card number: _____
Credit card expiration date: _____
Authorized signature: _____

- Send the completed application to the appropriate agency/office
  listed above during the period when they accept applications.
- Don't forget to enclose the fee, if any is required.
- Make as many copies of this form as you wish.

The Trailheads

Here are the descriptions for driving to all the trailheads used in trips in this book. At the beginning of each trip is a trailhead number, keyed to the numbers here. Shuttle trips have two trailheads, so the beginning trailhead number is given first in the trip, and the ending trailhead number is given second.

1. Oyster Creek Trailhead. Go 0.9 mile north of Silver Lake on State Highway 88 (0.1 mile past Oyster Creek Roadside Rest) to the bottom of the hill, where there are two hard-to-see dirt road entrances to the Horse Canyon Trailhead on the right (east) side of the highway. There is limited parking here; more is available at Oyster Creek Roadside Rest.

2. Plasse's Resort. Go east on State Highway 88 to the last downhill stretch before arriving at the shore of Silver Lake and turn right on a road signed PLASSE ROAD. Take this road down to the valley, past the resort, following signs to Stockton Silver Lake Camp. Just before the orange gate to the camp's parking area there are places to park a car, and the trail begins on the left (east) side of the road. There is a small sign marking the beginning of the trail, and more signs across the creek.

Alternatively, from Highway 88 at Tragedy Springs, a 4WD vehicle with high clearance can be driven on the Mud Lake Road past Allen's Ranch, to the trailhead on Squaw Ridge just south of Plasse's old trading-post site. Driving to the trailhead at the Mokelumne Wilderness Boundary will shorten the hike by over 3 miles each way.

3. Echo Summit. Go 0.3 mile south from Echo Summit (on U.S. 50) to the end of a graded summer-home-tract road.

4. Carson Pass. There are two trailheads at Carson Pass on State Highway 88. You *don't* want the one that's right at Carson Pass on the south side of the highway, though you'll find toilets, water, and a visitor center there. Instead, you want the more-westerly trailhead, so go 0.3 mile west of Carson Pass on State Highway 88 to a parking area on the north side of the highway.

5. Upper Blue Lake. Just 6.3 miles east of Carson Pass on State Highway 88 the Blue Lakes Road begins on the east side of the highway (on the right for those coming from Carson Pass). Head south up Hope Valley and over the Sierra crest 10.3 miles to a junction with the road to Lower Blue Lake. Continue ahead 1 mile and turn right at the Mokelumne Hydro Project. Go past Middle Blue Lake and at 13 miles from Highway 88 find a small parking area on the left, just below the spillway of Upper Blue Lake.

6. Upper Wolf Creek Meadows. About 2.5 miles south on State Highway 4 from State Highway 89, turn left and go southeast up Wolf Creek Road 3.3 miles to a fork left, where you could descend northeast to the north end of Wolf Creek Meadows. Continue straight ahead—south—1.5 miles beyond the fork to road's end at Wolf Creek Meadows Undeveloped Camping Area. The Wolf Creek Trail heads south up a creekside jeep road.

7. Wolf Creek Meadows. As for Upper Wolf Creek Meadows trailhead, above, follow Wolf Creek Road 3.3 miles to a fork left and descend northeast on it to the north end of Wolf Creek Meadows. In 0.6 mile from the fork, the road reaches a stock corral and a spur road heading southeast. Park here. This spur climbs a quarter mile to two adjacent trailheads. The two trailheads serve the High Trail and the East Carson River Trail.

8. Ebbetts Pass. This is the highest point on State Highway 4. The Pacific Crest Trail crosses State Highway 4 only 0.1 mile northeast of the pass; there is limited parking at the pass itself, and in another 0.3 mile northeast a short spur road veers right up to a PCT parking lot. A short spur trail up to the PCT leaves from the lot's south end.

9. Mosquito Lake Trailhead. From the east end of Lake Alpine go 6 miles northeast up State Highway 4 to the west end of Mosquito Lake, beside which is the signed trailhead. Toilet in Mosquito Lake Campground, across the highway.

10. Bull Run Lake Trailhead. From the east end of Lake Alpine go 4 miles northeast up State Highway 4 to a spur road branching right signed STANISLAUS MDW BULL RUN TRAIL. Follow this road 0.5 mile to its end, or just 0.3–0.4 mile if you don't have 4-wheel drive.

11. Lake Alpine. At the east end of Lake Alpine on State Highway 4 turn right 0.3 mile to the Silver Valley Overnight Campground. At the campground entrance is the trailhead for the Highland Creek Trail.

12. Rodriguez Flat. From the junction of State Highway 89 with U.S. 395, north of Coleville, go 5.5 miles south on U.S. 395 to Coleville, then another 2.2 miles to a road west, signed both LOST CANNON CREEK ROAD and MILL CANYON ROAD. Alternatively, from the State Highway 108/U.S. 395 junction, drive 13 miles north to Walker, then another 2.5 miles to Lost Cannon Creek Road. This dirt road west quickly becomes the Golden Gate Road. Go up it 6.3 miles; following LITTLE ANTELOPE PACK STATION signs. From the mountain crest junction at broad, open Rodriguez Flat, drive 0.5 mile south to road's end at signed Trail 1020.

13. Kennedy Meadow. On State Highway 108, 27 miles east of the Pinecrest **Y** (the turnoff from 108 to Pinecrest Lake, south of Strawberry) and 9.1 miles west of Sonora Pass, turn south onto the spur road to Kennedy Meadows and drive 1 more mile to Kennedy Meadows Resort. You can let passengers out at the resort and park there for a fee, or drive 0.5 mile back to a public parking area. Toilet, water, store, café at resort.

14. Gianelli Cabin. From the junction of State Routes 108 and 120 west of Sonora, go 33.5 miles northeast on 108 to tiny Cold Springs (east of Long Barn, west of the Pinecrest **Y**), and 1.2 miles east of Cold Springs turn right on signed Crabtree Road. Follow this paved road 6.8 miles to a junction just before a pack station. Go straight ahead onto dirt road and drive 2.6 miles to a junction. Turn left and go 4 miles to road's end.

15. Crabtree Camp. Proceed as above for trailhead 14 to the last-named junction, and go right 0.7 mile to the trailhead parking lot beside Bell Creek.

16. Sonora Pass. This is the highest point of State Highway 108, 67 miles northeast of Sonora and 15 miles west of the U.S. 395 junction.

17. O'Shaughnessy Dam (Hetch Hetchy Reservoir). Eastbound: go east on State Highway 120 4 miles beyond Buck Meadows and turn left at a signed junction; go 6 miles to another signed junction, turn right and go 6.5 miles to Camp Mather and then 9.5 more miles to the roadend. Westbound: go west on State Highway 120 through Yosemite and exit the Park at the Big Oak Flat entrance station; in less than a mile, turn east (right) onto Evergreen Road and follow it past Evergreen Lodge to a junction with Hetch Hetchy Road by Camp Mather; turn right onto Hetch Hetchy Road, re-enter the Park, pass Mather Ranger Station, and follow the road to its end. Toilet, water.

18. Leavitt Meadow. Go 8 miles east from Sonora Pass on State Highway 108, or 7 miles west from U.S. 395 on the same highway, to the Leavitt Meadow Campground backpackers parking area. Toilet, water.

19. Buckeye Roadend. Go 7 miles west from Bridgeport on Twin Lakes Road, which branches west from U.S. 395 in downtown Bridgeport, and turn north for 4 dirt-road miles at the junction signed BUCKEYE CAMPGROUND. Just beyond Buckeye Creek, turn left and go 1.1 miles, passing through a Forest Service Campground, to the end of the road. Alternatively, leave U.S. 395 3.8 miles north of Bridgeport and drive 6.0 miles to the same roadend.

20. Twin Lakes. Drive to hot, dusty, crowded Mono Village Resort at the end of paved Twin Lakes Road, 13.5 miles. There is a tiny, free hikers' parking lot just outside the resort's campground; if you can't find it, ask at the campground entrance kiosk. From the parking lot, on foot, follow signs generally westward through the campground to the Barney Lake Trail. Toilets, water, store, café at the resort.

21. Green Creek Roadend. From U.S. 395 south of Bridgeport and north of the junction with State Highway 270 to Bodie, turn west onto marked Green Creek Road and follow it to a junction with the Summit Meadows Road at 1 mile; go left here. Continue another 2.5 miles to a junction with a spur road southbound to Virginia Lakes; go right here. Continue another 5.2 miles, veering right to a parking loop at the trailhead (left takes you to the Green Creek Campground). Toilet, water.

22. Virginia Lakes Roadend. From Conway Summit on U.S. 395 turn west and go 6.2 miles on paved, then dirt, Virginia Lakes Road to the roadend by a lake. Avoid side roads. Toilet, water.

23. Saddlebag Lake. From State Highway 120 2.2 miles north of the Tioga Pass entrance to Yosemite, near Tioga Pass Resort, go 2.6 miles north up a part-paved, part-dirt road. Park at the roadend. Toilet, water, café, store, and ferry service (fee) at adjacent Saddlebag Lake Resort.

24. Lembert Dome Trailhead. From State Highway 120 in Yosemite's Tuolumne Meadows, just 7 miles southwest of Tioga Pass and just east of the bridge over the Tuolumne River, turn west on a dirt road and go 0.3 mile to a parking area near the stables. On crowded days you may have to park immediately off the highway at the Dog Lake trailhead parking lot.

25. Gibbs Lake Trailhead. From the junction of U.S. 395 and State Highway 120, which is just south of Lee Vining, go south 1.3 miles on 395 and turn west on a dirt road that's poorly signed HORSE MEADOW. Go up to 3.3 miles on this dirt road to roadend parking at Upper Horse Meadow *if your car can make it*; the road gets very rough beyond Lower Horse Meadow. If your car can't make it all the way, go as far as you can, park off the road as best you can, and walk the rest of the way to the trailhead; it's a nice stroll.

26. Tuolumne Meadows Campground. Just 7.2 miles southwest of Tioga Pass, and a short distance east of the Tuolumne Meadows store, café, and gas station, is the entrance to Tuolumne Meadows Campground. Turn south into the campground, stop at the

entrance station to get permission to go to the Elizabeth Lake
Trailhead, and then follow road signs toward the group-campground
loop. The trailhead is off the spur road to the group-campground
loop, the second *paved* turnoff left from the main campground road.
Follow the spur to a gate just before the signed Horse Camp; the
trailhead is here, another 0.4 mile from the highway. Park in the
adjacent lot. If the campground is closed, park outside it near the
entrance and walk through the campground. Toilet, water, when
campground is open.

27. Tuolumne Lodge. Following State Highway 120 in
Yosemite's Tuolumne Meadows, drive 0.5 mile east from the bridge
over the Tuolumne River, turn right on a paved road, and go 0.7 mile
to the roadend parking lot to let your passengers out. You must park
at one of the two backpackers' parking lots along this road.

28. Cathedral Lakes Trailhead. On State Highway 120 in
Yosemite, go 0.5 mile west of the Visitors Center in Tuolumne
Meadows, or 0.5 mile east of the west end of the meadows, to a
parking lot on the south side of the road.

29. Tenaya Lake. From State Highway 120 in Yosemite, at the
west end of Tenaya Lake, east of Olmstead Point and 15.8 miles west
of Tioga Pass, where signs indicate SUNRISE TRAILHEAD, drive a
very short way to a small parking lot. Toilet.

30. White Wolf. On State Highway 120 in Yosemite, go 14.5
miles northeast from Crane Flat or 32.3 miles west from Tioga Pass,
to the White Wolf turnoff, and follow that road one mile down to the
trailhead opposite White Wolf Lodge. Toilets, water, snack bar.

31. Happy Isles. In Yosemite Valley, take the Yosemite Valley
shuttlebus to Happy Isles, or park at Camp Curry and hike along a
trail 1 mile southeast to Happy Isles. Toilets, water, snack bar, nature
center.

32. Glacier Point. From the eastbound side of the main road
through Yosemite Valley, take the turnoff onto State Highway 41 to
Wawona and Oakhurst. Drive 9.3 miles south from Yosemite Valley
up 41 to its high point at Chinquapin junction, turn left onto Glacier
Point Road, and drive 15.5 more miles to a parking lot at road's end.
You can also get to Chinquapin junction by driving north up 41 from
Oakhurst and Wawona. Toilets, water, snack bar, souvenir stand.

33. Bridalveil Creek. Follow the directions for trailhead 32 to
Chinquapin junction, turn left onto Glacier Point Road, drive 7.6
more miles to the Bridalveil Campground road, branching right, and
follow this road through the campground to the southeast end of it.

34. Chiquito Pass Trailhead. First, get to Bass Lake; the road to
Bass Lake branches east from State Highway 41 3.5 miles north of
Oakhurst at Yosemite Forks, south of Yosemite National Park. From

the north shore of Bass Lake, drive northeast 20 miles up Beasore Road 434 (which becomes Road 5S07) to Globe Rock. There, turn left and drive 2.4 miles up Road 5S04 to a signed trailhead atop a small, flat ridge area.

35. Granite Creek Campground. From the north shore of Bass Lake (see the directions to Bass Lake for trailhead 34), drive northeast 20 miles up Beasore Road 434 (which becomes Road 5S07) to Globe Rock, then continue 9.8 miles along your road to the Minarets road, which goes south 52 paved miles to the town of North Fork. Still on Road 5S07, you reach the Clover Meadow Ranger Station in 1.7 miles, then continue past it 0.5 mile to Road 4S57. Branch right on this road and follow it 1.0 mile to a hikers' parking area in Granite Creek Campground. Road 4S57 may be undrivable as late as early July.

36. Fernandez Trailhead. From the north shore of Bass Lake (see the directions to Bass Lake for trailhead 34) drive 20 miles up Beasore Road 434 (which becomes Road 5S07) to Globe Rock. Continue on 5S07—the main road—for 8.0 miles, past Bowler Group Camp. Then, 100 yards beyond Ethelfreda Creek, veer left onto Road 5S05 toward the Fernandez Trailhead. This road climbs steadily for 2.3 miles to a turn-around loop at the trailhead.

37. Rush Creek. The June Lake Loop intersects U.S. 395 twice, once about 4 miles south of the State Highway 120-U.S. 395 junction on the outskirts of Lee Vining and again at June Lake Junction, about 6 miles farther south. Follow the June Lake Loop to the northeast end of Silver Lake (7.3 miles from June Lake Junction). The trailhead is on the west side of the road between the Frontier Pack Station and a mobile-home park. Toilet, water.

38. Agnew Meadows. Between Memorial Day and Labor Day, you may have to take a shuttlebus (fee) from Mammoth Mountain Ski Area to get to this trailhead as well as to the next two trailheads. At the Mammoth Lakes junction on U.S. Highway 395, take State Route 203 west through Mammoth Lakes to a signed junction at a traffic light, where going ahead (west) takes you into the Lakes Basin and going right (north) on 203 takes you to Mammoth Mountain Ski Area. Turn right and follow 203 north and west to the ski area. If the rest of the way is open to private cars, continue past the ski area and over the road's high point, Minaret Summit. From here to the spur road to Agnew Meadows, the road is steeply downhill, winding, and very narrow; be prepared to yield to oncoming traffic. At a hairpin turn near the bottom of the descent, 2.7 miles from Minaret Summit, turn right onto the spur road to Agnew Meadows and go another quarter mile to a parking area. There is an overflow parking area just beyond it. Toilet, water.

39. Devils Postpile. Follow the directions for trailhead 38 through Mammoth Lakes to Mammoth Mountain Ski Area. You may have to take a shuttlebus from Mammoth Mountain Ski Area. Otherwise, continue up 203 and over Minaret Summit. At the marked turnoff for Devils Postpile 6.7 miles from Minaret Summit, turn right and go 0.3 mile to a parking area at the spur road's end. Toilet, water, visitor center (maps, info).

40. Rainbow Falls Trailhead. Follow the directions for trailhead 38 through Mammoth Lakes to Mammoth Mountain Ski Area. You may have to take a shuttlebus from Mammoth Mountain Ski Area. Otherwise, continue up 203 and over Minaret Summit, then 8.1 more miles to a fork: left to Reds Meadow Resort, right on a dirt spur road 0.1 mile to Rainbow Falls Trailhead parking. You go right. Toilet, water.

41. Lake George. Follow the directions for trailhead 38 through Mammoth Lakes to the signed junction at a traffic light, where going ahead (west) takes you into the Lakes Basin and going right (north) on 203 takes you to Mammoth Mountain Ski Area. Go ahead on the road, now called Lake Mary Road, as it curves southwest into a basin of lakes. *Don't turn off to Twin Lakes.* Instead, stay on Lake Mary Road as it climbs to a **Y**-junction: right to Lakes Mamie and George and Horseshoe Lake, left to Lake Mary and Coldwater Canyon. Go right and skirt Lake Mary to a junction we'll call the *George-Mamie junction*: left to Lake George, right (ahead) to Lake Mamie and Horseshoe Lake. Turn left and drive between Lakes Mary and Mamie to a **T**-junction: left around Lake Mary's west shore, right to Lake George. Turn right and follow the road up to a parking area at Lake George, between Woods Lodge and Lake George Campground. Toilet.

42. Coldwater Campground. Follow the directions to trailhead 41, Lake George, as far as the **Y**-junction. Turn left and skirt Lake Mary on your right, Pine City Campground on your left. You shortly reach a junction with a spur road left into Coldwater Campground; turn left here and follow the road through the campground to a large parking area at the roadend. There are three trailheads here; the Duck Pass Trailhead, which you want, is the middle trailhead. Toilets, water.

43. Vermilion Campground. Take State Highway 168 northeast from Clovis (near Fresno) through the town of Shaver Lake. Eventually you reach a junction with a road left to the community of Lakeshore at Huntington Lake. *Lakeshore is your last sure chance for gas.* Bear right to stay on Highway 168, which soon becomes Kaiser Pass Road and which is rough, narrow, and winding after you cross Kaiser Pass and begin descending steeply. Be prepared to yield to oncoming traffic. It's a total of 81 miles from Clovis over Kaiser Pass to the Florence Lake/Lake Edison junction near the bottom of the descent, then 8 miles north on a mostly paved road to Vermilion Campground. The trailhead is at the east end of the farthest-east campground loop. Toilets, water in campground; store, café at nearby Vermilion Valley Resort.

44. Horseshoe Lake. Follow the driving directions to trailhead 39 as far as the George-Mamie junction. Go right (ahead) to a roadend parking loop next to Horseshoe Lake. Toilet, water.

45. McGee Creek Roadend. Go 32 miles north of Bishop or 8 miles south of the Mammoth Lakes Junction (with State Highway 203) to a turnoff to McGee Creek. Follow this paved, then dirt, road for 3.2 miles, across Crowley Lake Drive, past a turnoff to McGee Creek Campground, and past McGee Pack Station, to a paved, roadend parking loop. Toilet.

46. Hilton Lakes Trailhead. From U.S. Highway 395 25 miles north from Bishop or 15 miles south from the Mammoth Lakes junction, turn west on Rock Creek Road at Tom's Place, cross Crowley Lake Drive, and follow the road past Rock Creek Lake to a parking area on the right side of the road, 9.3 miles from 395. The Hilton Lakes trailhead is about 400 feet back down the road from here. Toilets and water in nearby Rock Creek Lake Campground; store and café at nearby Rock Creek Lakes Resort.

47. Mosquito Flat. Follow the directions for trailhead 46, above, but continue up Rock Creek Road to road's end at Mosquito Flat beside Rock Creek, 10.7 miles from 395. One-overnight backpackers' campground across creek from parking area, only for the night *before* you start your trip. You must show your legal permit for the trip out of Mosquito Flat to demonstrate your eligibility to occupy a campsite. Toilets.

Carson Pass

The Carson Pass area flanks the first trans-Sierra highway south of Lake Tahoe. As a recreational area, it boasts many lakes off the highway and a few beside the highway. The scenery is superb, mixing as it does volcanic rocks with granitic ones. You'll want a camera to catch the volcanic battlements north of Silver Lake rising above the granite bosses of the lake basin.

Some of the best flower displays in the entire Sierra grow alongside the trails in this part of *Sierra North*, such as the trails to Scout Carson Lake and Showers Lake.

Highway 88, designated a scenic highway, is the main gateway to the 105,165-acre Mokelumne Wilderness, enlarged in 1984 from 50,450 acres, when a number of new wilderness areas were created in California and many existing ones were enlarged.

To acclimate your body to the 8000-foot-plus altitudes, you could spend the night before hiking at Sorensen's, Kit Carson Lodge, Caples Lake Resort, or Kay's Silver Lake Resort—all near the pass and the trailheads. And there are plenty of campgrounds nearby.

1 Silver Lake to Scout Carson Lake

Distance	11 miles
Type	Out and back trip
Best season	Late
Topo maps	Caples Lake

Grade (hiking days/recommended layover days)

Leisurely	2/0
Moderate	Day
Strenuous	——
Trailhead	Oyster Creek (1)

HIGHLIGHTS   The mountains around Silver Lake are a startling amalgam of light-gray granite and dark-brown lava, the granite being gently rounded, but the lava arrayed in tiers of jagged cliffs. This trip follows a boundary between the two types of terrain, ascending gently southeast under the soaring lava cliffs of Thunder Peak and Thimble Peak to a lovely, small lake near timberline.

DESCRIPTION

1st Hiking Day (Silver Lake to Scout Carson Lake, 5.5 miles): From the east side of the small trailhead parking area our trail begins by heading northeast through a grove of aspen for a short distance before swinging southeast. Heading in this general direction, our route ascends gently in a forest of red fir, where we catch occasional views of the bizarre volcanic cliffs of Thunder Mountain. The trail then assumes a course roughly parallel to these golden-brown cliffs, passing several huge pieces of rock that have broken away from the mountain and come to rest far from the base of the cliff. Swinging to the east, our route steepens and we begin to encounter granite—at first in the form of glacially transported rocks and boulders, and then, as we climb higher into lodgepole-pine forest, as granitic bedrock, too. Here, we also find an increase in understory vegetation, including currant, deerbrush, huckleberry oak and chokecherry.

At 8200 feet elevation we ford our first perennial creek, turn north to climb alongside it, and then veer east and make a brief but steep climb onto an open hillside. As we contour along this hillside we have fine views across Silver Lake to the south and up to Squaw Ridge to the east. The trail then drops briefly to cross another unnamed, year-round creek and then climbs a sagebrush-dotted slope. Now at 8800 feet, our trail begins a level mile across an open, flower-dotted bench on the south side of Thimble Peak. To the east of the peak you'll notice the tops of some of the ski lifts at Kirkwood Meadows, which is in the next valley to the north and—thankfully— out of audio and visual range. This trail is, however, open to motorcycles, but they seldom come this far. After passing a hard-to-spot trail to Kirkwood Meadows, we ascend gently to a signed junction in a sandy meadow. Turn right here and stroll an easy ½ mile to Scout Carson Lake. Perched on a small bench, ringed by meadow, and surrounded by a forest of lodgepole pine, western white pine and mountain hemlock, this little lake is a sweet example of Sierra Nevada charm. Perhaps not so charming, though, are the many mosquitoes that live here till late season, and less charming still are the cows and their clanking bells that may be heard as they graze these meadows. To an extent, you can avoid both audio and epidermal distress by camping away from the meadowy lake shore, in the drier and rockier terrain to the west. It is disconcerting that private cattle can, for a nominal fee, degrade the backcountry environment on public lands. Scout Carson Lake supports a small but fat population of brook trout, which eat mosquitoes, and Emigrant Peak to the east is an easy climb whose summit offers superb, cow-free views of much of Mokelumne Wilderness.

2nd Hiking Day: Retrace your steps, 5.5 miles.

Brook trout caught in Long Lake

2

Silver Lake to Summit City Canyon

Distance	20 miles
Type	Out and back trip
Best season	Mid
Topo maps	Caples Lake, Mokelumne Peak

Grade (hiking days/recommended layover days)

Leisurely	4/1
Moderate	3/0
Strenuous	2/0
Trailhead	Oyster Creek (1)

HIGHLIGHTS   The first leg of this trip is a long traverse of very flowery open hillsides with fine views of the Silver Lake basin and its surrounding volcanic battlements. Then the trail enters a new stream valley and winds down through solitude-filled Horse Canyon to a variety of campsites along beautiful Summit City Creek.

DESCRIPTION (Leisurely trip)

1st Hiking Day: Follow Trip 1 to Scout Carson Lake, 5.5 miles.
2nd Hiking Day (Scout Carson Lake to Summit City Canyon, 4.5 miles): First we retrace our steps a short ½ mile to the Horse Canyon Trail and turn right onto it. Our sometimes muddy trail ascends moderately through a thinning tree cover almost to timberline, passing through upland meadows rife with flower color in early season. Approaching Squaw Ridge, we cross a set of little-used jeep tracks and in 100 yards arrive at an unnamed pass which is the border of Mokelumne Wilderness, a region of 105,165 acres where only foot travel is permitted and trails are generally kept up to a standard sufficient for walkers but not horses or mules.

The descent into steep Horse Canyon proceeds on a great number of switchbacks that zigzag down among tall, elegant western white pine trees past plentiful patches of daisies, groundsel, phlox, brodiaea, paintbrush and whorled penstemon, among other blossoms. At a natural overlook spot less than a mile down, the far-gazing hiker can see deep into Summit City Canyon and the Mokelumne River Canyon. It is hard to imagine, perhaps, that just under 150 years ago stalwart emigrants brought their covered wagons up this canyon, winching them from tree to tree when it was too steep for their straining livestock to pull them.

Swinging east briefly, the grade steepens as there are now fewer switchbacks. At 8100 feet we cross a creek and pass two immense, centuries-old red firs. Our sometimes faint trail descends grassy meadows and then, leaving cows behind, begins the final descent into Summit City Canyon. Now the views are open and we can see the U-shaped cross-section profile that characterizes glaciated canyons. Along this newer section of trail the brushy hillside supports a large population of chokecherry, whose late-season fruit grows in such abundance as to give a faint red tinge to the hillside at a distance. Small and bitter, it is no wonder they are called "choke" cherries. But for the industrious cook, these unlikely fruits make a most exquisite syrup.

At the forested canyon bottom we meet and turn right onto the Tahoe-Yosemite Trail. After an easy ¼ mile, just before seasonal Horse Canyon Creek, there is a good campsite near where Summit City Creek makes an S curve through a slot in granite bedrock. There is additional camping potential both up and downstream. Solitude is plentiful here in this canyon even though it's only 5 miles uphill to the nearest road at Forestdale Summit. Indeed, as Thoreau put it, "In wildness is the preservation of the world."

3rd and 4th Hiking Days: Retrace your steps, 10 miles.

3

Silver Lake to the Mokelumne River

Distance	31 miles
Type	Out and back trip (part cross-country)
Best season	Mid
Topo maps	Caples Lake, Mokelumne Peak
Grade (hiking days/recommended layover days)	
Leisurely	6/1
Moderate	5/1
Strenuous	4/0
Trailhead	Oyster Creek (1)

HIGHLIGHTS   The largest wilderness river in the northern Sierra is the goal of this trip. Cathedral forests here shade the cool, green river, brown trout often rise to the fly, and except at trail crossings solitude is plentiful.

DESCRIPTION (Leisurely trip)

1st and 2nd Hiking Days: Follow Trip 2 to Summit City Canyon, 10 miles.

3rd Hiking Day (Summit City Canyon to Mokelumne River, 5.5 miles): Some readers have complained that previous editions didn't mention the rattlesnakes in Summit City Canyon and along the Mokelumne River. Now they are mentioned. But we have yet to see one there.

Several hundred yards below the Horse Canyon Trail junction, our route, following the Tahoe-Yosemite Trail, easily crosses the Horse Canyon stream and then winds down Summit City Creek to cross Telephone Gulch. The main canyon narrows, but not so much as to force our path right next to the creek, and we follow a sandy duff tread across flats dotted with many lodgepole pines and aspens. The commonest flower here, as it has been since before we reached the floor of Summit City Canyon, is the pink-cupped sidalcea. The second commonest has been squaw root, also called yampa, with hundreds of little white flowers making up flattish flowerheads. Beyond Telephone Gulch our trail continues down Summit City Canyon, usually not next to the creek but not far from it. The descent is gentle as the trail crosses alternating moist, shady areas and open, dry areas. The trail is usually obvious, though growing fainter. About 2½ miles below Horse Canyon the trail comes to creekside where the creek leaves a shady flat and flows into a narrowing gorge of granite. Don't cross the creek here. The trail, which is blasted into the bedrock, continues along the west side of the creek a short distance and then ends. Continue along slabs and ledges above the creek, passing a campsite in a grove of Jeffrey pines, and after about another 200 yards cross the creek just above a narrow, steep-walled slot that the creek flows through. This crossing can be wet or possibly even dangerous during a time of exceptionally high runoff. To continue on the west side of the creek now would quickly become very steep and brushy. The trail resumes on the east bank, climbs about 30 feet and then turns right and continues downcanyon.

From here the trail is usually noticeable except when it crosses bedrock, but ducks will typically help guide the way. A few hundred feet beyond the creek ford we cross just such an area of bedrock. As the creek swings south here we simply parallel it. Beyond, we descend near the creek for a short distance, and then climb high above it over the west shoulder of a small dome. We descend steeply now past a smaller dome and then re-enter forest, meeting the first incense cedar. Our route is now separated from the creek by a low ridge, and the grade eases and then climbs onto slabs. Descend these slabs toward (but not to) a small creek on the left. At the bottom of these slabs the trail climbs down a steep notch toward the right and then comes again near Summit City Creek. Parallel Summit City Creek until the trail crosses the side creek just above its confluence with Summit City Creek. From here the trail leaves forest again and climbs very briefly onto an open, rocky slope. Continuing downcanyon, we cross more slabs, veering away from Summit City Creek. After several hundred yards the trail enters brushy huckleberry oak and manzanita. Staying mostly in brush, our route descends gently to a steeper, final slope down to the bottom of Mokelumne Canyon. Along this slope the views of the canyon open up and we can see the Tahoe-Yosemite Trail ascending the south side of the canyon below Mt. Reba. We descend several hundred feet, veer left on a flat area and then switchback down toward Summit City Creek. Don't cross the creek until it gets to the valley floor. The trail descends ledges, and at one point climbs a bit, to finally drop down through a cleft in the bedrock to creekside. The trail is faint as we cross the seasonal east channel of Summit City Creek via logs onto a shady, seasonal island. Go downstream to just above the confluence of the seasonal channel and ford the main branch on a log or rocks. If there are not available logs, then this ford can be wet or even dangerous during exceptionally high runoff.

The trail is now more distinct as we head southwest along the valley floor. Soon our trail climbs over a low ridge past several large ponderosa pines and enters a thick forest that shows signs of a ground fire. The forest cover opens briefly and we pass an enormous ponderosa pine that is more than 6 feet in diameter. Soon back in dense forest we meet other, larger giants: sugar pine—the largest pine in the world—grows exceptionally huge in this valley and we pass several towering monarchs that are over 7 feet in diameter at the base. Soon we meet the seasonal channel of the creek that drains Wester Park. The river is just to the left, and there is primitive camping along the river. Just below this tributary creek the river makes a bend and there is a long, deep pool whose tranquil waters beautifully reflect the cathedral forest towering above. This must be the kind of place that inspired the 19th century painter Albert Bierstadt to create his famous images of supernatural wonder. Beneath the surface of this mysterious pool dwell many fat trout.

4th, 5th, and 6th Hiking Days: Retrace your steps, 15.5 miles.

The Mokelumne River above Camp Irene

Silver Lake to Long Lake $\qquad$ **4**

Distance	14 miles
Type	Out and back trip
Best season	Mid
Topo maps	Caples Lake, Mokelumne Peak

Grade (hiking days/recommended layover days)

Leisurely	2/1
Moderate	2/0
Strenuous	——
Trailhead	Plasse's Resort (2)

HIGHLIGHTS   A viewful hike over rolling terrain leads to one of the area's loveliest lakes, just above which travelers will find campsites on granite benches that command spectacular views of the surrounding peaks.

DESCRIPTION (Leisurely trip)

1st Hiking Day (Silver Lake to Long Lake, 7 miles): From the obscure trailhead by Stockton Silver Lake Camp, our trail immediately crosses the creek, joins the trail coming in on the left from the pack station, turns right, and heads south up the valley. Soon the grade steepens and the wide, dusty trail winds uphill through a dense forest of mostly red fir. In ½ mile the grade eases and we veer east, passing the first of several beautiful, forest-fringed meadows. There are several trails that join and branch off from our route but it's easy to follow the main drag. This trail is not only open to stock travel, but also to motorcycles, which accounts for the deep dust.

At the head of the longest meadow we cross a small creek, passing between two large boulders of volcanic conglomerate, and then climb past the spring-fed source of this creek. On a low ridge just above, we meet the signed trail to Hidden Lake and turn right. We pass yet another verdant meadow, and then a huge boulder from under which issues a spring. We then make a last, hemlock-shaded climb to a divide between the American River and the Bear River drainages. Descending from this viewful ridge, we cross a drift fence and in less than 100 yards turn left onto a 4WD road. Traveling along the road, the grade is level as we pass Allen Ranch and then cross the seasonal headwaters of Bear River. Now ascending, we cross some perennial trickles, and just before a small creek we leave the road, veer right, and climb to re-meet the road on Squaw Ridge. Here we find a sign proclaiming a former site of Plasse's Trading Post. Raymond Plasse (pronounced pla-say) was a French immigrant who served and profited from the pioneers who traveled this emigrant trail. About 130 yard down from the ridge we leave the road and turn left into Mokelumne Wilderness.

The route is now on an old, rehabilitating road where it is no longer legal to drive since Mokelumne Wilderness was enlarged in 1984 from 50,165 acres to 105,165 acres. Just into the wilderness, we pass a little above Horse Thief Spring, which usually flows all year. Sadly, since there has been so much cattle grazing here, these springs are only a remnant of their former glory, but fill up anyway as this may be the last water before Cole Creek Lakes. Continuing south, the nearly level trail passes some long meadows and then joins a broad, volcanic ridge where we can see as far as the Carson-Iceberg Wilderness to the south. As the trail descends this ridge, we pass the faint, old trail to Cole Creek Lakes, and soon meet the junction with the trail heading left to Black Rock Lake. Now on granitic terrain, we cross another, viewful ridge where we have a closer look at Mokelumne Peak. Descending this rocky ridge, we pass a signed trail going right to Cole Creek Lakes. The grade is now level and we stroll through forest for ½ mile, and then briefly descend to the east shore of the southernmost Cole Creek Lake. From this lake's seasonal outlet, our trail descends gently south for most of a mile before gradually ascending to the signed junction with the trail to Long Lake. Here we turn left and in a short ½ mile arrive at the south shore of many-bayed Long Lake. The immediate lakeshore is overused by both people and cows, but nice camping is available by skirting the south shore and crossing one of the tiny dams that enlarge this lake and then heading east, away from the lake onto open granite benches. Within several hundred yards of the lake you can find level, dry, cow-free and mosquito-free campsites that have fabulous views to the southeast over Wester Park to the headwaters of the Mokelumne River and the peaks around Ebbetts Pass.

2nd Hiking Day: Retrace your steps, 7 miles.

Silver Lake to Camp Irene   **5**

Distance   26 miles
Type   Out and back trip
Best season   Mid
Topo maps   Caples Lake, Mokelumne Peak
Grade (hiking days/recommended layover days)
   Leisurely   5/1
   Moderate   4/0
   Strenuous   3/0
Trailhead   Plasse's Resort (2)

HIGHLIGHTS   The hiker taking this trip will stop overnight at
two highly contrasting places. Long Lake is at
8000 feet elevation, in the cool belt, and the green water is still, with
no visible inflow or outflow after early season. In contrast, the
Mokelumne River is a good-sized, clear-flowing river at an elevation of only 5000 feet, where middays can be very hot.

DESCRIPTION (Moderate trip)

1st Hiking Day: Follow Trip 4 to Long Lake, 7 miles.
2nd Hiking Day (Long Lake to Camp Irene, 6 miles): After
retracing the short lateral trail to Long Lake, this day's route turns left
(south) on the Cedar Camp Trail and rises gradually through a dense
forest of fir and pine. Many rivulets lace this slope into midseason,
and their courses are fertile growing grounds for lavender shooting
stars and other meadow flowers. As the grade levels off, the trail
swings eastward and soon arrives at green, sloping Munson Meadow,
where in late season you will find the first flowing water since Horse
Thief Spring. For northbound hikers, it is the first water since the
beginning of the long, unshaded climb up the manzanita-lined sandy
trail from the "oases" in the Mokelumne River canyon.

From Munson Meadow the trail wanders southeast over a forested plateau for a mile before it starts to descend in earnest into the river canyon. At first, the trail is rocky and dusty, shaded by a sparse forest cover of red firs. Then it steepens and becomes completely exposed to the sun as it leads down a series of long switchback legs on very sandy underfooting. Views across the canyon are quite expansive, and time passes quickly—for the descending traveler. Coming back is a very different story.

Nearly 2 miles from the start of the switchbacks, the trail, still steep, enters much more hospitable territory where all-year water allows alders, willows, aspens and a great panoply of wildflowers to flourish. About 100 yards below the first of these wet "oasis" areas is a flat spot where one could camp if he were up-bound and exhausted. The trail continues to descend, moderately to steeply, but it is well shaded much of the time, and it often crosses unmapped streams that flow all year. At these streams thirsty hikers can pleasure their mouths with the sweet water (purify it) and pleasure their eyes with the multicolors of orange tiger lily, pink columbine, yellow groundsel and white milfoil flowers, and the rich green of bracken ferns. After about four stream crossings—depending on the season—it is a steep 200-yard descent on a rocky-dusty trail to the junction of the unmapped trail up the river canyon and the trail down to Camp Irene.

Turning right here, our route descends to a stream not shown on the map and follows it down to the river, passing a 1974 burn shortly before reaching Camp Irene. This camping area has a sandy beach, fine granite slabs, lovely pools—and a lot of campers, since it is a popular overnight stop along the Tahoe-Yosemite Trail. Those who need solitude will find it up or down the river. Fishing in the Mokelumne is good for brown and rainbow trout (to 14").

3rd and 4th Hiking Days: Retrace your steps, 13 miles.

Silver Lake to   **6**
the Mokelumne River

Distance	28.7 miles
Type	Shuttle trip
Best season	Mid
Topo maps	Caples Lake, Mokelumne Peak
Grade (hiking days/recommended layover days)	
Leisurely	6/2
Moderate	5/1
Strenuous	4/0
Trailhead	Oyster Creek (1), Plasse's Resort (2)

HIGHLIGHTS   This tour visits examples of all the landscapes of the Carson Pass region—volcanic peaks, rounded granite domes, deep-cut river canyons and lake-dotted plateaus. Anyone in good condition who has the basic skills for hiking cross country will enjoy this long shuttle trip.

DESCRIPTION (Moderate trip; would be leisurely but for the 4th hiking day)

1st, 2nd and 3rd Hiking Days: Follow Trip 3 to the Mokelumne River, 15.5 miles.
4th Hiking Day (Mokelumne River to Long Lake, 6.2 miles): From the seasonal creek that drains Wester Park and Long Lake, we head west and soon begin climbing the 3000 vertical feet out of this canyon. On a hot summer day an early start will help, even though there is plenty of water for the first 1800 feet. At first we climb 200 feet onto a bench, where we pass the last of the extra-huge sugar

pines. Another steep, 200-foot climb brings us over a granite ridge
where we can look back over the stately-forested canyon bottom and
the large expanses of glaciated granite. We veer west and for a long
¼ mile the trail undulates up and down through a mixed forest of
oaks, pines, and cedars to the signed junction where the Tahoe-
Yosemite Trail goes left down to Camp Irene.

From here to Long Lake, reverse most of the 2nd hiking day, Trip
5, 5 miles.

5th Hiking Day: Reverse the 1st hiking day of Trip 4, 7 miles.

Mokelumne River near Summit City Creek

Carson Pass to Showers Lake 7

Distance	10.6 miles
Type	Out and back trip
Best season	Mid
Topo maps	Carson Pass, Caples Lake

Grade (hiking days/recommended layover days)

Leisurely	2/1
Moderate	2/0
Strenuous	——
Trailhead	Carson Pass (4)

HIGHLIGHTS   Showers Lake is one of the best camping places between U.S. 50 and State Highway 88, with numerous campsites and good angling for brook trout. En route, the trail through the upper Truckee Valley offers panoramic views of immense volcanic formations and promises potential close-up glimpses of many birds and mammals.

DESCRIPTION

1st Hiking Day (Carson Pass to Showers Lake, 5.3 miles): From the northwest corner of the parking lot (8560'), pick up the ill-marked trail. Amid dryland flowers, you head west over a seasonal trickle and past an information sign. The trail traverses between the highway to your left, below, and juniper-crowned gray granite cliffs on your right. The sandy trail reaches a junction at a little over ¼ mile: right (north) on a use trail that shortly peters out, left (southwest) on the Pacific Crest Trail. Go left, still traversing above the highway and aiming at the stark buttes beyond Caples Lake. You descend slightly as you veer northwest to excellent views of Caples Lake. At ⅔ mile you curve through a patchy lodgepole forest and emerge to a seasonally amazing flower display: a steep hillside thickly carpeted with bright yellow, daisy-like mule ears and sky-blue lupine.

Continue, crossing a pair of unmapped, seasonal streams, and begin switchbacking up a slope, heading for an obvious low point just west of Red Lake Peak. The grade eases as you reach a saddle with a lovely, unnamed lakelet at a little over 1 mile, to the west of a fence with a hiker's pass-through. Double ruts lead away into a high meadow spangled with blue iris, and spectacular views open up as you continue north, rising very gradually to a broad saddle: Lake Tahoe in the distance, peaks in Desolation Wilderness—Mt. Tallac, Dicks Peak, and Jacks Peak—granite slopes in Dardanelles Roadless Area, and a strange volcanic formation that towers over Round Lake. Nearby on the east, Red Lake Peak is topped by slablike volcanic outcroppings resembling a stegosaur's back plates. An easy scramble to its summit would yield panoramic views.

Down here, little runoff streams that spring from porous volcanic rocks trickle their water onto flower gardens of iris, yarrow milfoil, Mariposa lily, sulfur flower, lupine and paintbrush. Descending moderately to steadily from the summit, we cross three runoff streams (dry in late season), then a westward-flowing tributary, and finally the infant Truckee River—all via easy fords.

Just past another easy ford are the buildings of a cow camp, and near them the Round Lake Trail branches right. The meadows here are full of little gray Belding squirrels, commonly called picket-pins, and often a Swainson hawk soars overhead, hoping to surprise one of them. Continuing the level walk from the Round Lake junction, we pass an unsigned trail to Meiss Lake, visible as a meadow-fringed blue sheet in the northeast. Then one last time we ford the river, on boulders, and a few feet beyond the ford a use trail forks right toward Meiss Lake, as our route bears left.

We pass a trail to Schneider Camp (marked by a blazed S on the lodgepole), and ascend out of Dixon Canyon on a gentle grade. From the crest of this little ascent, the trail dips past a shallow, weedy pond and continues on the old two-track jeep road. After crossing two runoff streams (dry in late season), we begin a steady-to-steep ascent of ¼ mile, first up a wash filled with smoothed, round rocks, and then on a rocky-dusty trail, under moderate-to-dense forest cover of red fir, hemlock, western white pine and lodgepole pine. Sixty yards after the jeep tracks emerge from this forest onto a meadowy slope lush with lupine and mule ears, a trail veers slightly left and uphill from the tracks, and we take the trail. (The old jeep road also goes to Showers Lake.) This trail section traverses a bountifully flowered, meadowy slope to a forested saddle overlooking Showers Lake, from where it descends to the fair-to-good campsites on the west and east sides of the lake (8650'). Fishing is good for eastern brook (to 12"). From a base camp here, one may easily walk cross country to Four Lakes, where fishing and swimming are often good in mid-to-late season.

2nd Hiking Day: Retrace your steps, 5.3 miles.

Carson Pass to Echo Summit 8

Distance	12.8 miles
Type	Shuttle trip
Best season	Mid
Topo maps	Fallen Leaf Lake, Carson Pass, Caples Lake, Echo Lake

Grade (hiking days/recommended layover days)

Leisurely	2/1
Moderate	2/0
Strenuous	——
Trailhead	Carson Pass (4), Echo Summit (3)

HIGHLIGHTS   This trip offers one of the easiest ways in the whole northern Sierra to get away from the crowd, and it is an excellent choice for a two-party shuttle. With a minimum of effort, the hiker can traverse some high, scenic, little-used country, where the wildlife is as plentiful as the people are scarce.

DESCRIPTION

1st Hiking Day: Follow Trip 7 to Showers Lake, 5.3 miles.

2nd Hiking Day (Showers Lake to Echo Summit, 7.5 miles). Heading northwest from the southwest shore of Showers Lake, we soon find the trail, and then ascend gently for several hundred yards through mixed conifers. Coming out onto open slopes, we ford a year-round stream fed by the snow cornice that drapes the ridge of Little Round Top above. Where we cross this stream, its banks are lined with thousands of blossoms of the showy yellow flower Arnica chamissionis. In fact, this whole open bowl is laced with runoff streams and lavishly planted with colorful bushes and flowers: blue elderberry, green gentian, swamp whiteheads, mountain bluebell, aster, wallflower, penstemon, spiraea, cinquefoil, corn lily and columbine. As we walk around this bowl on the boundary between volcanic rocks above and granite below, we have good views of Stevens Peak and Red Lake Peak, both built up of layers of richly colored volcanic flows.

Finally, the trail ascends out of the bowl and enters a sparse cover of lodgepole and western white pine. At the crest of this ascent, the pine gives way to hemlock as we pass a cattle drift fence (close the gate) and level off through open high country. Reaching a willowy meadow, one may lose the trail momentarily, but it is easy to find if one continues straight across the meadow. A short distance beyond is a junction with a signed trail to Schneider Cow Camp, which leads west. One-third of a mile beyond this junction our route crosses, at right angles, an unsigned but well-grooved trail which is used by local stockmen, and then continues its almost level, winding course northward under a sparse-to-moderate mixed forest cover.

We then pass a collapsed stock fence and make a short, steep descent down a hemlock-covered hillside to a meadowy slope where marsh marigolds, their white and yellow petals set off by their rich green leaves, bloom in the wetness of melting snows until late in the season. Our sandy footpath soon passes a trail that winds down Sayles Canyon, and then we continue north to a summit from where views of the Crystal Range, including Pyramid Peak, are good. From here it is a gentle descent under hemlock and lodgepole and western white pine to Bryan Meadow. Here one may camp except in late season, when the stream is dry. A collapsed log cabin in the meadow sprawls near the confluence of routes leading to Showers Lake, U.S. 50 and Benwood Meadow.

Heading for Benwood Meadow, we ascend a gently rising sandy trail through meadowy, open stands of lodgepole pine, with some sagebrush. The alert hiker here may spot a red-shafted flicker on one of its characteristic undulating flights between trees. At the top of this sandy climb the trail levels off and becomes indistinct, but the route is well marked by blazes. A short, steep descent then brings us to a willow-filled bowl where an unnamed stream rises. We cross the young stream and on the far slope veer right, on a trail that soon switchbacks steeply down a red-fir-covered slope. At the foot of the slope is another willowy meadow, and shortly beyond that another steep downslope, also shaded by red fir, where following the route may require attention to the occasional ducks. The trail then levels out in a large meadow that was once a lake, skirting the west side of it.

The trail from this meadow to Benwood Meadow is sometimes indistinct, but there are sufficient blazes and ducks. At Benwood Meadow the flora is quite noteworthy: along the wet meadow margin the flower-spotter is kept busy by the plenitude of aster, corn lily, snow plant, alpine lily, monkey flower, penstemon, false Solomon's seal, squawroot, pennyroyal, groundsel, columbine, larkspur and mountain bluebell, to say nothing of the ferns, grasses and sedges.

Past Benwood Meadow, our nearly level trail meets a junction with a trail that goes left to a ski resort near Echo Summit. Then it dips to cross the outlet of a lily-filled pond, and ascends gently up a rather exposed slope, where a few mixed conifers partially shade a ground cover of huckleberry oak, pinemat manzanita and Sierra chinquapin. Finally, the rocky-dusty trail ends at a graded road (7520) that serves a small tract of summer homes ⅓ mile south of Echo Summit.

The "entrance" to Benwood Meadow

9   Upper Blue Lake to Grouse Lake

Distance	12 miles
Type	Out and back trip, part cross-country
Best season	Mid
Topo maps	Carson Pass, Pacific Valley, Mokelumne Peak

Grade (hiking days/recommended layover days)

Leisurely	2/1
Moderate	2/0
Strenuous	Day
Trailhead	Upper Blue Lake (5)

HIGHLIGHTS   This easy weekend trip is close to the Tahoe/ Reno/Carson City area. Nestled in a little-traveled corner of Mokelumne Wilderness, Grouse Lake sits high above Summit City Canyon. Requiring only modest effort, this hike offers both the spectacular scenery of sweeping vistas and the intriguing beauty of geological diversity.

DESCRIPTION (Leisurely trip)

1st Hiking Day (Upper Blue Lake to Grouse Lake, 6 miles): The Grouse Lake Trail begins just south of the campground by the overflow spillway of Upper Blue Lake. Crossing this seasonal channel, our trail then turns south into lodgepole-pine forest and descends briefly to a log crossing of the perennial outflow from Upper Blue Lake. Our trail is level for a bit as we pass an unsigned lateral to Middle Creek Campground. Swinging west, we ascend gently, and before long begin to get tree-shrouded views of some of the surrounding peaks, including Round Top. The grade eases briefly where we cross the Mokelumne Wilderness boundary. Continuing west, we skirt a small pond, and in about ½ mile swing next to the flower-lined, seasonal outlet of Granite Lake, which lies just above. Aptly named, Granite Lake is held in a small basin surrounded by weathered granite outcrops, and the coarse sand and gravel of disintegrating granitic rock, called grus, comes almost to the meadow-fringed shore.

Now out of range of road noise, we skirt the south shore of Granite Lake and turn left over a low ridge. Beyond the lake, we leave most dayhikers behind as our trail winds west for most of a mile through this weathered granite landscape, passing pockets of forest and a small creek. The trail then makes a short, very steep climb to a major viewpoint. Clockwise from the east you can see the Carson Range (in Nevada); dark, volcanic Raymond Peak; metamorphic Highland, Stanislaus, and Leavitt peaks; and the polished, light granite of deep Mokelumne River canyon.

From here, our trail descends gently past an old Mokelumne Wilderness boundary marker, crosses a meadow, and then begins a longer climb. After crossing several gullies we reach a sloping bench at 9200 feet, where light granite is overlain by dark volcanic bedrock. Where the granite meets the overlying volcanic rock there is typically a slope change because the overlying volcanic rock is softer and more easily eroded than granite. Along this bench we cross several spring-fed rills, indicating that the volcanic rock above holds more groundwater than the granite lying below this contact zone. As you take in the sweeping panorama, imagine almost all of this land covered by immense sheets of ice; indeed, this was the case many times during the Pleistocene Epoch, when even as recently as 13,000 years ago icecaps covered most of the High Sierra and valley glaciers flowed many miles down major canyons such as the Mokelumne.

From these spring-fed rills, descend west to a small creek, stay on the north side of the creek, and climb through low willows a short distance past the source of this creek. Continue climbing as the trail fades out on an open slope. Now following ducks, our route levels off and we contour northwest ¼ mile, to where the trail reappears briefly. Staying well above granite outcrops and a patch of willows, our trail fades out again before we reach a second patch of willows. Turn left and follow the small creek draining these willows. Very soon we pass some very large granite boulders, near which the trail appears again. Grouse Lake is now visible below, and the faint, ducked trail descends west 600 vertical feet to the moderately forested shore of this secluded body of water, which on a hot day can be a wonderful wilderness swimming pool. Nearby viewpoints offer looks into Summit City Canyon below to the west, and golden eagles, which traditionally nest in the canyon, can sometimes be seen riding thermals to dizzying heights above.

2nd Hiking Day: Retrace your steps, 6 miles.

Ebbetts Pass

The wilderness flanking Ebbetts Pass is probably the least-used area in the whole Sierra Nevada. One reason is that it doesn't have a lot of lakes. But it does have volcanic formations aplenty, and many year-round streams. The East Fork of the Carson River is a just-barely-discovered beauty.

Hikers who want to let their bodies acclimate overnight before hitting the trail can stay in style at Lake Alpine Lodge or at the accommodations in Bear Valley. Markleeville is not far away, and just south of Markleeville is the East Fork Resort—although these latter places are not as high as one might wish for acclimating.

Highway 4 provides the best access to the 160,871-acre Carson-Iceberg Wilderness, goal of most of the trips in this chapter. Few people know the name of this wilderness, and as a result you are likely to find solitude in it.

Mosquito Lake to Bull Run Lake 10

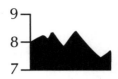

Distance	8 miles
Type	Shuttle trip
Best season	Mid
Topo maps	Pacific Valley, Spicer Meadow Res.

Grade (hiking days/recommended layover days)

Leisurely	3/0
Moderate	2/0
Strenuous	Day
Trailhead	Mosquito Lake Trailhead (9); Bull Run Lake Trailhead (10)

HIGHLIGHTS   Two of the better, scenic, trout-stocked lakes of the Lake Alpine area are visited on this easy hike. Dayhikers and fishermen may wish to hike only to Heiser Lake via the Heiser Lake Trail or only to larger Bull Run Lake via the Bull Run Trail, thereby avoiding the short 2½-mile car shuttle.

DESCRIPTION (Leisurely trip)

1st Hiking Day (Mosquito Lake to Heiser Lake, 2 miles): Head briefly south on the Heiser Lake Trail, almost immediately meeting a junction: right (west) to Lake Alpine on the Emigrant Trail (not on the topo), left (ahead, south) to Heiser Lake. Go ahead, curving around Mosquito Lake before veering south to begin a steep climb up the moraine south of the lake in moderate-to-sparse forest. Gaining the ridge at last, you begin a descent on a sandy trail and enter Carson-Iceberg Wilderness at nearly ½ mile. You continue, generally south-southeast, through forest relieved by a couple of small meadows and then, at a little over ¾ mile, climb up the next moraine.

On fresh-looking, glacially scoured rock we descend from the ridge and follow a winding route that takes the path of least resistance down slabs. After leveling off in deep forest, we climb ⅓ mile to a junction on a little flat. Tomorrow we'll head southwest from here down a creekside trail, but since our immediate goal is Heiser Lake, we turn east, hike a short ¼ mile uphill, then switchback and climb south over a low granitic ridge that hides the shallow lake. Dotted with several small islands of granitic rock, this conifer-fringed lake presents the fisherman with a picturesque distraction while he contemplates a meal of fresh brook trout. Campsites lie on the north and south shores under a pleasant canopy of red fir, lodgepole pine, western white pine, and mountain hemlock.

2nd Hiking Day (Heiser Lake to Bull Run Lake, 2.5 miles): First, retrace your steps ½ mile to yesterday's trail junction. From here our route, usually well blazed and ducked, takes us southwest to the brink of a rocky slope, and then down the slope via very steep switchbacks. We then stay fairly close to Heiser Lake's outlet creek, paralleling it west across a flat basin shaded by mountain hemlocks. Approaching the basin's west edge, we cross four closely spaced branches of a tributary that joins the outlet creek just south of the trail. After a brief climb west, our trail turns south and leads to a signed junction with the Bull Run Trail.

From the junction, this route almost immediately fords Heiser Lake's outlet creek, a ford that could require a little doing in early season when it is a small torrent of white water. After following an almost level granitic bench for ⅓ mile, this route angles south and crosses the first of many creeklets. Our winding route goes from slab to granitic slab as it climbs and gyrates up toward the lake. Were it not for a superabundance of blazes and ducks, some hikers would get off route. This climb is broken into distinct ascents, the first one trending southeast up and around a secondary ridge, the second one trending southwest past a trailside pond before it approaches Bull Run Lake's outlet creek and ascends near it to the lake's bedrock dam.

Although not large by Sierra standards, this popular lake can accommodate dozens of campers, particularly on the spacious flats beneath large red firs. Swimming in the lake is good in early August, and fishing is often good for brook trout.

3rd Hiking Day (Bull Run Lake to Stanislaus Meadow, 3.5 miles): After backtracking to the trail junction just west of Heiser Lake's outlet, our route stays on the Bull Run Trail as it winds, steeply at times, 350 vertical feet down rock slabs covered with lodgepole and western white pine, red fir and mountain juniper, well above the outlet creek from both lakes before it eases off in a shady flat. A short forest traverse brings us to a crossing of this creek, which in early season can entail a cold, wide, knee-deep ford. Beyond the ford we follow the creek a shady, long ⅓ mile to a refording of two branches of it, which will give early-season hikers another challenge. The trail from the ford maintains a westbound course for 100 yards to an even wider ford, the headwaters of North Fork Stanislaus

River. As usual, look for logs across the stream, which may make fording drier and perhaps much quicker.

Immediately beyond the North Fork we cross a seasonally dry wash before turning north and roughly paralleling the North Fork upstream. A wide path leads up this moderate grade, and, near its top, we may be greeted by a chorus of cowbells, which incessantly ring as their wearers munch away in Stanislaus Meadow. A fence keeps the cattle in the meadow and us in the forest while an easy ½ mile hike along its west side brings us to the Bull Run Lake trailhead.

Bull Run Lake

11   Wolf Creek Meadows to Soda Springs

Distance	20.5 miles
Type	Semiloop trip; part cross-country
Best season	Mid
Topo maps	Wolf Creek, Disaster Peak
Grade (hiking days/recommended layover days)	
Leisurely	3/1
Moderate	2/1
Strenuous	2/0
Trailhead	Wolf Creek Meadows (7)

HIGHLIGHTS   One can acquire a good feeling for eastside Sierra flora and geology on this trip, ideally suited for weekend backpackers. Because the landscape is viewed from a crest route going and a canyon route returning, the hiker sees it from two very different perspectives.

DESCRIPTION (Moderate trip)

1st Hiking Day (Wolf Creek Meadows to Soda Springs Guard Station, 9.5 miles): At the edge of a volcanic slope covered with sagebrush, mule ears and bitterbrush, the High Trail climbs upward into an open forest of Jeffrey pine and white fir. With the brief views of Wolf Creek Meadows behind us, we now enjoy the shade that the forest provides on this steep climb. Beyond a large split boulder and its surrounding mountain mahogany bushes, the High Trail parallels the ridge up to a level crest, then climbs steeply to a small, grassy flat. Just beyond this flat, we start an uphill traverse across a grassy, gentle slope that contains a curious combination of water-loving, white-barked aspens almost next to drought-resistant, mangy-barked junipers. Jeffrey pines, white firs, willows, mule ears and sagebrush complete the cast of principal plants. Here, taking a break, one can easily fall asleep to the soothing sounds of rustling aspen leaves.

Up these shady slopes we climb, and about ½ mile beyond the meadow, the steep trail eases up and then levels off as it comes to an open slope. Here the trail provides a momentary view of the Vaquero Camp buildings in the east, down in Silver King Valley, and more enduring views of the granitic Freel Peak area, in the northwest, beyond whose summits lies Lake Tahoe.

Along our short, open traverse we find a good exposure of a type of blocky volcanic rock that is common to this "land of fire and ice." It is called an autobrecciated ("self-broken") lava flow. From the middle Miocene epoch through the late Pliocene epoch, thick andesitic lava flows poured from summits that probably resembled today's Oregon Cascades, and they covered an area of the Sierra Nevada that extended from Sonora Pass north to Lassen Park and from east of the present Sierra crest westward to the Central Valley. When the thick lava flows cooled as they flowed along their downward paths, they became less and less able to move, particularly along their rapidly cooling edges, and eventually these edges solidified. But then the pressure of the still-flowing internal material fractured the edges, creating the broken-up texture we see here.

At the base of an autobrecciated flow decorated with vine maples, we enter a shady white-fir forest and encounter a refreshing, flowery, mossy, spring-fed creeklet. Beyond it our trail climbs moderately eastward, then descends slightly to a low knoll covered with ragged mountain mahogany. Leaving the knoll, we pass through a forest of pines and firs, and descend steeply south into two seasonal, parallel creeklets that drain Snowslide Canyon. Volcanic rocks give way to granitic ones as we leave this broad, brushy canyon, descend through a shady forest, round a jagged, granitic ridge, and then reach another seasonal creek.

One-fourth mile beyond this creek, our trail tops out at a bedrock saddle on a ridge above the East Carson canyon. From it, short switchbacks lead steeply down a brushy slope covered with huckleberry oak and manzanita; then our trail diagonals southwest down to a gentle slope on which we cross an unsigned east-west trail. Soon we reach a bubbling creek, and cross it only 90 yards before arriving at East Fork Carson River. If you don't like river fords, you can camp along or near the riverbank, and later backtrack ⅓ mile to the east-west trail and follow it east ¼ mile to another river ford. (Those who ford the East Carson southbound on this trip will reford it here.) Before mid-July, the river is usually waist-deep, about 50°F at most, and swift, but by Labor Day it has dropped to knee depth. A rope helps in an early-season traverse across the river's bouldery bottom, but it is unnecessary for the experienced backpacker, since there are no dangerous rapids downstream.

For those who fish this river, a likely catch is the mountain whitefish, which looks like a cross between a trout and a sucker. A small mouth on the lower part of its head is the sucker characteristic, but the presence of an adipose fin on the lower back identifies it as a close relative of trout and salmon. Like these fish, it is good to eat. This river also contains the Tahoe sucker, whose protractile mouth, on the bottom of its head, is ideally suited for scavenging the river bottom. Although bony, it is tasty.

Across the river, the High Trail ends in 80 yards at a signed junction with the East Carson River Trail—an old jeep road closed to motor vehicles. On this gravelly road we parallel the river ⅓ mile upstream to the north edge of a sagebrush flat. Here the river angles west, but our tracks head south through dense sagebrush. Reaching a dry wash debouching from a small, very bouldery gorge, we climb up it to a low bedrock saddle. From the saddle we make a short descent past a small, steep cliff, on the right, then reach a larger, longer, steeper one, on the left. This cliff we parallel southeast, then continue to three close-spaced Jeffrey pines in a sagebrush flat. From between the west and south pines, the main route goes 200 yards southwest to a ford of the East Carson, then south along jeep tracks through a shady forest to a refording of the East Carson one mile later. This refording takes place at the "bottom" (south) curve of a large meander, whose west half dries up late in the summer, when the lower river shoots directly east 150 yards to the ford (see the accompanying map). Eventually, the meander will disappear as the river establishes a more efficient, more direct course. About 250 yards south of this ford, in a field of granitic boulders left by a glacier, an indistinct trail heads east-southeast through the grass another 250 yards to Poison Creek, just beyond whose east bank is a path that leads south 300 yards to the Soda Springs Guard Station.

Most hikers, when they arrive at the three Jeffrey pines, will prefer not to ford and reford the East Carson, even though these two fords are considerably easier than the High Trail ford. For them there is a dry route to the Soda Springs Guard Station. After leaving between the south and east pines, follow a path south-southeast for 100 yards. If you're on the right path—there are many cow paths— it will bend south and soon reach a granitic cliff that plunges down to the East Carson only ¼ mile due south of the three pines. Once around the bouldery base of this small cliff, you have an easy, open walk southward that parallels the East Carson.

About ¾ mile beyond, the river bends west and you follow it on a faint trail through sagebrush to the northeast corner of the large meander mentioned in the alternate route. From this corner a set of jeep tracks leads southeast ⅕ mile across a flat to a signed junction with the Poison Flat Trail, just within forest cover. Trip 13 heads north along this trail, and trips 15 and 16 head south along it to this

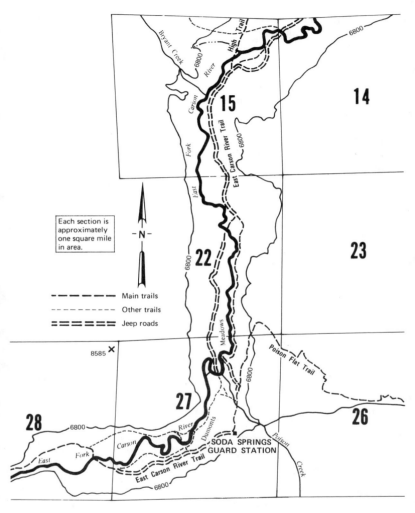

junction. We turn south, up-canyon, and follow the jeep tracks, which quickly reduce to a path in the 100 yards it takes to reach the first of as many as half a dozen distributaries of Poison Creek. Between two of them, the alternate route—a footpath from the west-northwest—ends at our broad path. A little beyond we meet the fenced-in compound around Soda Springs Guard Station. You can

camp by multibranched Poison Creek, or a small creek ⅓ mile along
the trail west of the guard station provides another possibility.

*2nd Hiking Day (Soda Springs Guard Station to Wolf Creek
Meadows, 11 miles):* First, retrace your steps 2¾ miles to the signed
High Trail junction. This day's route continues on a jeep road going
northeast from the junction, then quickly curves right as it rounds an
open flat. In 0.4 mile from the High Trail junction, we arrive at an
East Carson ford which is almost as difficult as the High Trail ford.
Our next segment of jeep road starts northeast up a flat and crosses
it, then is almost cut in two by a river's meander that has eroded
deeply into the flat. Beyond the meander, a traverse across an equally
long flat ends at the East Carson 1 mile below the High Trail junction.

Here, look for two large Jeffrey pines just north of you, between
which a barbed-wire gate marks the start of a trail. From the gate this
trail stays on the west side of the East Carson, paralleling the river at
first, but gradually veering away from it. We cross two long, but not
high, moraines—those bouldery, sandy ridges left by a glacier
before it retreated back up the East Carson canyon and into extinc-
tion. Beyond the second moraine is a seasonal creeklet which we
cross only 70 yards west of the East Carson. The trail now parallels
the river to a junction with some jeep tracks.

We follow these north almost ½ mile up to a low ridgecrest of a
rocky moraine that marks the northernmost extent of a former glacier
in Silver King Valley. Atop this moraine is a barbed-wire fence
across the jeep tracks. Our challenging route leaves the jeep tracks
atop the moraine, follows the fence west about 300 yards to a gate,
descends to the entrance of the gorge, and follows the river's west
side 2½ miles.

The difficulty of this gorge route varies, the hardest part occur-
ring in the scenic first half. When the water is low—after Labor
Day—you can walk along the river's edge, but in early season you'll
have to climb above it many times. Nevertheless, a rope is not
necessary. At first, you'll pass by impressive, deeply cut cliffs of
autobrecciated lava flows. Farther down, you're likely to see colum-
nar flows in addition. Campsites in this isolated gorge are plentiful,
but unfortunately the best ones are on the opposite bank. This route
ends at the official trail, which fords the East Carson at Gray's
Crossing, directly west of a low gap.

From the crossing, the East Carson River Trail heads west, then
climbs steeply up to gentler slopes above the river. Soon we reach a
gate, pass through it, and gradually curve westward into Railroad
Canyon. Up this canyon we hike, seemingly too long to be on the
right route, and then we cross its creeklet. From here, the last
permanent source of fresh water, our trail climbs north out of the

canyon, circles along the edge of a flat-topped autobrecciated lava flow, then traverses ⅓ mile northwest to the south tip of shallow Wolf Creek Lake (not the larger, better known Wolf Creek Lake at the east base of Sonora Peak).

From the lake's southeast corner, our trail climbs west up to the base of steep volcanic slopes, then ascends to the ridge above the trailhead, along which runs a fence. On the other side of its gate, we meet the end of a jeep road, and on it walk west a short distance to a saddle, recognizing that the large, scattered granitic boulders resting on the volcanic bedrock are "erratics"—boulders carried here by a large glacier that once flowed north down Wolf Creek canyon. From the saddle we can look up-canyon and imagine how impressive this canyon would have appeared about 6,000 years ago, when a river of ice, hundreds of feet thick, slowly flowed past this spot, quite likely reaching, and occasionally damming, the East Fork Carson River. After a moment's reflection on this subject, we leave the saddle and descend 100 steep yards to our trailhead, which is beside the trailhead of the High Trail.

12   **Wolf Creek Meadows to Wolf Creek**

Distance	24 miles
Type	Shuttle trip
Best season	Mid or late
Topo maps	Wolf Creek, Disaster Peak
Grade (hiking days/recommended layover days)	
Leisurely	3/0
Moderate	2/0
Strenuous	——
Trailhead	Wolf Creek Meadows (7), Upper Wolf Creek Meadows (6)

HIGHLIGHTS   This trip starts as a scenic crest route, then proceeds through parts of three glaciated canyons. Plenty of creekside campsites await anglers who would like to try their skill at trout fishing.

DESCRIPTION (Moderate trip)

1st Hiking Day (Wolf Creek Meadows to Murray Canyon Trail junction, 12 miles): First, follow Trip 11 to Soda Springs Guard Station, 9.5 miles. Leaving the shady campground at the guard station, we hike west on a jeep trail and after ⅓ mile cross a spring-fed creeklet. Just beyond this creeklet is a well-used campsite under lodgepole pines, only 20 yards downslope. Immediately below it is a trail coming from the larger meander mentioned in Trip 11 (see the map in Trip 11). Westward, this trail parallels our jeep trail, dying out in a grassy meadow. Our easy route through sagebrush reaches this meadow in ½ mile and the jeep tracks, like the trail, die out in it. They quickly reappear at the northwest end of the meadow and lead us 200 yards northwest to a wide ford of the East Carson.

Continuing northwest we arrive at an unsigned junction. From here our route goes 1½ miles over a trail that is often a multilane cowpath. The trail tends to stay away from the river as it ascends gently through Jeffrey-pine forest. After the canyon heads south, the trail emerges on the edge of a large, cow-infested meadow, on the northwest side of which is a signed junction about 50 yards beyond Murray Canyon creek. Several fair campsites can be found near the cottonwoods along the creek. This creek and the river provide fair-to-good fishing for rainbow and paiute-rainbow hybrid (to 10″).

2nd Hiking Day (Murray Canyon Trail junction to Upper Wolf Creek Meadows, 12 miles): At the signed trail junction, we leave the gentle gradient of the East Fork Carson River Trail and climb, steeply at times, up 15 switchback legs that lead high on a brushy, open-forested slope and then into Murray Canyon. Like virtually every tributary canyon of the East Carson above Soda Springs, this one usually had a glacier in it when there was one in the main canyon. Being much smaller, however, the Murray Canyon glacier was unable to keep pace with the tremendous excavating power of the East Carson glacier, which in this area was sometimes more than 800 feet thick. As a result, the East Carson glacier cut down faster, leaving Murray Canyon as a hanging valley—which we have just entered at the top of the switchbacks.

From the top of these switchbacks we go another 200 yards to the verdant banks of clear Murray Canyon creek. After 100 steep yards, the trail resumes a moderate grade and takes us past the first of many flower-lined creeklets. One-third mile up from the creek crossing, we pass through the gate of a cattle fence, then continue up the flowery path. At a trail junction where Murray Canyon splits in two, our trail, the main one, bends right and climbs steeply west up the canyon.

About ¼ mile above the junction is a permanent creek, lined with willows and alders; then in another ¼ mile the trail crosses a second creek. Beyond it the route steepens, on a few short switchbacks up a granitic slope. Talus that has fallen from volcanic formations above has buried much of the granitic bedrock, and it becomes very widespread as the grade eases and the trail enters a small gully flowered with mule ears. Beyond this gully, we climb steadily north ½ mile to a crest saddle, where, a few yards northwest of the actual crest, there is a junction with a fairly new trail. Trip 16, which has coincided with this hiking day up to this saddle, departs south along this crest path.

As we switchback northwest down rather open volcanic slopes, ahead is a flat-topped ridge composed of several thick, horizontal lava flows, below which lies a huge talus slope. This rocky slope was built up after the last glacier retreated up-canyon when water, freezing and expanding in the flows' cracks, pried off countless blocks.

At the bottom of the descent into deep, long Wolf Creek Canyon, we encounter a cattle fence, pass through its gate, and follow the trail as it widens to a jeep road. Joining this short stretch is a jeep spur from the south and, merged together, they head 100 yards northwest to a signed junction, near a conspicuous snow-depth marker, with the Asa Lake Trail. Our route, a jeep road for the remainder of this hike, starts north and quickly reaches a ford—usually a wet one—of Wolf Creek. Across the creek, we amble along an easy path ⅓ mile to a meadow and a signed junction.

Continuing northeast on the jeep road around the fenced meadow, we descend to a creeklet and then parallel Wolf Creek at a short distance, staying above the small gorge it has cut through volcanic rock. Small, tempting pools can be seen in the creek, particularly just before a gate on a low, descending ridge. Beyond the ridge gate, our route descends very steeply to a crossing of Bull Canyon creek, a wet ford except in late season. At this alder-lined crossing, granitic bedrock once again is evident and it becomes more abundant down-canyon.

Strolling down-canyon to Dixon Creek, we approach and veer away from Wolf Creek several times. A long, wide, rocky stream bed has formed behind a constriction in the canyon created by a prominent granitic ridge on the east side and by Dixon Creek's alluvial fan on the west. Dixon Creek has shifted its course to a more northern position down across this fan. For most of the summer Dixon Creek runs too high to ford without getting wet feet. Once across it, though, you'll keep your feet dry the rest of the way. The jeep road first parallels the creek, then veers northwest away from it, skirts a grove of aspens and cottonwoods, and curves east around a well-weathered granitic knob. From here it is an easy 1-mile stroll to the trailhead, the Wolf Creek Meadows Undeveloped Camping Area.

Wolf Creek Meadows to Sonora Pass 13

Distance	30 miles
Type	Shuttle trip
Best season	Mid
Topo maps	Wolf Creek, Disaster Peak, Sonora Pass

Grade (hiking/recommended layover days)

Leisurely	5/1
Moderate	4/0
Strenuous	3/0

Trailhead Wolf Creek Meadows (7), Sonora Pass (16)

HIGHLIGHTS One of the longest and deepest canyons east of the Sierra crest, the East Fork Carson River canyon at times contained glaciers up to 19 miles long. Our trip heads south up this spectacular canyon, stops at scenic Wolf Creek Lake, then passes through a sculptured volcanic "badland" on the south slope of Sonora Peak. This peak—the highest summit between State Highway 108 and Mt. Shasta—is easily climbed in a short side trip.

DESCRIPTION (Strenuous trip)

1st Hiking Day: Follow Trip 12 to Murray Canyon Trail junction, 12 miles.

2nd Hiking Day (Murray Canyon Trail junction to Wolf Creek Lake, 13 miles): Next to granitic bedrock just south of the Murray Canyon Trail junction is a fair campsite. At this campsite Murray Canyon creek blocks our path in early and mid season. During these seasons you may have to wade several yards downstream before you can resume your brief walk along the west side of this creek. In about

200 yards, Murray Canyon creek bends east and joins the meandering East Fork Carson River. Immediately south of the creek's bend, we join the main path from our starting point. This path, obvious to northbound hikers, makes four fords of Murray Canyon creek and, due to willows and grass, is difficult for southbound hikers to locate. Staying along the East Carson canyon's meadowy west edge, we now hike about ½ mile south to a usually flowing creek, cross a very low ridge, and make a very steep but short ascent, 200 yards to a junction. Here, a ¼-mile-long alternate route leads east to Carson Falls before turning south and rejoining the main route. Since both routes are equally strenuous, the more scenic Carson Falls Trail is certainly recommended.

Midway along this short trail you'll descend briefly to almost level granitic slabs near the lip of the river's gorge. Take your pack off here and then *cautiously* explore the falls and pools of the gorge. Over a period of thousands of years large potholes have been drilled into the bedrock as strong currents have swirled large boulders round and round. When the river's water is low, some potholes make brisk, invigorating swimming holes. If you climb to the top of an almost isolated granitic mass just downstream, you can get the best view of the main falls.

After the Carson Falls Trail rejoins the main trail, we walk through a flat that is being "logged out" by beavers. Entering an aspen grove at the edge of this flat, we curve southeast along a granitic base just above the sometimes swampy flat, and soon reach a ford of the East Carson. If you don't find any dry logs, cross at a wide, shallow place just downstream. A short ½-mile farther, where the river—trapped in a small gorge—turns abruptly west, we leave its company and hike up-canyon to a junction with the Golden Canyon Trail. From the junction our route curves southeast and quickly becomes a steep, brushy climb 400 vertical feet to the top of a granitic mass that has withstood repeated efforts of past glaciers to eradicate it. Leaving its southeast end, our route rollercoasters for ½ mile and touches upon a river meander just before it starts a fairly long climb.

This winding climb crosses a few creek beds before going south up the gully of a north-flowing seasonal creek. Beyond the top of the gully, junipers together with Jeffrey, lodgepole and western white pines are momentarily left behind as we descend into a shady red-fir forest, home of the red squirrel, or chickaree. Our path levels off at a year-round creek and beyond it we parallel the East Carson— usually at a small distance—for 3 miles upstream. The shady path crosses many creeklets as it progresses gently to moderately up-canyon, and along the way one has glimpses of the high cliffs along the canyon's east side.

At the south end of the cliffs, a descending ridge forces our route across the East Carson, which can be a slippery and wet ford in early and mid season. On the west bank, we hike south and in about 150 yards arrive at a junction with the Pacific Crest Trail. One mile from the PCT junction we cross the path of a recent avalanche which built up so much force on its descent of the west slope that it swept across the snow-covered East Carson River and knocked down trees on the east slope.

Beyond a second avalanche path we enter a forest of mature lodgepole pines and in it see more evidence of glaciation. Here, erratics—boulders transported by a glacier—were left behind as the glacier melted back some 12,000 years ago. The glacier that left these erratics was perhaps only 2½ miles long, a midget compared with the massive giant that flowed 19 miles down-canyon perhaps 60,000 years ago. The granitic bedrock over which the more recent one flowed is polished smooth and remains little changed from the day the glacier left it.

A ⅔-mile walk leads to a crossing of a permanent stream, tricky in early season. Then the trail's gradient increases noticeably. Unfortunately, when we sight the windswept saddle we're puffing up to, there is still ⅔ mile of climbing—now up a steep gradient—ahead. Whitebark pines and even late-season snow patches become evident as we make the final push. Finally struggling up to the 10,240-foot-high saddle, we take a well earned rest to pause and admire the view down the glaciated, U-shaped canyon of East Fork Carson River.

From the saddle, the Pacific Crest Trail leads southwest along Sonora Peak's northeast slopes, but this day's hike ends by descending ⅓ mile south to campsites at the west edge of the grassy, frog-inhabited meadow that contains shallow Wolf Creek Lake. A post marks the start of the ducked path down to the lake. In 200 yards along it you'll see the lake, and can take one of several ducked routes down a moderately deep slope to it. At 10,090 feet, the lake is usually pretty cold for swimming, and fishing would yield only frogs. The lake's serene setting, however, renews one's spirit, and while relaxing, you may be fortunate enough to see a large marsh hawk glide across the meadow.

3rd Hiking Day (Wolf Creek Lake to Sonora Pass, 5 miles): After retracing the steps back to the saddle, we follow the Pacific Crest Trail south. Winding among fractured granitic blocks, we reach a steep, conspicuous ramp. The ramp, unfortunately, is narrow, leaving the trail pitifully small latitude to switchback up it, and snow can obscure parts of this climb well into August. Emerging from it, we encounter two creeklets on a slope covered with wind-cropped willows. View-seekers wishing to climb Sonora Peak can leave the trail here for a stiff but technically easy 1000-foot climb up to its lofty, dark summit.

Granitic bedrock gives way to volcanic rocks and talus as we now traverse south along the east slopes of Sonora Peak. Along this easy stretch one can see how the whitebark pines have been reduced to shrub height by winter's freezing winds. To the east, the effects of glaciation are evident in Wolf Creek canyon, but they are negligible in the distant Sweetwater Mountains. At times, you may see camouflaged U.S. Marines from the nearby Mountain Warfare Training Center. In the field from May through October, these troops participate in war games in an area that includes the Sonora Peak environs, Wolf Creek canyon and Silver Creek canyon. From the saddle southeast of Sonora Peak, the high peaks on the Yosemite border are seen on the distant southeast horizon.

Our trail, now well graded, winds in and out of bleak gullies before coming to the tops of a conspicuous group of volcanic pinnacles that sit right on the Alpine-Mono county line. A 30-yard scramble south to one of their summits permits a sweeping panorama, north-to-east-to-south, of the Pacific Crest Trail and the slopes it traverses, and it also provides a panorama of the Sierra peak summits in the south.

More gullies lie ahead as we descend west. In ½ mile we reach a ridge and double back eastward. Then, hiking south near the crest, we again cross many gullies, so typical of this eroded volcanic landscape. Several of them have good water all year. The sunny slopes between are coated with sagebrush, mule ears, creambush, and a scattering of lodgepole and whitebark pines. Overhead, Clark nutcrackers flap and caw, and red-tailed hawks wheel and soar. Finally, we descend gently to a Pacific Crest Trail parking lot just north of where Highway 108 crosses Sonora Pass.

Wolf Creek Meadows to Poison Lake **14**

Distance	36.5 miles
Type	Semiloop trip
Best season	Mid
Topo maps	Wolf Creek, Coleville, Disaster Peak, Lost Cannon Peak

Grade (hiking days/recommended layover days)

Leisurely	5/1
Moderate	4/0
Strenuous	2/0
Trailhead	Wolf Creek Meadows (7)

HIGHLIGHTS Good fishing and swimming await hikers who backpack into Poison Lake. Along the way, they'll obtain numerous panoramas of large, glaciated canyons and visit several carbonate and soda springs.

DESCRIPTION (Moderate trip)

1st Hiking Day: Follow Trip 11 to Soda Springs Guard Station, 9.5 miles.

2nd Hiking Day (Soda Springs Guard Station to Poison Lake, 8 miles): From the campsites at Soda Springs Guard Station, we head north on the trail we hiked in on. In ¼ mile we arrive at a signed junction with the Poison Flat Trail. This trail we follow north as it hugs the east edge of Dumonts Meadows and then begins to climb above the canyon floor. Behind us, the west wall of the East Carson canyon becomes ever more impressive as we climb moderately to steeply up to a ridge just north of Poison Flat creek. From the ridge, we head east up toward a small exfoliating dome that at first resembles those of Yosemite, but closer up is seen to be volcanic.

Our trail's gradient eases off as it passes the dome and comes to a signed spur trail to Soda Cone, which is about 100 yards away on the south bank of Poison Flat creek.

The conifer-lined meadow that we follow beyond the Soda Cone spur trail is often inhabited by cattle, which give Poison Flat creek a disagreeable taste and odor. The hike through the meadow is an easy one up to a low, shady divide. Then, under the canopy of the forest's edge, we parallel the south side of the meadow eastward, cross an aspen-lined gully, and come to a barbed-wire gate, then another. Immediately beyond, we reach the signed Poison Lake Trail. Travelers who are hiking this trip at a very leisurely pace may want to descend 100 yards on the Silver King Trail to a junction with the Driveway Trail, near Silver King Creek. Between this junction and a crossing 300 yards upstream you can find many good, shady, creekside campsites beneath lodgepole pines. Along this creekside route Trip 15 descends before turning east up the Driveway Trail.

Our trail up to Poison Lake starts steeply, then eases as it climbs up to a ridgecrest. It stays on or near the ridge for about a mile. Where the ridge ends at the base of a steep slope, we climb steeply southwest to a minor ridge that provides a major, sweeping view of rounded hills in the north, granitic cliffs in the east, Silver King canyon in the south, and the ragged Sierra crest in the southwest. From the ridge our trail continues to climb through thick brush. Soon, short, very steep switchbacks lead up into the forest's shade once again, and the gradient becomes pleasant.

Another climb leads to a small, rocky flat, dense with sagebrush and bitterbrush, from whose south end we can look up-canyon into Lower Fish Valley, Upper Fish Valley and Fourmile Canyon. From the flat our trail makes an undulating traverse west toward a small canyon and nearly reaches it at its top. Here the trail turns northwest and goes past several meadows before leveling off on a broad ridge above Poison Lake. A short, steep descent down this ridge leads to the lake's willow-clad south shore. Good campsites lie under lodgepoles and hemlocks on its northwest shore and fishing is good for brook trout.

3rd Hiking Day: Retrace your steps to Soda Springs Guard Station, 8 miles.

4th Hiking Day: Follow the 2nd hiking day of Trip 11, 11 miles.

Rodriguez Flat to Lower Fish Valley 15

Distance	14 miles
Type	Semiloop
Best season	Mid or late
Topo maps	Coleville, Lost Cannon Peak
Grade	(hiking days/recommended layover days)
Leisurely	2/1
Moderate	2/0
Strenuous	——
Trailhead	Rodriguez Flat (12)

HIGHLIGHTS   A fine weekend selection, this two-day trip visits five subalpine valleys. The country traversed contains some of the largest Sierra junipers to be found anywhere. In addition, over half a dozen side trips can be made from the Silver King Trail.

DESCRIPTION

1st Hiking Day (Rodriguez Flat to Lower Fish Valley, 7.5 miles): Our trail, the Snodgrass Canyon-Fish Valley Trail, makes a moderate climb southwest and shortly passes two trails from the Little Antelope Pack Station. A forest cover of white fir, western white pine and lodgepole pine persists for the next ⅓ mile of steep ascent, then yields to sagebrush as the old, metamorphosed sediments of Rodriguez Flat give way to much younger volcanic rocks. The view here is quite spectacular, and on a clear day you can see desert ranges northeast well beyond broad, open Rodriguez Flat.

The short, open ascent soon curves around the base of a volcanic hill and gives us new views—of Slinkard Valley below in the north, and the Sierra crest in the northwest. A traverse across broad, gentle, sagebrush-covered slopes leads to a signed junction, at which the Driveway Trail—our returning route—forks right (southwest). Our trail, the smaller of the two, soon passes through a fence gate and descends moderately past sagebrush and bitterbrush to the well-used grazing lands of spacious Corral Valley. On the valley floor, we cross two branches of Corral Valley Creek. The north branch, which drains the area most used by cattle, tends to be muddy, but the south branch, which drains more-forested slopes, looks better. In it you'll see paiute trout, which, like those in Coyote Valley and upper Silver King Creek, are an endangered and protected species. Please, no fishing here!

Beyond Corral Valley Creek, our southbound trail goes into the forest, curves west, parallels the valley a short distance, and then climbs an ever-increasing slope up to a dry saddle. From here the descent into Coyote Valley is a steep one, but it is made easy by the cushioning effect of the deep gravel. Near the bottom of a gully, the trail crosses a seasonal creek and goes but a short distance southeast before coming to an enormous, two-trunked juniper. With a diameter of 12 feet and a girth of 36, this specimen just might be the largest juniper in the Sierra. Beyond it, our trail winds south down toward Coyote Valley, reaching its sagebrush-covered floor beside a large, five-foot-diameter lodgepole (the key landmark to look for if you're hiking this trail in the opposite direction).

On the valley floor we walk a level ¼ mile to an easy ford of Coyote Valley Creek. Beyond the ford, the trail veers away from the creek and gradually climbs south. Near the crest above Upper Fish Valley, the forest becomes more dense and the aspens more domi- nant. At the crest's broad saddle a fence greets us, and from its gate we descend, usually past grazing cattle, steeply down to Upper Fish Valley. On the valley floor, a signed trail junction lies near a tall, orange snow-depth marker. Our trip proceeds north about 300 yards beyond the junction to a meeting of three fences, each with its own gate. Go through the north gate and follow the path that parallels the west side of the north-northeast-heading fence. Our trail soon starts to curve northwest, climbs over a low moraine left by a retreating glacier, and then comes to within hearing range of unseen Llewellyn Falls, just southwest of us. Let your ears direct you to this significant 20-foot-high cascade.

Llewellyn Falls creates a barrier trout cannot get over. As a giant glacier slowly retreated up Silver King Canyon, perhaps 50,000 years ago, cutthroat trout followed its path. They were able to swim into Upper Fish Valley and higher valleys before Silver King Creek eroded away bedrock to form the falls. Once isolated, they evolved into a subspecies known as the paiute cutthroat trout (*Salmo clarki seleniris*), or simply paiute trout. These trout became endangered not through overfishing but rather through the introduction of Lahontan cutthroats and rainbows, which then bred with the paiutes to form hybrids. Once this miscegenation was discovered, Fish and Game workers removed purebreds and in 1964 treated Silver King Creek with rotenone to kill the hybrids. After the purebreds were reintroduced above the falls, their numbers grew from about 150 in the late 1960s to about 600 in the early 1970s. By 1975 the population had changed very little more, and it appears to be stable. Fishing, nevertheless, is strictly prohibited, for the paiute trout could be easily fished out of existence.

From Llewellyn Falls gorge, our trail descends briefly northeast into Lower Fish Valley. The trail approaches Silver King Creek several times before reaching the north end of this overgrazed grassland, where you can cross the creek (wet in early season) and camp among the trees wherever people and cattle have not made too much of a mess. Fishing along Silver King Creek is good-to-excellent for rainbow, paiute and rainbow-paiute hybrid (to 9").

2nd Hiking Day (Lower Fish Valley to Rodriguez Flat, 6.5 miles): Continuing downstream, we walk northwest toward a low ridge that hides the forested, little-visited valley of Tamarack Creek. Our path leaves Lower Fish Valley, turns northeast and climbs a low granitic saddle before entering the south end of Long Valley. To avoid springs and boggy meadows, take the trail that circles around the valley's east side. Partway down the flat valley, the trails join and then approach Silver King Creek. This creek meanders lazily through the glacial sediments that long ago buried its canyon's bedrock floor, and our trail approaches several of these meanders before leaving the valley's north end.

Following Silver King Creek, our trail passes its confluence with Tamarack Creek. After ½ mile of easy, shaded descent along the creek, we ford it about where granite outcrops force the trail to the north bank (wet in early season). About 200 yards downstream we meet the Driveway Trail near a large gate.

Our route then descends to cross Silver King Creek just below its confluence with Corral Valley Creek (wet in early season). Climbing steeply, we ascend a brush-covered slope where the thin soil supports only a few scattered junipers for shade. Soon the grade eases to moderate and then gentle, and after 2½ miles we reach a junction with the Snodgrass Canyon-Fish Valley Trail, from where we retrace the first part of the previous hiking day. Before hiking the last mile along this familiar trail back to the trailhead, stop and look at the oversized cairn just before this junction. Built seven feet high by careful hands, this cairn stands as a monument to the loneliness of the Basque shepherds who once tended flocks in the area. Called *arri mutillak*, or "stone boys," monuments like this were built by lonely shepherds for lack of any other way to pass the time. Today, hikers *seek* to be alone and *look* for places of solitude in this east Sierra landscape.

16 Rodriguez Flat to Ebbetts Pass

Distance	34 miles
Type	Shuttle trip
Best season	Mid
Topo maps	Coleville, Lost Cannon Peak, Disaster Peak, Dardanelles Cone, Ebbetts Pass, Wolf Creek

Grade (hiking days/recommended layover days)

Leisurely	5/1
Moderate	4/0
Strenuous	3/0

Trailhead	Rodriguez Flat (12), Ebbetts Pass (8)

HIGHLIGHTS   Ridges and canyons east of the Sierra crest wait to be explored along this scenic route. You'll encounter mammoth junipers, a rare trout, soda and carbonate springs, diverse scenery and good fishing. The last 11 miles are along the famous, ridge-hugging Pacific Crest Trail.

DESCRIPTION (Moderate trip)

1st Hiking Day: Follow Trip 15 to Lower Fish Valley, 7.5 miles.

2nd Hiking Day (Lower Fish Valley to Murray Canyon Trail junction. 9.5 miles): Follow the 2nd hiking day, Trip 15, to the Driveway Trail junction and walk 100 yards up the Silver King Trail to the Poison Lake Trail junction. From it, reverse the steps of the first half of the 2nd hiking day, Trip 14, to Soda Springs Guard Station, and then follow the 1st hiking day, Trip 12, to the Murray Canyon Trail Junction.

3rd Hiking Day (Murray Canyon Trail to Asa Lake, 10 miles): Follow the first part of the 2nd hiking day, Trip 12, up Murray Canyon to the crest junction. Our trail starts southeast from the crest, crosses a pebbly flat, and then returns to the crest to follow it a short distance. Through the thinning forest we see Highland Peak and other volcanic summits to the northwest, and in the southwest are the volcanic cliffs of Arnot Peak. Our trail soon leaves the crest and then contours ½ mile south across a brushy slope to a saddle just north of a low knoll. We cross the saddle, descend southeast, and gradually curve southwest through lodgepole forest over toward a grassy meadow south of the knoll. At the east end of this meadow our trail disappears, but you'll find it again at the west end. From here, you can look down across a large, open bowl. Our route, very vague, starts southwest down into the bowl, contours south just below the forest's edge, and then climbs southeast toward a saddle on the southwest side of a very prominent summit of highly broken volcanic rock. Just before the saddle, you'll reach a new segment of the Pacific Crest Trail.

Choosing the Pacific Crest Trail at the junction, we descend northwest along the west side of the bowl. As the bowl gives way to steeper slopes, the PCT circles west around a ridge, descends southwest, and momentarily enters and then leaves a small but deep side canyon before reaching the slightly cloudy east fork of Wolf Creek, flowing down a wide, rocky wash. The cloudy color is due to fine volcanic sediments suspended in the water. A ⅓-mile traverse west past caves and fingers of a cliff of deeply eroded volcanic deposits gets us to the wide, silty middle fork of Wolf Creek.

Leaving this stream, we curve west briefly, then climb steadily northwest up to several branches of the west fork of Wolf Creek. The Pacific Crest Trail climbs north up a slope just beyond the main, east-flowing branch, switchbacks west, and climbs more steeply through a thinning forest. Rather than traversing west to a forested saddle, our trail continues to climb northwest above its east end—a route designed to avoid cattle-grazing lands on the other side. On reaching the west slopes of summit 8960+, we diagonal northwest down them, then curve north down to a small, flat saddle that lies at the base of the summit's northwest ridge. Here, it is important that you not continue north and cross the saddle. Rather, head west down a small gully, then parallel a low ridge, staying on its southwest side. A large cow meadow will quickly appear below you, and you'll almost touch it just before reaching a small gorge. The meadow's creek joyfully cascades down the resistant, volcanic end of the gorge, then flows out into Lower Gardner Meadow. The Pacific Crest Trail descends to a jeep road at the east end of this meadow, and on this road Trip 15 parallels the creek westward. At this junction, situated on a broad, low ridge known as Wolf Creek Pass, the road curves north immediately into a grassy, boggy meadow.

From the jeep road, the Pacific Crest Trail climbs northwest up a low ridgecrest, then curves north above the boggy meadow. The trail crosses the old Asa Creek Trail, then in ¼ mile arrives at a small pond just southeast of unseen Asa Lake. A minute's walk upstream off trail from the pond leads to the lake's east shore, where it is apparent why this small lake stays full and clear even in late summer: refreshing springs rush from the volcanic rocks above its east shore, and with the aid of a canal, their water is continually channeled into the lake. Under shady red firs above its northeast shore are some good campsites, and brook trout await the skillful—or lucky—angler.

4th Hiking Day (Asa Lake to Ebbetts Pass, 7 miles): Get back on the Pacific Crest Trail by walking about 150 yards up-slope from Asa Lake's northeast corner. Once on the trail, follow it moderately to steeply up around a ridge, then through a small cove shaded by red firs. On the climb out of the cove, the forest of hemlocks and pines gives way to sagebrush as the trail traverses northwest toward a saddle. Tryon Peak looms ahead, and in the southwest, the large, popular Highland Lakes stand out clearly in their broad, glaciated canyon. At the often windy saddle we encounter whitebark pines, which, better than any other conifer in this area, thrive in the harsh winter climate of this high elevation (9300′).

We cross a crest-line fence, then follow a descending path that diagonals through tight clusters of whitebark pines and mountain hemlocks before crossing the willow-lined headwaters of Noble Creek to intersect the faint Noble Canyon Trail. Beyond this intersection the Pacific Crest Trail skirts above the east edge of a meadow and descends gradually southwest. Then our route curves north to a low saddle above the southwest corner of Noble Lake. Staying high above the lake, the route curves northwest across a low ridge. The trail here is vague over the next hundred yards. It quickly dies out, but can be found again on the east side of the small gully immediately below. From the gully, the trail curves east to Noble Lake's outlet creek, crossing it about 200 yards below the lake. Now the obvious trail heads north and soon switchbacks down a bizarre landscape of eroded, broken-up, *autobrecciated* lava flows (see Trip 11) that support only a few hardy junipers. We recross Noble Lake's creek, head west briefly to a ridge of glacial sediments, and follow it north ¼ mile to a fork. Here, just east of the ridge crest, the Noble Canyon Trail leaves the PCT.

The PCT rounds the ridge, descends to the bouldery main arm of Noble Creek, and begins a traverse northwest. After ⅓ mile it starts climbing in earnest and momentarily leaves volcanic rock behind as it approaches granitic knobs atop a northeast-trending ridge. Our trail climbs north to the ridge's crest, curves around one knob back to the crest again, and then starts southeast around a second knob. At its south side we cross the crest for good and commence a winding traverse west along the base of some impressive, deeply eroded, volcanic cliffs. Northeast across Noble Canyon is Silver Peak (10,774′), site of hectic mining activity beginning in 1863.

A brief climb north leads to the top of another northeast-trending ridge, this one just east of State Highway 4. Then a ¼-mile descent southwest from it brings the hiker to a junction, from which the PCT winds ⅓ mile southwest to a crossing of State Highway 4 only 200 yards north of Ebbetts Pass. From the junction, our route leads north and descends a spur trail ¼ mile to the Pacific Crest Trail parking lot.

Noble Canyon from above Noble Lake

17 Rodriguez Flat to Lake Alpine

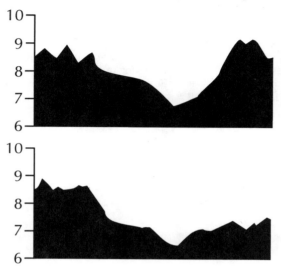

Distance	49 miles
Type	Shuttle trip
Best season	Mid or late
Topo maps	Coleville, Lost Cannon Peak, Wolf Creek, Disaster Peak, Dardanelles Cone, Pacific Valley, Spicer Meadows Res.

Grade (hiking days/recommended layover days)

Leisurely	8/2
Moderate	6/1
Strenuous	4/0
Trailhead	Rodriguez Flat (12), Lake Alpine (11)

HIGHLIGHTS   This exciting route traverses several major Sierra ridges along its westward course. As you progress west, the vegetation changes dramatically, sagebrush and juniper giving way to dense forests of pine and fir. Sections of two famous trails are hiked along this route: first, the 2600-mile-long Pacific Crest Trail, then later, the 180-mile-long Tahoe-Yosemite Trail.

DESCRIPTION (Moderate trip)

1st, 2nd and 3rd Hiking Days: Follow Trip 16 to Asa Lake, 27 miles.

4th Hiking Day (Asa Lake to Hiram Meadow, 9 miles): From Asa Lake, retrace your steps ½ mile south down the Pacific Crest Trail to the jeep road at Wolf Creek Pass. This road we take ½ mile west, following a creek through spacious, cow-inhabited Lower Gardner Meadow. Leaving the creek we traverse southwest across undulating country for another ½ mile to a north-flowing creek. In 150 yards we reach a signed fork, then turn northwest, and wind ¼ mile up to a gap, 100 yards beyond which our road is joined by a faint trail from Upper Gardner Meadow. In another 80 yards, this trail resumes its course, veering left. We follow it northwest ¼ mile up to a low crest, on which we cross a north-leading jeep road. From this junction the hiker will follow the trail about 200 yards to a reunion with the road 70 yards before a creek crossing. Draining lower Highland Lake, this creek can be a wet ford in early season. A trailhead parking lot is seen just above the west bank, and from it our road curves west 100 yards to the Highland Lake Road.

Wide, level Highland Lake Road contours around the west shore of lower Highland Lake, popular with fishermen for its population of brook trout. Beyond the lake, our road climbs gradually to Highland Lakes Campground, just north of the upper lake, which is divided into two camps. Backpackers will usually find quieter sites in the camp at the end of a short, eastbound spur road.

At the far end of upper Highland Lake the road ends and the well-signed Highland Creek Trail to Lake Alpine begins with a steep descent along the lake's outlet creek, then bends more westward away from it. Beyond a small knoll on the left, we descend west ½ mile down a steep, winding trail, passing a small gorge before we reach upper Highland Lake's outlet creek. In early season large boulders just downstream will make the crossing a dry one. Heading south, we pass through two small meadows, each with an abundant garden of corn lilies, then in ¼ mile approach an unnamed creek.

We follow the creek ¼ mile downstream, cross it near its union with Highland Creek, and in another ¼ mile come to a good campsite, under large cottonwoods, on the east bank of Highland Creek. At times, logs placed by hikers make this wide-creek crossing a dry one, but if you are here before mid-July, you can expect to wade. Then we round the base of a granitic ridge, enter a lodgepole flat, traverse the west side of a damp meadow, and return to forest cover as the trail and the nearby creek both bend south. In this part of the canyon, Highland Creek has several shallow pools that are ideal for a quick bath.

Our trail soon reaches a second ford of Highland Creek—just as wide as the first and a little deeper. Once across, we veer away from the creek on a minor climb, then descend to the stream that drains

Champion Canyon. Its ford is an easy one, and on a moderately descending trail we head down to the sunny flats of Hiram Meadow. Only 80 yards south of Highland Creek's union with Weiser Creek is a third, usually wet ford of the former.

Late-season hikers will note that this ford is a wet ford long after most Sierra snow has melted. This is because Highland Creek canyon and its tributary canyons have abundant volcanic sediments that act as a reservoir to hold water well into September. Good campsites lie across the ford on the west bank.

5th Hiking Day (Hiram Meadow to Rock Lake, 8.5 miles): About 100 yards west of the Highland Creek ford is a junction with the Weiser Trail. At the start of the deer-hunting season on the last weekend of September, hunters will descend this trail on motor-cycles, bringing noise and pollution with them. Plan accordingly. From the junction we hike west across wide, flat Hiram Meadow, re-enter lodgepole cover, and quickly arrive at a cabin. Our path turns southwest, soon reaches willow-lined Highland Creek, and then crosses some low knolls of highly fractured, fine-grained igneous rock. One mile southwest of Hiram Meadow the Highland Creek Trail briefly climbs away from the creek just before it turns south and cascades down a sizable gorge. Our trail parallels the watercourse at a distance as we descend steeply to a junction with the Woods Gulch Trail. This trail east—part of the Tahoe-Yosemite Trail—crosses Highland Creek in 60 yards, just north of its union with the creek from Jenkins Canyon. Westward, the next 13-mile stretch of the Tahoe-Yosemite Trail coincides with the Highland Creek Trail.

Leaving the junction, our route turns west and in a few minutes brings us beside some small, lovely Highland Creek pools. We follow the creek only momentarily, then gradually veer away and climb up a brushy, granitic slope to an open forest of Jeffrey pines. In it, we descend quickly to a shady flat from which our trail descends moderately to the canyon bottom, where we cross a usually trickling creek that originates in a small, shallow lake northwest of Hiram Meadow. Traversing around the east shore of this lake is the Bull Run Creek Trail, which we meet only ¼ mile west of the trickling creek. Although motor vehicles are allowed on this trail, few successfully make it up or down due to its excessively steep, very sandy nature. In 100 yards we cross refreshing Bull Run Creek, shaded by cottonwoods and white firs.

Now our route is on a trail segment built above the shore of the new Spicer Meadow Reservoir, which drowned Gabbott Meadow. Soon the trail climbs steeply northwest, but then turns southwest and almost levels off, giving one a chance to catch one's breath on the traverse through a shady forest of white fir and Jeffrey pine. Emerging from the forest, we begin to climb steeply again, this time up brushy slopes to a small gap in the granitic bedrock.

Almost immediately, we pass through a second gap, then start a short traverse southwest, from which we can admire the dark, volcanic formations called the Dardanelles. This monumental ridge, composed of lava hundreds of feet thick, is only a small remnant of a long lava flow that originated near Bridgeport, California, about nine million years ago. From that source it flowed about *100 miles* down-canyon, stopping at the western edge of the Sierra foothills. In the ensuing millions of years, the walls of the canyon it flowed down were eroded away while the canyon bottom it buried was preserved beneath the flow. Two million years of glacial attacks further eroded the Dardanelles landscape until the granitic floor of Highland Creek lay a good 1000 feet below the base of the Dardanelles. We can expect future glaciers to excavate Highland Creek's canyon even more. Visible up-canyon are Iceberg, Airola and Hiram peaks—all with volcanic summits but none of them related to the Dardanelles flow.

Crossing the crest, which stands 550 feet above Highland Creek, we hike southwest just west of the crest. That the last Highland Creek glacier was *at least* as thick as the crest is high is obvious from the fresh polish it gave the granitic bedrock here. The glacier was, in fact, about 1300 feet thick. At a point where one could head south cross-country 1 mile down to Highland Creek, our trail turns northwest and climbs to a glaciated saddle. Then, midway along the mile-long rollercoaster path to Wilderness Creek, we cross one of its tributaries. The ford of Wilderness Creek is difficult in early season, but the stream disappears in late season. Beyond this creek our trail passes the Sand Flat Trail, climbs north to a gravelly, barren flat, and then briefly parallels Wilderness Creek. Continuing a moderate-to-easy climb north, we reach the east end of Rock Lake in ¾ mile. Grassy and unappealing at this end, Rock Lake provides good swimming and fishing (brook trout) near its southwest end. Along its south shore are several forested campsites.

6th Hiking Day (Rock Lake to Lake Alpine, 4.5 miles): From the lake's end, our route starts northwest along the old Highland Lake Trail, and then, just out of sight of the lake, turns northeast and follows a new tread ¼ mile up a granitic ridge. Then, from the slightly higher main ridge, we curve north, cross a small, dry wash, and descend to a flat ¼ mile east of North Fork Stanislaus River. From it, a short climb north and then a steep descent bring us to the river (difficult ford in early season).

Beyond this ford we climb steeply northwest to cross a ridge, and then wind ½ mile down glacier-polished slabs to a large, forested flat with a trail junction. From here the old trail goes 1¼ miles west past the south shore of Duck Lake to a cabin-side junction with a jeep road. Through July and part of August the mosquitoes along this swampy route are almost unbearable. Turning right on the new trail, we immediately cross a creek, and wind west along the north edge of this forested flat. When the trail reaches a point about 200 yards north of Duck Lake, it abruptly turns north and climbs up a ridge. After 300 yards it turns abruptly west and then climbs more moderately ⅓ mile west up to a switchback in the jeep road that ascends northward from the Duck Lake basin. On this closed road we climb west briefly up to a saddle, pass through a gate, follow the crest southwest, and then descend ½ mile to the trailhead at the east end of Lake Alpine's Silver Valley Campground.

Rock Lake has good fishing and swimming

Sonora Pass

Southward from Tahoe, each highway pass over the Sierra crest is higher than the previous ones, and at Sonora Pass we are 9643 feet above sea level. Whatever the altitude, the scenery is magnificent. The volcanic reds and browns of Sonora Peak, Leavitt Peak, and Relief Peak contrast with the bright granite of Whitecliff Peak, Forsyth Peak and Tower Peak, and all over the area we find places where volcanic rocks and igneous rocks have collided.

The 117,596 acres of Emigrant Wilderness extend from the northern boundary of Yosemite National Park, north almost to California State Route 108. The eastern boundary abuts the Sierra Crest. Unlike the high, rugged, steep mountains and bare granite of Yosemite, Emigrant Wilderness offers the hiker gentle forested slopes at lower, less weather-beaten altitudes. Lakes and streams are more closely spaced here than anywhere else in the Sierra, offering the hiker legendary fishing, postcard photographs, and potential solitude, with an extraordinary abundance of wildlife, wildflowers—and mosquitoes.

Just east of the Sierra crest is a large area of *de facto* wilderness in the drainage of the West Walker River which some day, we hope, will be given wilderness status by Congress as an addition to either Emigrant Wilderness or Hoover Wilderness.

From State Route 108, we describe three trailheads which access Emigrant Wilderness. From west to east, these are Gianelli Cabin and Crabtree Camp, near the town of Pinecrest, and Kennedy Meadow. From each trailhead, a wealth of trails provides a large number of out-and-back and semiloop trips, lasting from a day or two to the entire summer. Further, the three trailheads are interconnected, so that longer shuttle trips also allow you to explore the myriad lakes along the way. Of the nearly infinite number of possible trips, we describe 16. Their length is arbitrary—you can easily add or subtract a lake or two. The gentle terrain and the abundance of lakes invite you to design your own trip.

Three main routes run west-to-east from Gianelli Cabin and

Crabtree Camp to the cluster of Deer, Buck, and Wood lakes and their neighbors. The most northern and most beautiful route originates from Gianelli Cabin (see Trips 22, 23, 25, 26, 27), passes granitic Powell Lake, visits lovely Whitesides Meadow, and then veers south to Deer Lake at 16 miles. A close second in beauty but considerably more direct route begins at Crabtree Camp (see Trip 24), passes Camp Lake, exciting Lily Pond Lake, and Gem and Jewelry lakes to reach Deer Lake at 11.3 miles. The third path, lowest in elevation and most southern, also originates at Crabtree Camp, but follows Buck Meadow Creek in its canyon. The first two routes are described in detail. There are multiple connections among all three, as well as countless side trips to lakes and peaks from each of them.

Several routes from the north also access the cluster of Deer-Buck-Wood lakes, starting from the Kennedy Meadows trailhead. The most direct passes through lower and upper Relief valleys and joins the Gianelli Cabin Trail at Salt Lick Meadow just north of Deer Lake. A somewhat longer route follows the Summit Creek Trail and turns south at Lunch Meadow to Emigrant Lake, the largest lake in the Wilderness. From there the route goes west into the Deer-Buck-Wood cluster of lakes. A third route, exploring the most elevated and eastern end of the Wilderness, follows the Summit Creek trail through Brown Bear Pass to Emigrant Meadow Lake. From there you can travel to Emigrant Lake and the Deer-Buck-Wood cluster. The second and third of these routes from Kennedy Meadow are described in detail (Trips 19, 20).

If you are planning a Pinecrest shuttle trip, we recommend that you begin at Gianelli Cabin and end at Crabtree Camp: over the many ups and downs of your trek, you will gradually descend (rather than ascend) 1400 feet. Similarly, if you choose the longer shuttle between Kennedy Meadow and Gianelli Cabin or Crabtree Camp, begin in the east—high—and end in the west.

Considering the altitude, it would be well to spend a night before hiking at a campground or at a resort such as Kennedy Meadows, to allow your red-blood count to increase. Have fun!

Kennedy Meadow to Summit Creek

18

Distance	13.6 miles
Type	Out and back trip
Best season	Early or mid
Topo maps	Sonora Pass, Emigrant Lake

Grade (hiking days/recommended layover days)

Leisurely	3/0
Moderate	2/0
Strenuous	Day
Trailhead	Kennedy Meadow (13)

HIGHLIGHTS   A part of this route follows the historic Emigrant Trail used by the pioneers in crossing the Sierra from the area around Bridgeport to Columbia and points west. Relief Peak was a major landmark for these early travelers, and the terminus of this trip lies in this unusual formation's shadow. The scenery along the way is an absorbing study in glacial and volcanic terrain. The route from Kennedy Meadow to Emigrant Meadow Lake (Trip 19) receives very heavy packer use.

DESCRIPTION (Moderate trip)

1st Hiking Day (Kennedy Meadow to Summit Creek, 6.8 miles): The trailhead (6400′) is located alongside Middle Fork Stanislaus River at Kennedy Meadows Resort. Amid a dense forest cover of Jeffrey pine, incense-cedar, sugar pine, juniper and white fir, the trail crosses a small ridge to Kennedy Meadow itself and skirts the east side of the meadow, offering sweeping views of the lush grasslands. Beyond the meadow, the trail crosses the river on a footbridge to reach a junction where a use trail branches right and your main trail curves southeast along the base of a handsome granite dome. The trail, blasted out of the granite, soon becomes steeper and quite rocky, with views of the infant Middle Fork Stanislaus River, under very sparse forest cover. Look for a series of steep cascades near the point where Kennedy and Summit creeks meet and for more foaming cascades where the trail crosses Summit Creek on another footbridge. Beyond the footbridge there's a false junction, where the left fork is an old, abandoned trail; you take the right fork to stay on the main trail.

The route continues climbing through patchy forest to a junction with the Kennedy Lake Trail: left (east) to Kennedy Lake, right (south) to Relief Reservoir. You go right and soon pass a PG&E dam-maintenance station. Beyond the station, you continue past use trails branching west, and past a rusty old boiler, to a splendid overlook of Relief Reservoir.

Our route then contours high above the east side of Relief Reservoir. The trail section paralleling the shore offers excellent views to the south and west before it descends to the timbered shallow at the Grouse Creek ford. From Grouse Creek, the trail ascends steadily over a series of rocky switchbacks, and then veers southeast to pass the Lower Relief Valley Trail after one mile. Then we begin a steady-to-steep uphill climb as it leaves the shaded riparian zone and enters the brush-covered volcanic rubble above Summit Creek. Near the top of the ascent, the trail passes above a pocket meadow with a campsite. The steady ascent is relieved when the trail drops into the wet little bowl called Saucer Meadow, where there are one or two poor campsites on the meadow's extreme edges.

The section of trail beyond this point was part of a major trans-Sierra route, used during the middle of the 19th century—the Emigrant Trail. With the many-hued volcanic rock of Relief Peak on the left, and white, glaciated granite on the right, the trail climbs along Summit Creek to several fair campsites between 8200 and 8300 feet. Some formerly popular campsites on the creek side of the trail are closed for recovery. Others are still open, and yet more campsites can be found uphill of the trail, in sandy flats among large granite slabs. There are other campsites along the trail from here to Lunch Meadow, including heavily used Sheep Camp (see Trip 19). Fishing along the creek is poor.

2nd Hiking Day: Retrace your steps, 6.8 miles.

Kennedy Meadow to Emigrant Meadow Lake

19

Distance	25.2 miles
Type	Out and back trip
Best season	Mid or late
Topo maps	Sonora Pass, Emigrant Lake
Grade (hiking days/recommended layover days)	
Leisurely	4/1
Moderate	3/0
Strenuous	2/0
Trailhead	Kennedy Meadow (13)

HIGHLIGHTS Scenically, this route splits the terrain into two distinctly different parts. To the north, the basaltic and pumice slopes vividly disclose the vulcan overlay that gives the country its colorful reds and blacks. To the south, in contrast, glaciers have polished the granite into shining mirror slabs.

DESCRIPTION (Leisurely trip)

1st Hiking Day: Follow Trip 18 to Summit Creek, 6.8 miles).

2nd Hiking Day (Summit Creek to Emigrant Meadow Lake, 5.8 miles): Our level trail continues up-canyon on red-fir-dotted slopes for a mile, then makes a rocky 400-foot ascent to a little saddle which is the portal of the hardened camping area called Sheep Camp. The main trail curves away from Sheep Camp, skirting granite outcrops, to meet Summit Creek again and trend eastward past an unnamed meadow with a forested campsite beyond its east end. Leaving timber cover, the trail crosses a pumice slope above huge, multilobed Lunch Meadow. This large meadow is subalpine, dotted with sparse stands of lodgepole and mountain hemlock. At the east end of Lunch

Meadow there is a junction: left (ahead, east) to Emigrant Meadow Lake, right across the creek (south) past a campsite to Emigrant Lake. Go left. North of our trail, red and black volcanic columns thrust up from the otherwise smooth, red, pumice slopes, and punctuate the skyline with their tortured shapes. Directly to the east the traveler can discern the shallow saddle that is Brown Bear Pass.

The trail to the pass is a gradual but steady ascent offering colorfully contrasting views of Granite Dome and Relief Peak to the west. At the summit of Brown Bear Pass (9750'), the grassy expanses of historic Emigrant Meadow begin to present themselves, and the serenity of the view is enhanced by placid tarns.

The trail descends from Brown Bear Pass on a long traverse into a vast, grassy, granite-walled basin. As your route swings around the top of Emigrant Meadow Lake (9407'), you pass a trail to the left to Grizzly Meadow and Snow Lake. This gigantic basin often is swept by gigantic winds. You can find sheltered camping among the boulders and battered trees on the saddle just south of the lake. Exposed, Spartan sites also exist on the rocky knolls to the northeast. Fishing for rainbow (8-13") is good, with a midseason slowdown.

3rd and 4th Hiking Days: Retrace your steps, 12.6 miles.

Looking east from Brown Bear Pass to Emigrant Meadow

Kennedy Meadow to Emigrant Lake **20**

Distance	26.8 miles
Type	Out and back trip
Best season	Mid or late
Topo maps	Sonora Pass, Emigrant Lake

Grade (hiking days/recommended layover days)

Leisurely	4/1
Moderate	3/1
Strenuous	3/0
Trailhead	Kennedy Meadow (13)

HIGHLIGHTS   A long-time favorite of anglers, Emigrant Lake is often used as a base camp for short fishing trips to the numerous lakes that lie close by. This route to Emigrant Lake allows the traveler to take in the geological variety of the country. Lush alpine meadows surrounding isolated melt-off tarns contrast with vast slopes of red pumice and fields of polished granite.

DESCRIPTION (Leisurely trip)

1st Hiking Day: Follow Trip 18 to Summit Creek, 6.8 miles.

2nd Hiking Day (Summit Creek to Emigrant Lake, 6.6 miles): First follow Trip 19 to the trail junction at the east end of Lunch Meadow. Here our route branches right (south), fords Summit Creek, and ascends moderately steeply from 9000 to 9300 feet through a sparse mountain-hemlock cover to a long, low saddle. Views along this segment of trail present a wide range of colors. The superimposed vulcanism of Relief Peak and the ridge to the east are a potpourri of pastel shades of reds, blacks, yellows and ochres. Black Hawk Mountain to the west is granite in varying shades of dun, gray, and buff-brown.

The trail now winds through a long saddle composed of a series of granite fields that are delightfully broken by tiny, wildflower-filled meadows. Many of these meadows are further enhanced by small melt-off tarns. The long, shallow valley on the other side of the saddle contains a tributary of North Fork Cherry Creek. There are excellent views across the Cherry Creek watershed south to Michie and Haystack peaks.

The trail descends on the east side of this tributary for ½ mile and then fords to the west side. (From this ford, the angler may wish to head east cross country to reach Mosquito Lake, which has pink-fleshed rainbow trout.) Continuing down the east bank, we ford a little tributary and then recross the main stream to the west side. As you descend through moderate forest cover, several trails of use lead off to the right to tree-protected campsites well above Emigrant Lake. Our trail descends to the large meadow at the inlet to large (230-acre) Emigrant Lake (8827'). Here we encounter a trail junction. The trail to the left leads upward to Blackbird Lake; we continue straight ahead to the good-to-excellent campsites at the inlet, on the north side, and at the outlet. This popular lake is glacial in character, with a sparse forest cover, and fishing for rainbow (8-18") is good (excellent in early and late season).

3rd and 4th Hiking Days: Retrace your steps, 13.4 miles.

Camp above Emigrant Meadow Lake

Kennedy Meadow to Cow Meadow Lake   **21**

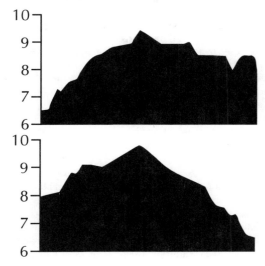

Distance	46 miles
Type	Semiloop trip
Best season	Mid or late
Topo maps	Sonora Pass, Emigrant Lake

Grade (hiking days/recommended layover days)

Leisurely	7/2
Moderate	5/2
Strenuous	4/2
Trailhead	Kennedy Meadow (13)

HIGHLIGHTS   This is a fine choice for a midseason fishing trip, as it circles the lake-dotted Cherry Creek watershed. A day's walking from one or another base camp will permit the fisherman to sample almost 100 lakes. The route tours some of the finest scenery in Emigrant Wilderness, and the gentle terrain is ideal for the beginning backpacker.

DESCRIPTION (Leisurely trip)

1st and 2nd Hiking Days: Follow Trip 20 to Emigrant Lake, 13.4 miles.

3rd Hiking Day (Emigrant Lake to Cow Meadow Lake, 7 miles): From the trail junction at the inlet to Emigrant Lake, we walk along the long, timbered north side of the lake, about 2 miles. In a flat, meadowed spot the trail turns north, away from the lake, pasing a junction with a faint, unmarked and unmaintained trail to Cow Meadow Lake via North Fork Cherry Creek. It then crosses a low, forest-covered saddle and descends through a rich, varied forest of very large trees to ford Buck Meadow Creek. The trail now turns south, and for a mile we traverse the long meadow at the north end of upper Buck Lake (8318'). The trail circles the west side of that lake, passing a trail to Deer Lake, crosses the isthmus separating the two lakes, and follows the east side of lower Buck Lake, often being back in the trees away from the lakeside. Upper Buck Lake is a good-sized (50-acre) glacial lake with numerous excellent campsites around the isthmus and the east shore. Camping is not allowed on the west shore. In late season, deer greatly outnumber campers here. Fishing for rainbow (to 18") is good. Lower Buck Lake is somewhat deeper and rockier, though about the same size, and fishing is usually about the same as at the upper lake. About ¼ mile beyond the south end of Lower Buck Lake at the end of a saddle, the trail passes the Wood Lake lateral. We pass through a gate (please close it) and amid a nice forest cover of lodgepole descend steeply (600') to an unmarked, complex trail junction at North Fork Cherry Creek. Our well-traveled route crosses the creek and at once turns southward (right) toward Cow Meadow Lake. If we turn right before we cross the creek, we are carried down to the west side of the lake. If we bear left, we pick up the poorly maintained, faint trail up to Emigrant Lake. Our route, now level, passes through forest cover along the north side of lovely Cow Meadow Lake (7780'), where there are several excellent, well used campsites. This 55-acre lake is connected by lagoons with overhanging banks. A DF&G dam at the south end keeps the water level fairly constant, and fishing for rainbow and some brook is excellent (8–18"). Angling on the stream above the lake is good.

4th Hiking Day (Cow Meadow Lake to Maxwell Lake, 7.5 miles): From the east side of Cow Meadow Lake, the trail ascends 560 feet via a frequently blasted, usually cobbled trail to a signed trail junction. The main route, marked LOWER HUCKLEBERRY, leads to the right. Your route, HUCKLEBERRY—ROUGH TRAIL, heads left and approaches a western tip of serene, deep Letora Lake (8351'). This 25-acre lake offers only fair angling for brook and rainbow (7–13"). From the west end of Letora Lake this route veers south and then east and descends over a very rough trail to the northeast end of large

(200-acre) Huckleberry Lake (7856'). In late season, large numbers of ducks live among the grasses in the lake. This subalpine lake provides good fishing for brook and rainbow (8-18"), and East Fork Cherry Creek above the lake often provides excellent angling.

From the meadows at the northeast end of Huckleberry, the trail heads upstream and passes a junction with the Lower Huckleberry Trail. Here there are many hardened campsites under moderate forest cover. The route soon fords East Fork Cherry Creek and ascends the canyon. Views of the unusual granite island known as Sachse Monument dominate the northern skyline as the trail passes an abandoned tungsten mine. At this point the trail joins the mining road, and then it refords the stream before passing the Twin Lakes Trail lateral. At the south end of Horse Meadow our trail branches northwest up a timbered slope to 46-acre Maxwell Lake (8662'). This emerald-green gem with a tufty meadow fringe affords excellent angling for brook trout (8-14"). The polished granite of Sachse Monument towers over the south side of this charming lake, and the choice campsites on the north side of the lake have an uninterrupted view of both the lake and the peak.

5th Hiking Day (Maxwell Lake to Emigrant Meadow Lake, 5.5 miles): From Maxwell Lake the trail climbs by a series of switchbacks through a moderate forest cover of lodgepole pine and then winds through a long, rock-lined meadow past several beautiful lakelets to Blackbird Lake (9042'). Excellent camping may be found on all sides of the lake. At the northwest tip of Blackbird Lake the main trail heads west toward Emigrant Lake. Your route, unmarked and hard to find, heads north, then east around the top of the lake past several small tarns that are usually dry by late season. The trail soon becomes faint, since this lateral is unmaintained.

This footpath ascends along the south side of wandering North Fork Cherry Creek for about 1½ miles, and then fords the creek. From the ford onward, the trail is rutted into meadowy turf, but has become overgrown due to lack of maintenance. There are spectacular camping sites along the creek. The trail becomes a little steeper just south of Middle Emigrant Lake, and then levels out at the wet meadows at the foot of the lake. Anglers who wish to try their luck on this fair-sized, granitic lake will find the fishing fair-to-good for rainbow (7-10"). The trail rounds the west side of the lake, fords the inlet stream (this crossing is both difficult in footing and hard to see, as the route is densely willowed), and crosses a low, rocky ridge to the Emigrant Meadow Lake basin (9407'). This huge meadow was the traditional stopping place for emigrant trains on the first leg of their Sierra crossing. While fair, exposed campsites lie on the south

end of Emigrant Meadow Lake, the prudent choice is among the
boulders and stunted trees in the saddle between Middle Emigrant
and Emigrant Meadow lakes. It's a distance from water, but gale
winds occur suddenly and frequently here. Fishing in Emigrant
Meadow Lake is good for rainbow (8–13").

6th and 7th Hiking Days: Reverse the steps of the 2nd and 1st
hiking days of Trip 19, 12.6 miles.

Co-author Jason Winnett fishing in Maxwell Lake

Gianelli Cabin to Y Meadow Lake

22

Distance	10 miles
Type	Out and back trip
Best season	Mid or late
Topo maps	Pinecrest, Cooper Peak
Grade (hiking days/recommended layover days)	
Leisurely	2/0
Moderate	——
Strenuous	Day
Trailhead	Gianelli Cabin (14)

HIGHLIGHTS   Except for the short distance from Gianelli Cabin to Burst Rock, this trip is within beautiful Emigrant Wilderness, and the route parallels a segment of the historic Emigrant Trail. En route to Y Meadow Lake, anglers can try their luck on two small but fairly productive lakes, and early-trip views, from Burst Rock, are panoramic.

DESCRIPTION

1st Hiking Day (Gianelli Cabin to Y Meadow Lake, 5 miles): At Gianelli Cabin (8560'), a hunting cabin dating back to the beginning of the 20th Century—now only part of the log cabin's base remains—the trail begins in a meadow and soon ascends a steep slope covered with red fir and lodgepole and western white pine. After the first mile, the trail follows the mountain spine, and you can look down a thousand feet into the valley below, and perhaps see the remains of a shattered pioneer wagon. The trail tops the ridge at Burst Rock (9161'), a landmark for the old Emigrant Trail, and crosses the Emigrant Wilderness boundary (no motorized vehicles allowed). This vantage point offers excellent views to the north of Liberty Hill, Elephant Rock, the Dardanelles, Castle Rock, and the Three Chimneys. You can see as far as Mt. Lyell on the southeast border of Yosemite Park. As the trail bears east along the ridge, the traveler also has excellent views of the Stanislaus River watershed to the north and the Tuolumne River watershed to the south.

The trail descends gradually to a low saddle overlooking granitic Powell Lake. This small lake offers fair fishing for brook trout in early and late season, and the fine views to the northeast make this an attractive spot for a lunch break. Excellent camping is found among the beautiful boulders and trees surrounding the lake. The trail then crosses a small ridge, descends through a forest of lodge-pole, fir, and mountain hemlock, and arrives at the open stretches of meadowy Lake Valley, which offers a spectacular display of flowers even in late season. A faint fisherman's trail (0.7 mile) to Chewing Gum Lake turns south through the meadow. Anglers with a yen will want to try the fair-to-good fishing for brook on this small (5-acre) lake before continuing. From Lake Valley it is 1½ miles across another broad ridge to the turnoff to Y Meadow Lake. Here our route turns south for one winding mile to the fair campsites at the north end of Y Meadow Lake (8400'). Unfortunately, the water level fluctuates so much that the lake cannot support fish life. However, anglers accustomed to cross-country walking may elect to try the waters of Granite Lake (0.7 mile south) for the good fishing for brook (8–13"). There are some poor-to-fair campsites at Granite Lake.

2nd Hiking Day. Retrace your steps, 5 miles.

Remains of Gianelli Cabin

Gianelli Cabin to Wire Lakes 23

Distance	24.8 miles
Type	Out and back trip
Best season	Mid or late
Topo maps	Pinecrest, Cooper Peak

Grade (hiking days/recommended layover days)

Leisurely	4/1
Moderate	3/0
Strenuous	2/1
Trailhead	Gianelli Cabin (14)

HIGHLIGHTS This round trip penetrates the heart of Emigrant Wilderness as it wends through a delightful series of meadows and over high, open ridges. Wire Lakes, the destination for this trip, is a stepladder set of three memorable high-mountain lakes that afford excellent angling and several fine choices for secluded camping. Layover days allow visits to many lakes, some of which you'll have to yourself.

DESCRIPTION (Leisurely trip)

1st Hiking Day: Follow Trip 22 to Y Meadow Lake, 5 miles.

2nd Hiking Day (Y Meadow Lake to Upper Wire Lake, 7.4 miles): First retrace your steps from Y Meadow Lake to the trail junction of the Gianelli Cabin/Whitesides Meadow Trail. Here our route turns right (northeast) toward very large Whitesides Meadow. Travelers should be prepared for the probability of seeing summer-grazing cattle on these broad expanses (Forest Service Multiple-Use land program) but these bovine occupants should not detract too much from an appreciation of this subalpine grassland. At the north end of this meadow, several aspens bear the etched names of pioneers who were buried here. At the east end of the meadow our route passes the Eagle Pass Trail, and then ascends, through an astonishing wildflower chute, the moderately timbered slope at the northeast end. On this ascent our rough path passes a trail left to Upper Relief Valley and Kennedy Meadow, and an unsigned one right to Toejam Lake after 1½ miles of descent. Then it dips down to ford West Fork Cherry Creek (sometimes dry in late season) at Salt Lick Meadow (8520').

From here the trail climbs to a tarn-dotted bench and then descends past several picturesque tarns to Spring Meadow. Tiny lakes sprinkle the green expanse of the meadow, and early-to-mid season trailpounders will find the grassland areas spiced with lupine, paintbrush and buttercup. Anglers will find the fishing for brook trout fair-to-good along the tributary (Spring Creek) flowing through Post Corral Canyon. A short mile farther southeast, a signed trail leaves the main trail and winds the remaining 0.4 mile along a ridge, past a large devastated expanse of trees blasted by a lightning strike, to the excellent campsites on the northwest side of upper Wire Lake (8720'). More isolated sites are on the east side. Equally good campsites may also be found at Banana Lake (middle Wire Lake), 0.3 miles southwest via a cross-country route. Fishing on the Wire Lakes is good-to-excellent (with a midseason slowdown) for brook (8–14"). Campers will find any of the several secluded campsites on these high montane lakes an idyllic setting for a base camp from which to explore the many lakes nearby.

3rd and 4th Hiking Days: Retrace your steps, 12.4 miles.

Upper Wire Lake

Crabtree Camp to Deer Lake **24**

Distance	22.6 miles
Type	Out and back trip
Best season	Mid or late
Topo maps	Pinecrest, Cooper Peak

Grade (hiking days/recommended layover days)

Leisurely	4/2
Moderate	4/0
Strenuous	——
Trailhead	Crabtree Camp (15)

HIGHLIGHTS Deer Lake is a worthy destination for anyone who likes to be surrounded by lakes. There are dozens of lakes and lakelets within 2 miles of Deer Lake, offering excellent fishing and/or swimming, and Deer Lake itself is prime fishing water.

DESCRIPTION

1st Hiking Day (Crabtree Camp to Piute Creek, 6.4 miles): Leaving the moderately forested flats of Crabtree Camp (7160'), we hop Bell Creek, making sure that our water bottles are full for the waterless climb to Camp Lake, and quickly come to a junction with the Chewing Gum Lake Trail (not on the topo) on a sandy bench. Our route ascends dustily through open mixed conifers, then contours south, undulating gently, to reach a segment of older trail. Here we assault a steep, much abused path, fortunately well-shaded, which levels out under aspens and lodgepoles at a lateral trail to Pine Valley. Open stands of mature Jeffrey pine, lodgepole pine, black oak, red fir, and Sierra juniper allow a viewful traverse above deeply forested Pine Valley; then the trees close in as we follow a red-fir corridor around a grassy pond and gently ascend to the Emigrant Wilderness boundary. Four hundred yards later we reach the west end of shallow, green Camp Lake (7590'). This sparsely forested, sorely trampled lakelet supports a harried population of brook trout. Hardened, very public camping is possible. At a saddle just past Camp Lake the trail to popular Bear Lake takes off to the left. There, on the west side of the lake, further hardened campsites exist, and there's the opportunity of an invigorating swim.

From the junction, the steep, dusty trail switchbacks down on deep sand flanked by dense manzanita and ceanothus to an easy ford of Lily Creek. Densely mosquitoed campsites on dense carpets of pine needles are to the south, just west of the stream. Swinging southeast through a meadow sporting corn lilies, lungwort and groundsel, our path soon comes to a granite headwall, and makes a steep, rocky ascent. Now above most of the trees, we see, in the south, Pine Valley and the chaos of white domes in the Chain Lakes region. A parade of switchbacks leads to a lengthy traverse that passes through meadows south of black-streaked granite outcrops, and we soon reach Lilypad Lake, not named on the topo map, and much larger than shown on the map, speckled with Indian pond lilies and backdropped by dancing aspens and lichen-dappled granite. Its clear, shallow waters support a thriving population of yellow-legged frogs. There is good camping to the south, above the trail.

After a short climb east of this tarn, we survey large Piute Meadow in the east, dome-guarded Toms Canyon in the north, Groundhog Meadow below in the southeast, and, on the eastern horizon, Bigelow Peak and the jutting prominence of Tower Peak. Bone-jarring dynamited switchbacks, esthetically ameliorated by a profusion of wildflowers, lead down to a sidehill traverse in glacial boulders west of Piute Meadow.

Keeping to the trees south of the willowed west arm of Piute Meadow, we pass a small campsite; then, where our route bends south to easily cross Piute Creek, many unpleasant campsites lie among the trees just to the north. This popular rest stop is also heavily used by packers and stock. Only yards after Piute Creek the unsigned Groundhog Meadow spur trail comes in from the south.

2nd Hiking Day (Piute Creek to Deer Lake, 4.9 miles): The dry slabs and lodgepole pines demarcating the lower margin of Piute Meadow are left behind when our path bends upward, switchbacking rockily up the east slope of Piute Creek canyon to a broad saddle southwest of Piute Lake. The trail then descends to the meadowed fringes of tiny (2-acre) Piute Lake (7865') and the good campsites on the north side. Fishing for rainbow (8–12") in this shallow lake is fair to good.

From Piute Lake the trail drops to ford West Fork Cherry Creek and then strenuously ascends a steep, rocky, washed-out section to an overlook just above warm little Gem Lake (8224'). There is limited camping to the north and a few sites on the lake's south side. Less steep than the previous climb, the trail from Gem to Jewelry Lake is nonetheless a rocky ascent. Our route skirts the north side of the meadow fringes surrounding Jewelry Lake (8399'), and anglers will want to try their luck for the fair-to-good fishing for rainbow (to 10″) in the lake and the lagoons around the inlet. Hardened, vandalized sites are on the west end of the lake. From the east end of Jewelry Lake, it is a short mile by rocky, gently ascending trail to the excellent campsites on the north side of Deer Lake (8461'). This long, granite-bound lake has nice meadow fringes on the north side. The forested campsites look out over the lake's island- and rock-dotted surface. Swimming is excellent, and fishing for nice-sized rainbow (8–16″) is good-to-excellent on both the lake and the inlet stream.

3rd and 4th Hiking Days: Retrace your steps, 11.3 miles.

Jewelry Lake: rainbow trout waters

25 Gianelli Cabin to Crabtree Camp

Distance	34.3 miles
Type	Shuttle trip, part cross-country
Best season	Mid or late
Topo maps	Pinecrest, Cooper Peak
Grade (hiking days/recommended layover days)	
Leisurely	7/3
Moderate	6/0
Strenuous	4/0
Trailhead	Gianelli Cabin (14), Crabtree Camp (15)

HIGHLIGHTS   This shuttle trip visits a large number of the most beautiful lakes in Emigrant Wilderness. The lakes differ in character from granitic, dramatic, isolated Kole Lake, barely nestled in a mountain summit, to densely forested, popular Pingree Lake. Incomparable beauty is to be found at every step.

DESCRIPTION (Moderate trip)

1st Hiking Day: Follow Trip 22 to Y Meadow Lake, 5 miles.

2nd Hiking Day (Y Meadow Lake to Deer Lake, 8.6 miles): Follow Trip 23, 2nd hiking day, to the signed turnoff ("a signed trail") to Wire Lakes. Your route continues straight ahead on the main trail. In 1.5 miles you reach the north shore of lovely Deer Lake (8461') and the junction with the Buck Lakes-Crabtree Camp Trail. You will find excellent camping to the east; there is more private, off-trail camping on the south side of the lake. Deer Lake offers superb swimming, good fishing, and an ideal site for a layover day. From this base camp you can explore eastward to Buck Lakes, close by, or more distant Emigrant Lake.

3rd Hiking Day (Deer Lake to Pingree Lake, 6.5 miles): From the north shore of Deer Lake your route goes east about a half mile to a trail junction. Straight ahead over a low saddle (east) the trail

Luther Linkhart

Deer Lake

continues to Buck Lake; your route turns right (south) toward Wood
Lake. You pass a small tarn on the right and cross several small
streams, which will be running in early summer, stagnant in
midseason, and often dry at summer's end. Most of the descent is
gentle, with several brief stretches of steep switchbacks. The final
approach to Wood Lake (8270′) is through a meadow, across which
the heavily wooded lake is tantalizingly visible. The trail branches
in this meadow, allowing travel around the lake in either direction.
The branch to the left leads to good camping, but you bear right. Your
initially severely-eroded trail crosses a low shoulder and then travels
along the north shore of Wood Lake on a high, smooth granite slab
with good views. The trail then drops, crosses the outlet stream, and
goes downstream (west) a short distance to a junction with the Buck
Meadow Creek Trail. Here you turn back (east), passing good
camping at the west end of Wood Lake, and then travel along the
south shore. Just east of the point where the shores compress the
waters to a narrow neck, you reach the signed junction with the trail
south to Karls Lake.

Turn right at this junction and ascend a short, steep saddle. Next, you make a moderate descent over granite slabs (the trail is often indistinct) and re-enter a forest cover with a floor of corn lilies. After you pass a packer camp you find excellent camping along the very beautiful and irregular northwestern shore of Karls Lake (8290'). Even better camping may be found at the narrows halfway along the northwest side of the lake. There are many more granite islands than are shown on the topo, and the entire lake is bordered with lodgepoles, also contrary to the impression given by the topo.

From the northwest shore of Karls Lake your cross-country route soon becomes indistinct as you cross the scant ¼ mile of land separating Karls from the northmost tip of Leighton Lake (8280'). Leighton Lake encoffins many dead trees, creating an eerily beautiful wasteland. The patterns of the trunks make a photographer's paradise. Many birds have found their homes here; their cries add to the strangeness of this stark landscape. There is no camping. In mid to late season, when the water level is low, the best route around Leighton Lake is along the north side at the water's edge—you will have to leapfrog across dead trees. In early season you will need to go a bit higher over huge granite boulders. There is no visible trail either way.

To leave the lake, go to its extreme western tip and then ascend west directly up the easy granite slabs. Be sure to look back into the lake basin during your climb to observe the cracks in these slabs, which are filled with seedling lodgepoles that are slowly breaking up the mountainside. Eschew the obvious lower saddle to the southwest, and aim slightly north to the 8600-foot saddle just northeast of Kole Lake. If you hanker for dramatic vistas, take a brief stroll up to the knob ½ mile southwest of Kole Lake. There is nothing higher than this point west all the way to the Pacific Ocean, and you have visual access to the entire western end of Emigrant Wilderness, much of Yosemite to the south, and as far beyond as the atmosphere permits.

Kole Lake (8384') is unusual in that you ascend to the lake: it lies in a small hollow in a crest. Its shores are gently forested in lodgepole and carpeted with ferns and wildflowers. Granite slabs lead into the water, inviting you in for a swim. Wonderful unused camping is available on all sides of the lake.

The 1½-mile cross-country route from Kole to Pingree Lake starts with a rapid descent down the granite slabs at the west end of Kole Lake and then levels out as it crosses gigantic slabs laced with streams. Stay to the north side of this flat, relatively close to the underside of the cliff to the north. The final part of the descent is over irregular but easy terrain. A use trail appears in the meadows

bordering the east side of Pingree Lake (8093') and continues around
the north side. Superb camping surrounds the lake. The shore of this
large lake is very irregular, offering privacy for a swim, and the many
granite islands tempt the swimmer to sunbathe.

4th Hiking Day (Pingree Lake to Gem Lake, 4.7 miles): From
the northwest side of Pingree Lake the very visible but unmaintained
and highly eroded trail leads west, crosses a flat shelf and drops
sharply 250 feet to the drainage between Pingree and Rosasco lakes.
At the low point, you pass on the left the unsigned trail to Big Lake
to the south, and almost immediately come to another trail junction.
Here you turn right (north) to hike toward the Buck Meadow Creek
Trail. Your trail first slopes gently up along slabs and multiple
watercourses, then steepens occasionally and enters sparse forest.
After a mile, the trail turns east, in thicker lodgepole forest, and
follows the base of a vertical rock wall for another mile, where it
suddenly turns north to meet the unsigned Buck Meadow Creek
Trail. You turn left (west) onto this trail and drop quickly to Buck
Meadow Creek. The stepping-stone crossing to the north side of the
creek may be difficult in early season. A short climb up the north wall
soon brings you to a trail leading north to Gem Lake. This is a choice
point. If you continue west on the Buck Meadow Creek Trail, you
can reach Crabtree Camp more directly. We describe a bit longer,
more scenic route: turn north and follow the trail uphill to Gem Lake.
Much of the very beautiful, very steep ascent is over open granite
slabs where no trail is apparent. Aim for the obvious saddle 200 feet
above you and walk up your chosen slabs. Gem Lake (8224') sits in
the saddle and has fair camping.

5th Hiking Day (Gem Lake to Lilypad Lake, 4.4 miles): Your
trail becomes distinct as it passes the east side of Gem Lake, and soon
meets the signed Deer Lake-Crabtree Camp Trail, which hugs the
north side of Gem. Turn left onto this main trail. The next part of your
journey reverses the 2nd hiking day, Trip 24, west from Gem Lake
to Piute Creek.

In 3.1 miles you reach Piute Creek, with abundant, heavily used
camping, and the junction to Groundhog Meadow and the Buck
Meadow Creek Trail. You continue straight west toward Camp Lake
and Crabtree Camp. In 1.3 miles you reach Lilypad Lake (6960'), the
long, skinny lake not named on the topo. The trail passes along the
south shore of this lake. Good camping may be found on the lightly
treed shoulder south of the trail.

6th Hiking Day (Lilypad Lake to Crabtree Camp, 5.1 miles):
Reverse the first part of the 1st hiking day, Trip 24.

26 Gianelli Cabin to Crabtree Camp

Distance	27.3 miles
Type	Shuttle trip
Best season	Mid or late
Topo maps	Pinecrest, Cooper Peak
Grade (hiking days/recommended layover days)	
Leisurely	5/1
Moderate	4/1
Strenuous	3/0
Trailhead	Gianelli Cabin (14), Crabtree Camp (15)

HIGHLIGHTS   This route has proved popular with angler, naturalist, photographer and hiker alike. High, coldwater lakes and streams vie with deep fir forests and alpine meadows for the attention of the visitor. The shortness of the shuttle for this trip makes it a near-loop.

DESCRIPTION (Leisurely trip)

1st and 2nd Hiking Days: Follow Trip 23 to Upper Wire Lake, 12.4 miles.

3rd Hiking Day (Upper Wire Lake to Piute Lake, 5.5 miles): From upper Wire Lake the traveler has the option of circling to Deer Lake by the longer trail route or descending through the Wire Lakes basin and going cross country to the west end of Deer Lake. The trail route, after retracing the short angler's lateral, rejoins the Spring Meadow/Deer Lake main trail and turns south. Almost immediately the route passes an unsigned trail to the left. (This 45-minute sidetrip to Long Lake is worthwhile if you want a more isolated campsite or a lake to yourself for a while.) After a slight climb, the remaining distance to Deer Lake is a steady descent over a forested streamcourse that passes several small, unnamed lakes. At Deer Lake this route passes the Buck Lakes trail (your entry route if you are hiking from Kennedy Meadow to a Pinecrest trailhead) and turns right (southwest) toward Jewelry Lake.

The cross-country route from upper Wire Lake to this point first leads southwest to Banana Lake (middle Wire Lake), where all semblances of trail vanishes. The easiest descent from here is to take the clear route through the meadowed area east of Banana Lake and then descend via the usually dry streamcourse to reach the Jewelry Lake/Deer Lake Trail about 0.3 mile west of Deer Lake. The trail from Deer Lake to Jewelry Lake is a ½-mile rocky descent that brings the traveler to the pleasant meadow fringes surrounding Jewelry Lake. This lake has placid lagoons forming its inlet which provide fair-to-good fishing for rainbow (to 10″). Crossing the inlet stream, the route descends a rocky trail to warm little Gem Lake (8224′). From this viewpoint the trail descends steeply to a ford of West Fork Cherry Creek and then climbs gently to tiny Piute Lake (7865′). Fishing for rainbow (8–12″) in this shallow lake is fair-to-good.

4th and 5th Hiking Days: Reverse the steps of part of the 2nd and all of the 1st hiking days, Trip 24, 9.4 miles.

Casting for trout in Deer Lake

27   Gianelli Cabin to Kennedy Meadow

Distance	33.3 miles
Type	Shuttle trip
Best season	Mid or late
Topo maps	Pinecrest, Cooper Peak, Emigrant Lake, Sonora Pass

Grade (hiking days/recommended layover days)

Leisurely	5/2
Moderate	4/2
Strenuous	3/2
Trailhead	Gianelli Cabin (14), Kennedy Meadow (13)

HIGHLIGHTS   This trip journeys through a cross section of Emigrant Wilderness. The route touches some justly popular base-camping lakes, and from these points the traveler has access to the unusual and exciting surrounding country. Taken at Leisurely pace, this route affords one of the best possible week-long excursions in the region.

DESCRIPTION (Leisurely trip)

1st and 2nd Hiking Days: Follow Trip 24 to Upper Wire Lake, 12.4 miles.

3rd Hiking Day (Upper Wire Lake to Emigrant Lake via Deer and Buck Lakes, 7.5 miles): The traveler going to Deer Lake has a choice of going by trail or cross country. The trail route entails retracing the short fisherman's trail to its junction with the main trail from Spring Meadow. There our route turns right (south), and descends gently past several unnamed tarns to Deer Lake (8461') and the signed intersection with the Crabtree Camp-Buck Lakes Trail. Turn left (east). The cross-country route goes south through the Wire Lakes basin to Banana Lake (middle Wire Lake), and then veers east a short distance through a meadowed basin. At the end of this meadow a long, usually dry streamcourse descending to the south gives access to the Crabtree Camp-Buck Lakes Trail 0.3 mile west of Deer Lake (8540′). This is a large, granitoid, meadow-fringed lake offering good-to-excellent fishing for nice-sized rainbow (to 16″), and anglers who have had an early start will want to try these waters.

The trail to Buck Lakes continues east, passes the signed lateral to Wood Lake, crosses over a low rocky ridge with several tarns, and then descends steeply to join the Emigrant Lake/Cow Meadow Lake Trail on the west shore of Buck Lakes. At this junction our route turns left (north) along the west side of upper Buck Lake, and follows Buck Meadow Creek as it crosses the long meadow at the lake's north end. Our route then veers east, fords Buck Meadow Creek, and crosses the steep, low ridge separating the Emigrant Lake and Buck Lakes basins. At Emigrant Lake (8827′) the trail follows the long north shore to the several good-to-excellent campsites near the inlet. Emigrant Lake is the largest lake (230 acres) in this Wilderness, and is a long-time favorite of fishermen because of the good-to-excellent rainbow fishing (8–18″) in its deep waters. Those who prefer stream fishing will find the lagoons near the inlet exciting sport, but the fish are smaller.

4th and 5th Hiking Days: Reverse the steps of the 2nd and 1st hiking days, Trip 20, 13.4 miles.

Lower Buck Lake   *Luther Linkhart*

28   Kennedy Meadow to Gianelli Cabin

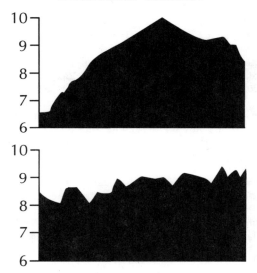

Distance	43.1 miles
Type	Shuttle trip
Best season	Mid or late
Topo maps	Cooper Peak, Emigrant Lake, Sonora Pass, Pinecrest

Grade (hiking days/recommended layover days)

Leisurely	7/3
Moderate	5/2
Strenuous	4/2

Trailhead   Kennedy Meadow (13), Gianelli Cabin (14)

HIGHLIGHTS   After visiting the north side of Emigrant Wilderness, this route turns south and traverses the beautiful, lake-dotted country of the Cherry Creek watershed. At Emigrant Meadow the trail joins the old Emigrant Trail, and history buffs will have the opportunity of seeing this historic crossing as the pioneers did.

DESCRIPTION (Leisurely trip)

1st and 2nd Hiking Days: Follow Trip 19 to Emigrant Meadow Lake, 12.6 miles.

3rd and 4th Hiking Days: Reverse the steps of the 5th and 4th hiking days, Trip 21, 13 miles.

5th Hiking Day (Cow Meadow Lake to Deer Lake, 3.5 miles): Leaving Cow Meadow Lake, the trail passes a junction with a trail from East Fork Cherry Creek and then ascends steeply 600 feet amid a dense, predominantly lodgepole forest cover to a junction with the Wood Lake lateral. Ahead, lower Buck Lake (42 acres) is a rocky, deep, glacial lake that is separated from upper Buck Lake by a narrow isthmus. Fishing on both lakes for rainbow (to 18″) is good. Our route crosses the isthmus and turns north to strike the Deer Lake Trail. Here our route turns left (west) and climbs steeply for ½ mile. Then it descends more gently for a mile past the Wood Lake Trail to the excellent campsites on the north side of Deer Lake (8540′). This long lake has the same kind of subalpine meadow fringing as upper Buck Lake. The fine campsites, situated in small stands of lodgepole, look out across the lake's island-dotted surface. Fishing for rainbow (8–16″) is good-to-excellent.

6th Hiking Day (Deer Lake to Y Meadow Lake, 9 miles): From the trail junction at the middle of Deer Lake's north shore, our route climbs north beside an unnamed stream and past a series of inviting tarns. About 1.7 miles from Deer Lake we pass the Wire Lakes Trail going left (west) and then descend a densely forested slope to the east end of Spring Meadow. This meadow is a vast, lakelet-dotted grassland that is lush with buttercups, lupine and paintbrush. One frequently sees cattle grazing here, allowed by the National Forest multiple-use land program.

From Spring Meadow the trail crosses a small ridge containing more tarns and then descends moderately-to-steeply through a wooded section to Salt Lick Meadow, where it crosses tiny West Fork Cherry Creek (sometimes dry in late season). Then the route ascends through lodgepole pine and mountain hemlock, passing the first of two trails leading north to Upper Relief Valley and Kennedy Meadow and, 0.6 mile later, an unsigned trail leading south to secluded Toejam Lake. Our trail tops the ridge and then descends to sprawling Whitesides Meadow. At its head we pass another trail to Upper Relief Valley and, soon after, a trail to Cooper Meadow, both leading north. The green expanse of this meadow is broken by the flow of an unnamed tributary of South Fork Stanislaus River. Our trail touches this stream at the meadow's west end, then veers away southwest to the Y Meadow Lake Trail junction. Here we branch left and walk one winding mile to the fair campsites in the timber fringe at the north end of Y Meadow Lake (8600′).

7th Hiking Day: Reverse the steps of the 1st hiking day, Trip 22, 5 miles.

29 Leavitt Meadow to Fremont Lake

Distance	18 miles
Type	Out and back trip
Best season	Mid or late
Topo maps	Pickel Meadow, Tower Peak

Grade (hiking days/recommended layover days)

Leisurely	3/1
Moderate	2/0
Strenuous	——
Trailhead	Leavitt Meadow (18)

HIGHLIGHTS   You visit several lovely lakes on this beautiful semiloop route. An ideal three-day weekend for the beginner, this trip offers off-trail excursions to further lakes for the more advanced backpacker. Photobugs and anglers alike can look forward to a fine time.

DESCRIPTION (Moderate trip)

1st Hiking Day (Leavitt Meadow Campground to Fremont Lake, 9 miles): The trail leaves the Leavitt Meadow Campground (7120′) via a metal bridge across the West Walker River. Beyond the bridge the trail ascends briefly and in ¼ mile reaches a junction just beyond a mountain juniper on the left and a Jeffrey pine followed by an uprooted stump on the right. Here we veer right onto the West Walker River Trail on a sagebrush-covered arid slope where we descend moderately steeply, and traverse over to the wide valley of Leavitt Meadow. Far up the river canyon Forsyth Peak stands majestically on the border of Yosemite.

As we ascend gently for several miles, we look down onto the West Walker River, which forms sensuous curves in the valley floor. There we can also see the pack trail from Leavitt Meadow Pack Station. Close beside the trail we may observe many tall specimens of a bush-tree called mountain mahogany. Despite its dry, tough appearance, the foliage of this desert plant is relished by the local mule-deer population. The plant is particularly striking in the early fall, when the styles (part of the flowers) are white, silky, 3-inch-long plumes growing by the hundreds on each bush.

On this steady ascent we meet several trails, coming upward at acute angles, that lead back north to the pack station in Leavitt Meadow. After the meadow disappears from sight and after the route has clearly converged with the pack trail, just beyond a pond, we pass the Poore Lake Trail branching left . (Note this junction: on your return trip you will take the northward fork and follow the main trail toward Poore and Secret lakes.) Now on the main trail, you continue southward to the shore of algae-bottomed Roosevelt Lake, ringed with a sparse fringe of Jeffrey pines. There are some undistinguished campsites on the west side of the lake, and sometimes fishing is good for brook trout (to 13″).

Our trail leads next over a granite shoulder and down to the outlet of Lane Lake, nearly a twin of Roosevelt and only a few yards from it. This outlet usually dries up by midsummer, but the dead lodgepole pines southwest of the ford are testimony to flooding earlier in the season. From the ford, the trail ascends briefly southeast and then levels off as it passes several lovely aspen groves, some with lush grass floors even into late season.

Over a mile from Lane Lake, we descend to the willow-lined banks of the river, crossing a small but vigorous tributary and in ⅛ mile reach the main stream. We ascend gently near the riverside for ¼ mile through a cool forest of mixed conifers, aspens and cotton-woods, then veer away on a steeper ascent that fords another tributary. Now on the rocky-dusty trail we climb steeply to surmount a saddle crested with junipers and Jeffrey pines, which offers fine views up the West Walker valley to Forsyth Peak and the Sierra crest. Descending over a sandy trail, we pass the signed turnoff to Hidden and Red Top lakes, and then resume the moderate ascent along the east bank of the West Walker River. This rocky stretch of trail alongside the river gives access to many pleasant, granite-bottomed potholes. Here the river tumbles along in a series of small falls and cascades that have carved a narrows through the white granite that typifies the middle of the West Walker River valley. The upper walls are of barren, metavolcanic rock that ranges the color spectrum from black to reds and yellows.

Where the narrows opens out onto a forest flat, rife with mosqui-toes in early season, you find yourself on the east side of the West Walker River. The trail to Fremont Lake leaves from the west side. You pass several potential log crossings. For the easiest, continue until you come to an unsigned trail junction a bit inland from the river, just off the Pickel Meadow topo map. Turn right, follow this trail to the riverbank, and find a good log crossing less than 100 yards downstream. Across the river are many well-used campsites, and we stroll downstream past several to reach the signed Fremont Lake Trail continuation. This we follow westward, ascending steeply to cross a saddle topped with juniper and Jeffrey pine. This saddle offers V'd views south to Tower Peak. The trail then descends gently, passes the trail to Chain of Lakes, and in 100 yards reaches Fremont Lake (8240'). The forest cover around this generous-sized lake is moderate-to-dense lodgepole and juniper. Around the south end of the lake in the timber are fair campsites, and fishing for rainbow (to 12") and eastern brook (to 10") is good. A layover day here allows you to explore, cross country, nearby Red Top and Hidden lakes; or to make an on-trail loop to the south around the Chain of Lakes and Long Lake.

2nd Hiking Day (Fremont Lake to Leavitt Meadow, 9 miles): Retrace your steps past the junction with the pack trail on your left, and continue past several leftward laterals, including the one on which you came. At the signed junction with the trail to Poore Lake, turn left toward Secret Lake. Surrounded by trees, Secret Lake has several excellent campsites. Beyond the lake, the trail ascends and then follows the crest. Expansive views in all directions invite us to linger; many of the trees we pass are stunted and hauntingly shaped by wind. Finally the trail descends to the junction with the West Walker River Trail, from which we retrace our steps to the campground.

West Walker River

Leavitt Meadow to Cinko Lake 30

Distance	28 miles
Type	Out and back trip
Best season	Mid or late
Topo maps	Pickel Meadow, Tower Peak
Grade (hiking days/recommended layover days)	
Leisurely	4/1
Moderate	3/0
Strenuous	2/0
Trailhead	Leavitt Meadow (18)

HIGHLIGHTS This interesting route traces West Fork West Walker River to its headwaters cirque beneath the Sierra crestline. From the sagebrush and Jeffrey pine belt it ascends to the Boreal belt, passing through three life zones. Of the several trips in this drainage, this offers one of the best exposures to the geological, topographical and biological features of this country.

DESCRIPTION (Moderate trip)

1st Hiking Day: Follow Trip 29 to Fremont Lake, 9 miles.

2nd Hiking Day (Fremont Lake to Cinko Lake, 5 miles): After retracing our steps back to the Chain of Lakes junction described in Trip 29, we turn right (south) and ascend steadily near, but out of sight of, Fremont Lake. This ascent steepens as it crosses open, granite-sand slopes with only a few junipers and pines for shade. Near the top of this ascent one has uninterrupted views to the south of Forsyth and Tower peaks, and one encounters the first western white pines of this trip. The first of three large granite domes that tower over the east side of Chain of Lakes comes into view, and the trail crosses to the north of it. Then, on a gently descending path through an increasingly dense forest cover, we pass the marked trail to Walker Meadows and arrive at the first of several tiny, green, lily-padded lakes. These lakes reflect the verdant forest cover that extends to their willow-lined shores, and by late summer their shallow depths teem with the biota that typifies near-stagnant waters.

The trail leaves the last and largest of the Chain of Lakes and ascends gently over sand and duff through a moderate forest cover of lodgepole and western white pine past a small, unnamed lake north of Lower Long Lake. A few yards past this lily-padded lake, the trail veers right, around the north side of Lower Long Lake. The "blancoed" rock in the center of the lake is a favorite midday resting place for the sandpipers that inhabit the area. Fishermen seeking the pan-sized rainbow here will enjoy the sandpiper's low, skimming flight, which seems to trim the fringe of rushes. Fair-to-good campsites dot the north and west sides of the lake. More extensive campsites are found a few yards farther up the trail, at Upper Long Lake.

The trail jogs around the lower end of Upper Long Lake, fords the intermittent outlet stream and meets the Piute Meadows lateral, going left. Our route turns right past a picturesque tarn to the banks of West Fork West Walker River. Here at another junction our route branches left alongside this tumbling stream. Good campsites dot both sides of the West Fork near the junction, marred only by the cowflops incident to the Multiple-Use grazing permit for nearby Walker Meadows. Occasional hemlocks with their gracefully bowed tops occur along the pleasant, granite-ledged, timber-pocketed ascent from the campsites. Many wildflowers, including shooting star, penstemon, bush lupine, aster, columbine, goldenrod, heather, Mariposa lily, wallflower, woolly sunflower and fleabane, decorate the stream's edge and complement the cheerful splashing of the nearby stream.

This gentle-to-moderate climb continues along the southeast side of the stream to the foot of a large, white granite dome, where it fords via boulders to the northwest side of the creek. Contrasts of the dark volcanic rock and the white granite underlayment of this part of the Sierra are nowhere more marked than in this valley, and the viewer is assailed with dark battlements of multihued basalt, and sheer escarpments of glacially smoothed batholithic granite. William H. Brewer, head of the Brewer Survey party that passed near here in July 1863, took note of the volcanic surroundings, saying ". . .in the higher Sierra, along our line of travel, all our highest points were capped with lava, often worn into strange and fantastic forms—rounded hills of granite, capped by rugged masses of lava, sometimes looking like old castles with their towers and buttresses and walls, sometimes like old churches with their pinnacles, all on a gigantic scale, and then again shooting up in curious forms that defy description."

This ascent takes the traveler to timberline and to alpine climes as the surrounding forest cover becomes stunted and comes to include occasional altitude-loving whitebark pines. At a signed junction our route turns southeast along a clear trail to Cinko Lake. This trail fords West Fork West Walker River and passes a charming meadow with a tiny tarn in its upper reaches. Then it makes a brief moderate ascent to the intermittent north outlet of arrowhead-shaped Cinko Lake. There is another outlet on the south side of the lake. The trail emerges at the lake's edge (9194′), adjacent to the north outlet, where there are several good campsites. Fishing for rainbow and eastern brook (to 12″) is good.

3rd Hiking Day: Retrace your steps, 14 miles.

West Walker River above Leavitt Meadow

31 Leavitt Meadow to Dorothy Lake

Distance	34 miles
Type	Semiloop trip
Best season	Mid or late
Topo maps	Pickel Meadow, Tower Peak
Grade (hiking days/recommended layover days)	
Leisurely	6/1
Moderate	4/1
Strenuous	3/1
Trailhead	Leavitt Meadow (18)

HIGHLIGHTS   Touring the headwaters of the West Fork West Walker River and the headwaters of Cascade Creek and Falls Creek would be an ambitious undertaking in any one trip, but this trip boasts more. Near Dorothy Lake, the culmination of the trip, the visitor can take in the unusual Forsyth Peak "rock glacier."

DESCRIPTION (Moderate trip)

1st and 2nd Hiking Days (Leavitt Meadow to Dorothy Lake, 18 miles): First follow Trip 30 to Cinko Lake, 14 miles. From the southeast side of Cinko Lake our trail winds down a lodgepole-and hemlock-clothed hillside to the unpopulated banks of an unnamed stream. Then it climbs slightly, veering east away from the water. A very short, steep descent then takes the hiker to a beautiful lakelet. About ⅛ mile past the lake, we reapproach the stream and then veer away again eastward. In another ⅛ mile the trail crosses this persistent tributary on a wooden bridge, then ascends for a moment, levels off, and passes three snowmelt tarns on the right. Continuing level through a tarn-filled saddle here, our southbound trail soon meets the Dorothy Lake Trail, which is also the Pacific Crest Trail here, and we turn right (south), following the trail on a gentle ascent through a thinning forest cover of lodgepole, hemlock and whitebark pine.

One-half mile from the junction we cross Cascade Creek on a large log near a large east-bank campsite, and in another ⅓ mile ford the outlet of Lake Harriet. After this ford the trail ascends more steeply, and becomes rocky after passing island-dotted Lake Harriet. This ascent levels through a meadowy section and fords the stream joining Stella and Bonnie lakes. Ahead, the low profile of Dorothy Lake Pass is fronted by another moderate, rocky ascent, and the trail then levels past the grassy north arm of Stella Lake. At the northeast end of this arm, a ducked cross-country route to Lake Ruth and Lake Helen departs from our route.

The long, low saddle on which Stella Lake sits terminates at Dorothy Lake Pass, where there is an excellent view of Dorothy Lake (9400'). To the southeast, the hiker has V-notched views of Tower Peak, and to the south, the granite grenadiers of multi-turreted Forsyth Peak dominate the landscape. From the pass, the trail descends steadily over a rocky slope that is the territory of numerous conies and marmots.

As the trail skirts the north side of this beautiful lake, it winds through lush grass and willow patches with spots of color provided by shooting star, elephant heads, goldenrod, paintbrush, whorled penstemon, pussy paws and false Solomon's seal. This stretch of the north shore was not so lush when the first recorded explorer of this lake walked here. Lt. N.F. McClure, of the 4th Cavalry, came this way in 1894 noting, "Grazing here was poor, and there had evidently been thousands of sheep about." The trail passes three windy campsites along the north shore before arriving at the good campsites at the west end of the lake. Fishing for rainbow and occasional eastern brook is good-to-excellent except during a midsummer slowdown. This lake makes an excellent base-camp location for exploring and fishing the nearby lakes in the upper Cascade Creek basin, and for viewing the Forsyth Peak "rock glacier."

This phenomenon can be viewed from the unnamed lake south of Dorothy Lake. Seen from here, it is a prominent "river" of rock flowing in a long northwest-curving arc. This arc begins on the northeast face of Forsyth Peak, then curves down the easternmost ravine and points its moving head toward Dorothy Lake. Composed of coarse rock that tumbled from Forsyth Peak's fractured face, it hides an underlayment of silt, sand and fine gravel, and it depends upon ice caught between larger boulders for its mobility.

3rd Hiking Day (Dorothy Lake to Fremont Lake Trail Junction, 8 miles): First retrace the steps of the previous hiking day as far as the Cinko Lake Trail. Then continue to descend on the north side of tumbling Cascade Creek. Switchbacks are needed to convey the hiker down past the cascades of this namesake creek. Near the bottom of this descent the forest, now including stately red firs, becomes thicker. As the trail nears the West Walker River, the moderate descent levels, and then the route fords near an old corral. Beyond the wading ford is a **Y** junction, and here our route turns left (downstream). The trail continues north along the east side of the West Walker River, fords an unnamed tributary of the river, and skirts a large meadow before beginning a gentle-to-moderate ascent. The sand-and-duff trail then crosses a saddle and descends to ford Long Canyon Creek. About ¼ mile beyond this stream is the Fremont Lake Trail junction, and we take this trail across the river to the campsites passed on the first hiking day. Alternatively, one may continue downstream on the east side of the river to other good campsites. Fishing in the deeper holes of this section of the river is good for rainbow (to 11″).

4th Hiking Day: Reverse the steps of most of the 1st hiking day, Trip 29, 8 miles.

Dorothy Lake and "rock glacier" on Forsyth Peak

Leavitt Meadow to Tower Lake **32**

Distance   40 miles
Type   Semiloop; part cross-country
Best season   Mid or late
Topo maps   Pickel Meadow, Tower Peak
Grade (hiking days/recommended layover days)
   Leisurely   7/2
   Moderate   5/2
   Strenuous   4/2
Trailhead   Leavitt Meadow (18)

HIGHLIGHTS   The cross-country segment of this trip makes it a choice for experienced backpackers only. The strenuousness of the route guarantees the walker a proportionate measure of solitude, and views of the alpine crest on this trip are seldom seen by anyone except the cross-countryer.

DESCRIPTION (Moderate trip)

1st and 2nd Hiking Days: Follow Trip 31 to Dorothy Lake, 18 miles.

3rd Hiking Day (Dorothy Lake to Tower Lake, 5 miles): From the campsites at the west end of Dorothy Lake, retrace the steps of the previous hiking day to Stella Lake, to where the ducked cross-country route to Lake Ruth rounds the northeast end of the lake. This route ascends over a rock-and-grass ledge system along the east side of the intermittent stream joining Stella Lake and Lake Ruth, and arrives at the outlet end of Lake Ruth. Here, nestled in the sparse whitebark-pine fringe of the lake, are good campsites that make a fine alternative to the more crowded environs of Dorothy Lake. The route from the outlet skirts the east side of the lake for a short distance and then ascends a long, gentle swale to the southeast. Several small melt-off tarns mark the crossover point to the Lake Helen drainage. Keeping to the south side of this large, granite, circular lake, the route fords the tiny but noisy southwest inlet, and then crosses the rocky slope directly south of the lake.

At the southeast inlet our route fords and ascends moderately to a lovely grass bench. The remaining ascent to the obvious saddle in the southeast crosses steeper sections, and route-picking is best accomplished on the left (north) side of the cirque wall. This steep pitch brings one to a sparsely dotted whitebark-pine saddle offering incomparable views. Included in the views are, from north to west, Wells Peak, White Mountain, Sonora Peak, Stanislaus Peak, Leavitt Peak, Kennedy Peak, Relief Peak and Forsyth Peak. To the east and southeast the view encompasses, from east to south, Flatiron Butte, Walker Peak, Buckeye Ridge, the Kirkwood Creek drainage, Grouse Mountain, Hunewill Peak, Hawksbeak Peak, Kettle Peak, Cirque Mountain and Tower Peak. From the summit of this saddle one can also see most of the lakes of the Cascade Creek drainage, as well as Tower Lake at the foot of Tower Peak. Tower Peak, the most spectacular peak of the North Boundary Country but not the tallest, is the goal of most climbers in this region. Visible from most of the drainages to the south, it has served mountaineers as a landmark for more than a hundred years.

Descending from the saddle on the southeast side entails crossing rock and scree to a rocky bench, and thence a grass-and-ledge system to a small lakelet just north of Tower Lake. The route then rounds the south nose of a granite ridge to the willowed outlet of Tower Lake, where it fords to the fair campsites, centered in the only stand of timber found here on the east side of the outlet (9600'). There is fair-to-good fishing for the golden trout (to 11") that inhabit this lake. Good alternative campsites can be found ½ mile down the outlet stream.

4th Hiking Day (Tower Lake to Fremont Lake Trail Junction, 9 miles): From Tower Lake the trail descends over a rocky slope close to the north side of the outlet stream. This steep, rocky descent affords a view of a dramatic avalanche chute that slices the slope on the northeast side of Kirkwood Creek canyon. To the rear, back toward Tower Peak, the view is dominated by the climactic, phalluslike northern extension of Tower Peak. This classic white-granite pinnacle soon obliterates views of Tower Peak itself, and it stands as mute testimony to the obdurate granite's resistance to glacial erosion.

The rocky descent soon reaches timberline, where hemlock and lodgepole pine appear, and then refords the outlet stream in a willowed section at the confluence of the Tower Lake outlet and the tiny stream draining the glacier at the foot of the granite column to the south. This new section of trail from Tower Lake keeps to the east side of the creek as it descends gently over duff and rock, and fords an unnamed tributary.

Beyond the ford, the new trail rejoins the old trail, winding through a dense forest cover of lodgepole and hemlock. Then the trail refords Tower Lake's outlet stream and ascends above the narrowing canyon. These narrows show almost vertical granite walls, between which the stream becomes a plummeting ribbon. Ahead, the valley of the West Walker River can be seen through the trees, and a short, easy descent over a duff trail soon brings us to a trail junction just north of the confluence of the Tower Lake outlet and Kirkwood Creek.

Our route turns right, fords the West Walker River, and then skirts the oxbows of the river where it serpentines through Upper Piute Meadows. At the north end of the meadows the sandy trail passes a turnoff to Piute Cabin, a Forest Service trail-maintenance station, and then veers away from the river as it continues to descend gently. The cattle seen in some years in Upper Piute Meadows are part of the Forest Service's "Multiple Use" administrative concept. Cowflops have been reported as far away as the head of Thompson Canyon— and it may be logically assumed that they were a result of allowing grazing here. After jogging around a marshy section, the trail again comes within sight of the river, and then joins the trail from Dorothy Lake. From the junction we proceed as described in the 3rd hiking day, Trip 29.

5th Hiking Day: Reverse the steps of most of the 1st hiking day, Trip 29, 8 miles.

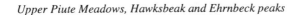

Upper Piute Meadows, Hawksbeak and Ehrnbeck peaks

33 Leavitt Meadow to Buckeye Creek

Distance	39.9 miles
Type	Shuttle trip; part cross-country
Best season	Early or mid
Topo maps	Pickel Meadow, Tower Peak, Buckeye Ridge

Grade (hiking days/recommended layover days)

Leisurely	7/2
Moderate	5/2
Strenuous	4/1
Trailhead	Leavitt Meadow (18), Buckeye Roadend (19)

HIGHLIGHTS   Using two major eastside drainages this trip circumnavigates Walker Mountain and Flatiron Ridge, and is about evenly split between high country and lower, forested areas. This is a superlative choice for the novice who has a couple of shorter trips behind him, and who is looking for a longer trip with some of the challenge of cross-countrying.

DESCRIPTION (Moderate trip)

1st, 2nd, and 3rd Hiking Days: Follow Trip 32 to Tower Lake, 23 miles.

4th Hiking Day (Tower Lake to Buckeye Forks, 7.5 miles): First, descend to Upper Piute Meadows as described in the 4th hiking day, Trip 32. Just below the confluence of Kirkwood Creek and the creek draining Tower Lake, ford to the northeast side of the stream and turn right, up Kirkwood Creek. Here at the southernmost extension of Upper Piute Meadows our route ascends moderately through a dense forest cover of lodgepole and occasional western white pine that sees the inclusion of hemlock near the top of the climb. This route passes below the spectacular avalanche chute noted on the previous hiking day. On a moderate ascent that steepens as it turns east and then northeast, the trail rises to the saddle marking the divide between the Walker River and Buckeye Creek. The startling eminence of Hawksbeak Peak to the south vies for the traveler's attention with the rich volcanic reds and blacks of the slopes to the north. After reaching a small pond at the headwaters of Kirkwood Creek, the trail descends moderately on duff and rocky surfaces to the head of North Fork Buckeye Creek. This descent through a sparse-to-moderate forest cover of lodgepole, hemlock, and occasional whitebark and western white pine crosses back and forth over the splashing creek. Then, in a final steep descent, the trail drops to "Buckeye Forks," where it meets the trail descending from Buckeye Pass to the south.

Here at the forks is a meadow-set snow-survey cabin of log-tenon construction. It is believed that this well-made cabin was constructed in 1928, and is the oldest U.S. Snow Survey shelter. When built, the cabin was surrounded by open meadow, which has since been overgrown with the ubiquitous lodgepole and willow. This dense growth is undoubtedly due to the strong evolutionary contribution of the nearby colony of beavers. As is clearly seen just downstream, these beavers have repeatedly flooded this section between Buckeye Forks and The Roughs, and the consequent buildup of sediments and high water table were conducive to forest reproduction. However, what the beaver giveth he also taketh away. Were this dense forest to be flooded again, these healthy trees would be drowned. That happened downstream, where the bleached white ghost snags make skeletal reminders of the beaver's potent niche in the evolutionary web. Of the mammals, excepting man, the beaver is far and away the greatest single alterer of the natural environment.

There are good campsites near the old cabin, and fishing in Buckeye Creek is good for rainbow and eastern brook (to 9").

5th Hiking Day (Buckeye Forks to Buckeye Roadend, 9.4 miles): From the cabin, the trail continues to descend steadily over alternating duff, sand and rock. On each side, gnawed and fallen aspen show the beaver's dietary preferences, but despite this rodent's industrious efforts (some naturalists would say "because of it") the forest cover along the creek is dense, and it serves as a foraging grounds for all manner of birdlife, including flickers, chickadees, juncos, robins, Williamson's sapsuckers, hummingbirds and nuthatches.

As the canyon narrows between high, glacially polished granite walls, the trail enters the section known as The Roughs. Here the sometimes swampy trail winds along the left bank of Buckeye Creek, overshadowed by sheer, rounded granite to the north and polished spires to the south. Good campsites can be found in The

Roughs. The first one is one mile from the forks, and there is another ¼ mile farther. Then, ¼ mile beyond, we make a steep 200-yard ascent over black metasedimentary shale to a juniper-topped saddle and the boundary of the Hoover Wilderness. From just beyond the saddle views down Buckeye Canyon are spectacular. The lush grasslands of Big Meadow provide a soft counterpoint to the ruggedness of Flatiron and Buckeye ridges.

A few hundred steep yards down beyond the saddle, we ford the vigorous creek that drains the basin between Ink Rocks and Hanna Mountain, and the tumultuous sounds of the cascades above and below the ford furnish soul-satisfying background music for a fine rest stop. From this viewpoint the trail descends over a rocky, exposed slope on a long traverse to rejoin the trail shown on the topo map just upstream from the confluences of Buckeye Creek and the tributaries draining the slopes of Hunewill and Victoria peaks. This steady descent is the last of the precipitous terrain, and the remainder of the walk is over long, gradual slopes covered with sagebrush, mountain mahogany, bitterbrush and mule ears. Occasional clumps of aspen occur where the trail crosses a tributary or where it veers close to Buckeye Creek, and they provide welcome shade on a hot mid-summer afternoon. In these well-watered sections the traveler also encounters colorful clumps of monkey flower, goldenrod, lupine, shooting star, paintbrush and penstemon.

Big Meadow itself is a charming two-mile-long grassland replete with Belding ground squirrels and morning-feeding deer. At one time, around 1870, this meadow rang with the sounds of axes and the whirring of a sawmill blade. Here the Upper Hunewill mill operated to provide mining timber. Near the fence at the bottom of the meadow, the observant passerby can make out the signs of an abortive effort to construct a flume to carry water from Buckeye Creek to Bodie.

We pass through a gate in this fence and immediately head right, downhill, for the ford of Buckeye Creek, marked by two posts about 6 feet tall, about 30 yards downstream from the fence. This ford can be difficult in early season. From the creek our trail leads up a small ridge and then undulates over several more ridges, generally within sight of the stream. Beyond a viewpoint for seeing a beaver dam, the trail traverses along a hillside clothed by many head-high aspen trees and many flowers (in season), including scarlet gilia, with its red, trumpet-form blossoms. After crossing two little runoff rills, we can look through the trees down upon a large meadow, which we skirt on a level trail under aspen, juniper, red-fir and lodgepole-pine trees. About ½ mile farther we cross the tip of a tongue of that meadow, and an unmapped stream that flows late into summer. Soon the trail becomes a two-track abandoned vehicle way, and we stroll through a sagebrush field squeezed between the lodgepole pines that border the creek and a large stand of aspen trees on the nose of a ridge that protrudes onto the canyon bottom.

The next section of trail passes through alternating green meadows and gray sagebrush fields, with constant good views of the towering north and south walls of Buckeye Canyon. Past one last, fairly large meadow we come to a fence with both a hiker's gate and a stock gate, where we begin the last mile of this 5-day journey under the shade of Jeffrey and ponderosa pines, red firs and quaking aspens. This last mile is a gentle downhill stroll that ends at a parking area just up-canyon from a Forest Service campground.

Yosemite

Yosemite—a magic name, famous world-wide.

But when most people think of Yosemite, they think Yosemite Valley, which is all too crowded. Hardly anyone knows that it is possible to spend a week in the backcountry of northern Yosemite and not see anyone. We don't guarantee you would see no one, but it is possible, especially if you spend the week off-trail somewhere in the drainage of Rancheria Creek, Piute Creek, Stubblefield Canyon or Thompson Canyon.

Most of the acres in Yosemite National Park are officially declared wilderness, where people are only visitors and their works are absent. You should take advantage of that fact. Almost a thousand miles of trail will help you do so.

Those who would prefer a little bit of civilization in the backcountry can reserve—far in advance—a bed in a tent plus dinner and breakfast at any or all of the five High Sierra camps run by the Park concessionaire. These camps form a loop that makes a good week-long itinerary. (For reservations, write High Sierra Camps, Yosemite National Park, CA 95389.) Each camp also has a backpacker camping area near it.

Of course there are plenty of places to stay in the Valley, but its elevation of 4000 feet won't do much to acclimate you for hiking. Prefer the campgrounds at Bridalveil Creek or Tuolumne Meadows for hikes near those places.

Twin Lakes to Peeler Lake   **34**

Distance	16 miles
Type	Out and back trip
Best season	Mid or late
Topo maps	Buckeye Ridge, Matterhorn Peak

Grade (hiking days/recommended layover days)

Leisurely	——
Moderate	2/1
Strenuous	——
Trailhead	Twin Lakes (20)

HIGHLIGHTS   Despite a stiff 2500-foot climb, this trip makes a fine choice for the city-weary hiker with a "long weekender" trip-selection problem. An early start will allow the hiker to enjoy the morning freshness on the steeper uphill parts, and to be in camp soon enough for a pleasurable swim or some afternoon angling. Peeler Lake, as a destination, is a delightfully unique Sierra experience in that one camps literally on top of the mountain chain, for this lake pours its waters down both sides of the Sierra.

DESCRIPTION

1st Hiking Day (Twin Lakes to Peeler Lake, 8 miles): This trip begins in the Mono Village Campground at the west end of Twin Lakes. First, follow signs saying Barney Lake through the campground to find the wide, level, shaded trail. Travelers setting out in the fall season should take a few minutes at the outset for a side trip to view the colorful Kokanee salmon spawning in the shallows of Robinson Creek south of the campground.

Beyond the campground our sandy trail winds through a moderate-to-dense forest of Jeffrey pine, juniper, lodgepole pine, aspen and cottonwood along Robinson Creek. In late summer, cottony catkins from the cottonwood trees here litter the initial section of trail, leaving the ground surface the gray-white of spring snow. Crossing several small tributaries, the trail then ascends gently, and within ¾ mile encounters the first fir trees, but the forest cover soon gives way to a sagebrush-covered, gently sloping bench, from where one can see the great headwall of the valley in the west.

As you make you way up this open bench through thigh-high sagebrush, rabbitbrush, chamise and mule ears, you have unobstructed views of Victoria, Hunewill and Robinson peaks on the right, and some ragged teeth of the Sawtooth Ridge on the left. About halfway up this bench the trail passes a "ghost forest" of drowned trees caused by beaver dams downstream. Beavers still share this fine Sierra stream with us. On the right, somnolent marmots are likely to be seen dozing among piles of scree that flow from the feet of the avalanche chute scarring Victoria Peak; on the left, the dramatic, unbroken granite wall of Blacksmith Peak at the top of Little Slide Canyon dominates the view. A sign here proclaims this area as part of Hoover Wilderness. On the left, Robinson Creek becomes a willow-lined cascade that is frequently heard but seldom seen.

About ½ mile into the wilderness, the ascent resolves into switchbacks that ford several small tributaries. In their moist banks one encounters monkey flower, monkshood, red columbine, swamp onion and shooting star scattered among clumps of bracken fern. Along the drier stretches of trail the severity of the rock is alleviated by colorful patches of Indian paintbrush. Mariposa lily, scarlet gilia, yarrow milfoil, whorled penstemon, pussy paws, streptanthus and goldenrod.

After the ascent levels out, the trail veers south, fords another tributary, and arrives at the outlet point of arrow-shaped, overused Barney Lake (8258′). Anglers wishing an interlude of fair-to-good fishing for eastern brook and rainbow trout will want to tarry around the deeper east and northeast shores of the 9-acre gem. Others may elect to take a cool, quick dip, or merely to lie on the sandy beach and watch the play of the local water ouzels.

This trail skirts the west side of the lake in a steady, long, hot ascent that takes one onto the canyon wall well above the "ghost forested" delta inlet of Barney Lake. Once above the wetter sections of the delta, the trail descends to a wildflower-decorated ford of Robinson Creek. Here amid the willows can be found lavender swamp onion, red columbine, orange tiger lily and yellow monkey flower. The moderate forest cover now shows the transition to higher climes with the introduction of hemlock and some western white pine.

About ¼ mile upstream the trail refords Robinson Creek, and after fording the outlet creek from Peeler Lake just above its confluence with Robinson Creek, it rises abruptly by steep, rocky switchbacks. Leveling off somewhat, it then comes to a bench junction with the Crown Lake Trail. Here our route turns right and ascends moderately for about ½ mile near the south outlet from Peeler Lake, and then steeply up the draw just northeast of the lake, to reach this outlet. Beautiful Peeler Lake (9489′) sits astride the Sierra crest, contributing water to Robinson Creek on the east and Rancheria Creek on the west. Large (about 60 acres), it has abrupt, rocky shores, and the deep-blue color characteristic of deeper Sierra lakes. There are good-to-excellent campsites almost all around the lake. The best lie on the east shore, reached by leaving the trail where it starts to descend to cross the south outlet. Fishing for eastern brook and rainbow trout (to 14″) is sometimes good.

2nd Hiking Day: Retrace your steps, 8 miles.

Crown Point over Barney Lake

35 Twin Lakes to Crown Lake

Distance	16 miles
Type	Out and back trip
Best season	Early, mid or late
Topo maps	Buckeye Ridge, Matterhorn Peak
Grade (hiking days/recommended layover days)	
Leisurely	——
Moderate	2/1
Strenuous	——
Trailhead	Twin Lakes (20)

HIGHLIGHTS Like the previous trip, this one entails considerable "up," but it is still a good two-day trip selection. This route follows Robinson Creek all the way to Crown Lake, and in its course exposes the traveler to some of the finest east-side scenery available anywhere along the Sierra. Crown Lake itself is set in the heart of the Sierra crest, and consonant with its name, it forms a royal diadem of blue in a regal setting of forest greens.

DESCRIPTION

1st Hiking Day (Twin Lakes to Crown Lake, 8 miles): First follow Trip 34 to the junction of the Peeler and Crown Lake trails. From this junction our route leads south, undulating gently between large outcroppings of glacially polished granite. As the trail ascends moderately below Robinson Lakes, it winds through one near-pure stand of hemlock—unusual for this part of the Sierra. Just before you reach Robinson Lakes is an inviting natural, deep pool that is colored bright aqua. Robinson Lakes are two small, shallow, placid lakes with a sparse forest cover of lodgepole pine, western white pine and hemlock, separated by an isthmus.

The trail rounds the south side of the larger Robinson Lake, fords Robinson Creek, and turns south on a steady ascent. Just below Crown Lake we reford the creek and then switchback up to the good campsites (9440') just downstream from the lake along the outlet, where there are excellent views of Kettle Peak and Crown Point. Fishing for rainbow and some eastern brook (to 9") is fair.

2nd Hiking Day: Retrace your steps, 8 miles.

The Sierra Crest over Crown Lake

36 Twin Lakes to Upper Piute Creek

Distance	23 miles
Type	Out and back trip
Best season	Mid or late
Topo maps	Buckeye Ridge, Matterhorn Peak
Grade (hiking days/recommended layover days)	
Leisurely	——
Moderate	4/1
Strenuous	3/1
Trailhead	Twin Lakes (20)

HIGHLIGHTS   This trip is a satisfying one for the hiker who has viewed the Sawtooth Ridge from the north side only. Following Robinson Creek nearly to the crest of the Sierra, this route circles the west end of the Sawtooth Ridge, and then drops down into the scenic upper reaches of Piute Creek. For those who appreciate spectacular mountain scenery of alpine character, this trip is almost a must.

DESCRIPTION (Moderate trip)

1st Hiking Day: Follow Trip 35 to Crown Lake, 8 miles.

2nd Hiking Day (Crown Lake to Campsites, Upper Piute Creek, 3.5 miles): From Crown Lake's outlet the trail ascends along the west side, offering fine views of the meadowed inlet. The ascent soon steepens as the trail begins a series of short, rocky switchbacks that terminate just east of Crown Point. Here the trail levels out in a willowed meadowy area with several small lakelets, and meets the Snow Lake Trail just beyond. Our route turns left (south), fords the stream draining Snow Lake, and climbs over an easy talus-and-scree pile. This rocky ascent levels briefly within sight of another small lakelet; then the trail cuts across a bench and ascends steeply by rocky switchbacks. In most years there is a large snowbank across this slope well into summer, and one should exercise some caution here. After one more bench this ascent terminates at a tundra-topped saddle on the divide north of Slide Mountain. Here sparse whitebark pine and hemlock stoop to alpine climes, and the traveler taking a well-deserved breather at Mule Pass is likely to hear the scolding of a disturbed cony.

From this pass the trail stepladders down through a series of sandy tundra pockets, serpentining its way north and then east before beginning the long traverse down to Piute Creek. This traverse strikes timberline just below the cross-country turnoff to Ice and Maltby lakes, which is at the ford of the stream draining the swale that gives access to Ice Lake. Fishermen will find the excellent fishing for eastern brook in these two lakes worth the side trip. On the lodgepole and hemlock that line the trail, one will encounter the historic **T** blaze typical of the older trails in Yosemite National Park—a sign emblazoned on these trails by the U.S. Cavalry in the early part of the century, when it was their responsibility to patrol the Park.

This hiking day terminates at the campsites upstream from the turnoff to the cross-country route down Slide Canyon, located on Piute Creek (9600′) along the first ½ mile after the trail comes within sight of the creek. Fishing for eastern brook (to 8″) is fair. This location makes a fine base-camp location for exploratory trips down Slide Canyon or over into Matterhorn Canyon, and it is a traditional base camp for climbers making ascents of Matterhorn Peak and other climbs along the Sawtooth Ridge.

3rd and 4th Hiking Days: Retrace your steps, 11.5 miles.

37 Twin Lakes to Buckeye Creek

Distance	22.4 miles
Type	Shuttle trip
Best season	Mid or late
Topo maps	Buckeye Ridge, Matterhorn Peak
Grade (hiking	days/recommended layover days)
Leisurely	4/1
Moderate	3/1
Strenuous	3/0
Trailhead	Twin Lakes (20), Buckeye Roadend (19)

HIGHLIGHTS   This circle trip around Buckeye Ridge visits nearly the entire range of Sierran environments, from the sagebrush-scrub of the east side to the subalpine grassland of Kerrick Meadow. In between, it winds through pure stands of hemlock, past water-loving clumps of quaking aspen and amidst windblown, gnarled whitebark pine. In its variety it is indeed an "everything trip for everyone."

DESCRIPTION (Moderate trip)

1st Hiking Day: Follow Trip 34 to Peeler Lake, 8.0 miles.
2nd Hiking Day (Peeler Lake to Buckeye Forks, 5.0 miles): From Peeler Lake the trail descends along the lake's west outlet, crossing and recrossing this outlet as it flows down into the marshy upper reaches of Rancheria Creek in Kerrick Meadow. In the meadow, we meet the Kerrick Canyon Trail, turn right (north) on it, and then ascend a gentle slope above the north end of the meadow. A moderate forest cover of mostly pines lines the rest of the gently ascending sand-and-duff trail to the summit of Buckeye Pass. This pass (9572′) in a small, lodgepole-encroached meadow is on the Yosemite Park boundary.

Then the duff trail drops down the northeast side of the pass, and soon fords the infant rill of Buckeye Creek. From here to the next ford, this descent skirts a series of charmingly meadowed steps on the northwest side of the creek. These pockets of grasslands have rich gardens of flowers whose full, splashy colors invite the passerby to linger and enjoy the aster, goldenrod, paintbrush, penstemon, shooting star, larkspur, lupine, buttercup, columbine and monkey flower. Owls hunt these meadows at night, and the daytime traveler should keep a lookout for large convocations of agitated birdlife. At the core of such gatherings, frequently, is a large owl seeking protection in dense foliage.

The series of meadows terminates at a ford where the trail crosses to the east side of the creek. About ¼ mile beyond this ford is a snowcourse, and from it an unmaintained trail takes off over the ridge bound for Barney Lake. For the next ½ mile our trail continues to descend moderately through an area where the trees are much avalanche-broken, and then we jump across an unnamed tributary that tumbles down from Hunewill Peak. In another ½ mile we reach the first of several fair and good campsites located at places where the trail periodically touches the stream. Then a steep descending section followed by two less steep inclines bring us to the flat where the North and South Forks of Buckeye Creek conjoin. In this quiet flat we cross the South Fork on a log and 200 yards farther on wade the North Fork. There are good campsites in the vicinity of a snow-survey cabin here, and the junction with the main east-west trail is just beyond. Fishing in the forks for rainbow and brook (to 9″) is good.

3rd Hiking Day: Follow the 5th hiking day, Trip 33, 9.4 miles.

(Just 1.1 miles down the road toward Bridgeport a side road goes south across Buckeye Creek, but if you go straight ahead 0.4 mile and then park in a used-looking area beside the road, you can walk a few yards downhill to Buckeye Hot Springs. Here, right beside the singing brook, you can soak away the trip's dirt in a natural hot spa.)

38 Twin Lakes to Kerrick Meadow

Distance	22.5 miles
Type	Semiloop trip
Best season	Mid or late
Topo maps	Buckeye Ridge, Matterhorn Peak

Grade (hiking days/recommended layover days)

Leisurely	5/1
Moderate	3/1
Strenuous	3/0

Trailhead   Twin Lakes (20)

HIGHLIGHTS   To use a business metaphor, this trip gives a great return for a minimum investment. From the outset this route is enveloped in magnificent scenery. Along Robinson Creek, the skyline and the immediate surroundings are those of rugged grandeur, consonant with the physical expenditure of effort required on the uphill. As the trip circles Crown Point, it "levels out" both in physical terrain and in emotional impact. The ruggedness gives way to sweeping meadows and rounded summits, providing the traveler an opportunity to absorb some of the impact of this land of contrasts.

DESCRIPTION (Moderate trip)

1st Hiking Day: Follow Trip 35 to Crown Lake, 8 miles.

2nd Hiking Day (Crown Lake to Peeler Lake, 6.5 miles): Rounding the rocky west side of Crown Lake, the trail rises out of the lake basin by steep, rocky switchbacks that offer fine views back of the clear blue lake. This ascent levels out as it crosses a granite-flanked saddle and meets the Rock Island Pass Trail just west of a lakelet in a sandy-meadowed section. Our route turns right (southwest) and begins a long, steadily traversing climb toward Snow Lake. This traverse gives way to switchbacks midway up the hill, and jogs southwest under Crown Point before resuming its southward course on more switchbacks by a little stream. Looking back from the top of this climb, we have fine views to the east of the soldier-tipped summit of Kettle Peak and the west end of the Sawtooth Ridge (called Blacksmith Peak). Snow Lake itself, like Peeler Lake to the north, is a crestal lake perched atop a divide, but in angling circles it is best known for its fishery of golden trout. As the trail rounds the rocky north edge of the lake, we see the meadowy lake fringes, which are most extensive at the southwest end. Here the meadows extend from the lake's edge to the low-profiled saddle called Rock Island Pass (10,240').

From Rock Island Pass the trail descends into the Rancheria Creek drainage. The descent witnesses a change from sparse whitebark pine to a conglomerate forest of lodgepole, hemlock and western white pine. After traversing above a sandy meadow, the T-blazed trail here rises sharply over a sandy ridge and then drops moderately on switchbacks through dense forest cover to Kerrick Meadow and a ford of Rancheria Creek.

On the northwest side of the ford, the trail meets the Kerrick Canyon Trail, where our route turns right and ascends gently up Kerrick Meadow. Rancheria Creek winds its oxbowing way through these sandy grasslands, and on the right we can see large crestal sand accumulations indicating where the living stream has moved across the meadow floor, leaving its spoor. The meadow bottlenecks briefly into a canyon narrows, where the creek tumbles over a silver cascade, and then opens into a beautiful, open, wetter section near the headwaters. In the middle of this marshy section the trail fords one arm of the creek, and then continues on to meet the unsigned Peeler Lake Trail at the meadow's head, where our route turns right (east). From this junction the trail crosses the open meadow and winds through a broken, moderate forest cover of lodgepole. This route crisscrosses back and forth over the west outlet stream from Peeler Lake and arrives at the good campsites along the west shore of this large and beautiful lake (9489'). These campsites offer fine views to the east of Cirque Mountain, Kettle Peak and Crown Point, and the deep waters near the west shore offer fine bank fishing for eastern brook and rainbow (to 14"). Other good campsites lie on the east shore.

3rd Hiking Day: Reverse the steps of the 1st hiking day, Trip 34, 8 miles.

39   Twin Lakes to Benson Lake

Distance	37.2 miles
Type	Out and back trip, part cross-country
Best season	Mid or late
Topo maps	Buckeye Ridge, Matterhorn Peak, Piute Mountain

Grade (hiking days/recommended layover days)

Leisurely	8/2
Moderate	6/1
Strenuous	4/1
Trailhead	Twin Lakes (20)

HIGHLIGHTS   This long trip penetrates to the heart of the North
Boundary Country. In its course it surmounts the
Sierra crest and traces a westside watershed to the Shangri-la basin
of Benson Lake. Because of its moderate climes and its remote
location, this lake is a favorite layover spot for parties traversing the
Pacific Crest Trail, and its popularity is well founded.

DESCRIPTION (Moderate trip)

1st Hiking Day: Follow Trip 34 to Peeler Lake, 8 miles.
2nd Hiking Day (Peeler Lake to Arndt Lake, 5 miles): Leaving
Peeler Lake beside the west outlet, the trail drops down gently as it
crosses back and forth over the outlet stream. This descent soon
leaves the moderate forest cover and enters the north edge of Kerrick
Meadow. At the head of this open, rank grassland the trail meets the
Buckeye Pass Trail, where our route turns left (south) and begins a
long, gentle descent. The trail on the west side of twisting Rancheria
Creek is a narrow, sandy track lined with a wildflower collage of
shooting star, penstemon, paintbrush, aster, goldenrod, buttercup,
lupine, Douglas phlox, and pussy paws. In a timber-lined bottleneck,
the meadows narrow briefly and then reopen. On the left one can see
sand banks that were stranded when the oxbowing stream altered
course sometime in the geologic past. The broad grasslands are alive

with the scurrying and piping of alarmed Belding ground squirrels.

The trail then passes the Rock Island Pass Trail and continues to descend to a second timbered narrows. This brief stretch of lodgepole pine opens to yet another long meadow that is flanked on the southwest by the granite heights of Price Peak. On the descent through this meadow the canyon starts to narrow, and where the trail starts a gentle 200-yard ascent, our route leaves the trail.

Our short cross-country segment strikes out southward, fords Rancheria Creek, and ascends beside the tundra-lined outlet of Arndt Lake (9234′). A good route to the north shore of hidden Arndt Lake is via the saddle in the granite just east of where the outlet leaves the lake.

One will find good campsites at the outlet and around the north shore of Arndt Lake (9234′). Those with a tolerance for cool mountain water will enjoy the swimming off the granite that drops into this lake. Views of the polished granite domes flanking the south and east sides of the lake are soul-satisfying, and beckon the explorer to further investigation and discovery.

3rd Hiking Day (Arndt Lake to Benson Lake, 5.6 miles): From Arndt Lake our route retraces the cross-country segment of the previous hiking day to the Kerrick Canyon Trail, and then continues down through a narrow, rocky canyon. The unseamed white granite canyon walls in this narrows show the glacial polish, smoothing and sculpting that reflect the geologic history of the canyon. Rancheria Creek on the left bumps and splashes down through a series of fine potholes offering swimming and fishing spots. Like all the older trails in the Park, this one is T-blazed, indicating that it was once a U.S. Cavalry patrol route—a route blazed when the Army was responsible for the integrity of the Park lands.

The sparse-to-moderate forest cover of mountain hemlock and whitebark and lodgepole pine in the narrows gives way to another meadow as the trail continues to descend. This meadow is surrounded by several magnificent examples of glacial domes—all unnamed. The clean, sweeping lines of the dome to the west are particularly impressive, and the passerby cannot help but feel the awesome power of the natural forces that created it. Near the foot of the meadow, the trail fords to the east side of Rancheria Creek, where it hugs the sheer, water-stained granite wall. Both the trail and the creek make an exaggerated Z before straightening out on a westward course and reaching the Pacific Crest Trail.

At this junction, it's left (southwest) to Benson Lake. and ahead (right, west) to continue down Kerrick Canyon. Go left to climb steeply under a moderate forest cover of hemlock, through three meretricious but beautiful gaps. As you approach a tarn in the first gap, the trail veers abruptly away to climb steeply to the second and highest gap, passing a pair of tarns and then a sandy campsite overlooking a little meadow. As the forest grows increasingly sparse, the trail drops to the little meadow before attacking the third gap, beyond which is Seavey Pass (9150′), 30 feet lower than the second gap before it.

From the glacially polished granite setting of Seavey Pass the trail drops past another stately rockbound tarn just below the pass, and finally plummets down over steep, eroded pitches alongside a riotous unnamed stream that feeds the Benson Lake alluvial fan. This descent is rocky going, requiring a "grunt and bear it" attitude of the downhill-weary traveler, alleviated only by the fine views of Volunteer Peak across Piute Creek and of the splashing waterfall springing from the ridge south of Piute Mountain.

Where the trail levels out on the valley floor, it crosses the sandy alluvial sediments, and witnesses some drastic changes in the flora. The initial contact with the valley floor, with its solitary-standing specimens of Jeffrey pine towering amid gooseberry, gives the traveler the impression of sandy aridity. But within a few yards, the atmosphere changes as the trail becomes immersed in bracken fern, overflow freshets and dense forest. The trail is sometimes difficult to follow because of the rank growth and quagmire conditions of the valley floor. Two trails cut through this fertile area to Benson Lake, which offers the only good camping in the vicinity. One, an unsigned, overgrown use trail that is hard to spot and follow, turns right to skirt an outcrop just after you enter the valley floor. The other departs just before the ford of Piute Creek. This lateral winds along the northwest bank of Piute Creek through fields of corn lily and bracken fern, with occasional clumps of tiger lily and swamp onion, to the good campsites along the east shore of the lake (7581′). Anglers can look forward to good fishing for rainbow and eastern brook trout (to 14″). Except in mosquito season, this lake makes a fine spot for a layover day.

4th, 5th and 6th Hiking Days: Retrace your steps, 18.6 miles.

Benson Lake

Twin Lakes to Smedberg Lake **40**

Distance   49.6 miles
Type   Semiloop trip
Best season   Mid or late
Topo maps   Buckeye Ridge, Matterhorn Peak, Piute Mountain
Grade (hiking days/recommended layover days)
   Leisurely   8/3
   Moderate   7/2
   Strenuous   5/1
Trailhead   Twin Lakes (20)

HIGHLIGHTS   Making a grand loop through the center of the
North Boundary Country, this trip traces three
major watersheds, visits six major lakes, and views the finest scenery
in the region. Layover days taken on this long route provide the
opportunity of visiting any of the nearby lakes, over a dozen, or
making side trips into any one of several other watersheds. It is a long
trip with many stiff climbs that make it advisable for the hiker to first
prepare himself by taking one or more shorter trips.

DESCRIPTION (Leisurely trip)

1st, 2nd and 3rd Hiking Days: Follow Trip 39 to Benson Lake,
18.6 miles.
4th Hiking Day (Benson Lake to Smedberg Lake, 4.5 miles):
There is an old saying among those who have visited Benson Lake,
"Everywhere from that hole in the ground is up," and one contemplating this hiking day must agree. Retracing our steps over the short
lateral to the main trail, the route then fords Piute Creek and begins
a long, steep climb through a moderate forest cover of lodgepole
laced with occasional western white pine. Crisscrossing back and
forth over the outlet stream from Smedberg Lake, the trail then

circles beneath the steep west facade of Volunteer Peak, and finally crosses over the shoulder of this peak past the first of two trail junctions to Pate Valley. On the north side of Volunteer Peak the trail drops to the south shore of Smedberg Lake (9220'), where excellent campsites may be found all along the south shore and along the southeast inlet about 200 yards from the lake. Fishing for rainbow and occasional eastern brook (to 13") is excellent. As a layover point this picturesque, island-dotted lake makes a fine central location for excursions to nearby Surprise and Sister Lakes.

5th Hiking Day (Smedberg Lake to Matterhorn Canyon, 6.5 miles): From the narrow valley holding Smedberg Lake, the trail is a steady climb to Benson Pass. It first follows up an inlet of Smedberg Lake on a southeast, meadowed course, then swings east on a stepladdering climb through moderate, then sparse, forest cover to an upper meadow above the main drainage feeding Smedberg Lake. After this brief respite the trail resumes its steep, rocky, upward course to Benson Pass (10,139'). The last climb is up a narrow, meadowed draw with a trickling stream and then over a heavily eroded surface through sparse whitebark pine and hemlock. Excellent views to the northeast present themselves at the pass, and one can see Whorl Mountain, Twin Peaks, some of the pinnacles making up the Sawtooth Ridge, and the granite divide between Matterhorn Creek and Piute Creek.

From Benson Pass the trail drops steeply to a newborn tributary of Wilson Creek, where a sandy meadow at 9780 feet provides campsites as long as the water holds out. The grade eases, then grows steep again, as the trail drops to cross splashing Wilson Creek and wind down through an increasingly dense forest into Wilson Canyon. Then the downgrade is gradual along the banks of Wilson Creek to the lip of Matterhorn Canyon. In this section the trail winds back and forth over Wilson Creek through an increasingly dense forest cover of lodgepole, with occasional whitebark pine near the top and western white pine near the bottom. Finally, the path is steep again to the floor of Matterhorn Canyon. On the canyon floor, Matterhorn Canyon Creek is a meandering stream flowing alternately through willowed meadows and stands of lodgepole mixed with western white pine. Our trail turns north, passing some good campsites, and follows the stream a mile, then fords it to several campsites 200 yards downstream from the junction with the trail to Tuolumne Meadows. These canyon campsites (8480') boast several fine swimming holes just upstream in granite potholes. Fishing for eastern brook and rainbow trout (to 12") is good.

6th Hiking Day (Matterhorn Canyon to Campsites, Upper Piute Creek, 8.5 miles): From these campsites our route goes northeast and leaves the Pacific Crest Trail behind. The route ascends moderately through alternately sandy and rocky sections. On both sides of the canyon, glaciated gray granite shoulders drop to the valley floor, and the black water-staining on their broad surfaces, particularly on Quarry Peak, makes eerie configurations. In a wet, muddy section where the trail fords several small tributary runoffs, it winds through wildflower displays that include lupine, elephant heads, monkey flower, paintbrush, goldenrod, aster and Mariposa lily. The trail then fords to the west side of Matterhorn Canyon Creek and then refords to follow the east bank through the latter part of the canyon narrows and well beyond. About ½ mile above a meadow it refords back to the west side.

From this ford the trail keeps to the west side of the creek, winding through meadow and tundra sections on a moderate ascent. Ahead, the pointed tops of Finger Peaks come into view, and later the massive granite of Whorl Mountain and Matterhorn Peak. Scattered lodgepole and hemlock trees dot the trail as it progresses up to the sky-parlor meadows of the upper basin. Some clumps of trees hold campsites (their protected location is testimony to the wind that often sweeps through the canyon), and the tree clumps are interspersed with stretches of grassland laced with sagebrush and willow.

Now the trail passes the last stand of trees, and ascends steadily on a long traverse below Finger Peaks. Views across the barren upper basin of Whorl Mountain are awesome, and its rugged massiveness contrasts sharply with the delicate wildflowers found underfoot as one nears Burro Pass. Here, scattered among sparse whitebark pines, one enjoys the spots of color provided by primrose, scarlet penstemon, wallflower and Douglas phlox. The final climb to the divide is accomplished via rocky switchbacks that terminate on the low saddle of Burro Pass (10,560'). Fine views of both the Matterhorn and Piute Creek canyons are to be had, but overshadowing all are the soldier-topped summits of the Sawtooth Ridge to the north.

The first recorded crossing of this pass was made by Lt. N.F. McClure in 1894. Today's travelers can compare their observations of the pass and its surroundings with those of McClure, who said,

> The route now led for five miles through little meadows on each side of the stream, until a comparatively low saddle was seen to the left of us and near the head of the canyon. Investigating this, I found it was a natural pass. The scenery here was truly sublime. I doubt if any part of the main chain of the Sierra presents a greater ruggedness . . .

As the trail descends on the north side of the pass, it affords fine views of the tiny, barren lakes at the foot of Finger Peaks. The basin of the pass is usually wet, and sometimes covered with snow, thereby making route-picking an instinctive matter. Here Piute Creek is a far cry from what was seen two hiking days ago. A mere stripling of a stream, it tinkles through meadow grass, and the traveler fords to the north side by an easy step. Belding squirrels pipe one's passage through the grassy tundra stretches, and the call of marmots on the nearby scree is a cacophonous accompaniment to the gentle descent into the moderate forest cover of lodgepole and hemlock. This hiking day ends at the good campsites (9600′) found along that stretch of Piute Creek where the trail touches the creek banks northeast of Finger Peaks. Here fishing for eastern brook (to 8″) is fair.

7th and 8th Hiking Days: Reverse the steps of Trip 36, 11.5 miles.

In Kerrick Canyon near Peeler Lake

Green Creek to East Lake   **41**

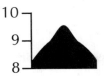

Distance	8 miles
Type	Out and back trip
Best season	Early, mid or late
Topo maps	Dunderberg Peak

Grade (hiking days/recommended layover days)

Leisurely	2/0
Moderate	Day
Strenuous	Day
Trailhead	Green Creek Roadend (21)

HIGHLIGHTS   This is a fine beginner's weekend hike. East Lake offers one of the most colorful backdrops for a camping scene to be found in any wilderness. The trilogy of Gabbro, Page and Epidote peaks is composed of rocks varying in hue from vermilion reds to ochre, and these colors are set in metavolcanic blacks for contrast. Nearby Nutter, Gilman and Hoover lakes offer good fishing to supplement the angling in East Lake, and the general spectrum of scenery along the trail rounds out a rich diet indeed.

DESCRIPTION

1st Hiking Day (Green Creek Roadend to East Lake, 4 miles): Amid moderate-to-dense Jeffrey, juniper, lodgepole and aspen forest cover, the trail ascends gently to a small step-across spring runoff. A ground cover of sagebrush, mule ears, serviceberry, western blueberry, wild lilac, lupine, wallflower, paintbrush, pennyroyal and buckwheat lines the trail in the initial drier stretches, and along the wetter spots one may find tiger lily, penstemon, shooting star, monkshood, monkey flower, columbine, rein-orchid and aster. The ascent then becomes steeper as it crosses an easy rocky ridge, and finally it begins a long series of steady switchbacks.

Crossing several intermittent runoff tributaries coming down from Monument Ridge, the trail keeps to the northwest side of West Fork Green Creek. While the creek itself is never out of hearing, it is often obscured visually by the sheath of willows that line its bank. Ahead, on the left, one can make out Gabbro Peak, and on the right the stream that falls from the hanging valley containing West Lake. Added to the wildflowers to be seen along the trail here are iris, corn lily, cow parsnip, stickseed, gooseberry, Douglas phlox and pussy paws.

The trail then climbs another dry slope by moderately ascending switchbacks to a junction just before Green Lake where the right fork leads to another trail junction in $\frac{1}{5}$ mile (from this second junction, it's left to campsites at the head of Green Lake and beyond into Glines Canyon, and right to West Lake, which has few campsites). Anglers may wish to tarry here for the good fishing for rainbow and eastern book (to 14"). At your present junction, take the left fork to descend to a deep ford of West Fork Green Creek just below Green Lake (8945'). Hunt for easier crossings; a use trail leads up to the lake's half-ruined, low dam for a possible crossing. Green Lake is large (about 50 acres), with a campsite or two below it and a few more on its east shore, but virtually none on its west shore. A mixed timber cover of lodgepole, hemlock and occasional western white pine surrounds most of the lake except for the meadowed inlet delta.

Our route, the left fork, fords West Fork Green Creek just below the lake. After fording the creek, the trail switchbacks up to ford the outlet stream from East Lake for the first time. This outlet stream is a vigorous watercourse that follows the natural ravine shown on the topo map just north of East Lake. The trail makes a long loop away from the stream and then veers back to a second ford. Beyond, the trail ascends by long, gradual switchbacks as it continues on to ford the two meadowed outlets of East Lake (9458'). There are a fair campsite between the outlets and fair-to-good campsites east of the trail as it rounds the lake's east shore. Fishing for rainbow trout on this 75-acre lake is good. This lake makes a fine base-camp location for forays to nearby Nutter, Gilman and Hoover lakes.

2nd Hiking Day: Retrace your steps, 4 miles.

Green Creek to Tuolumne Meadows

42

Distance	26.7 miles
Type	Shuttle trip
Best season	Mid or late
Topo maps	**Tuolumne Meadows**, Dunderberg Peak, Matterhorn Peak, Falls Ridge, Tioga Pass

Grade (hiking days/recommended layover days)

Leisurely	4/1
Moderate	4/0
Strenuous	3/0
Trailhead	Green Creek Roadend (21), Lembert Dome Trailhead (24)

HIGHLIGHTS   Three quarters of this scenic route travels remote sections of Yosemite National Park that are not frequented by day walkers. Solitude-seekers will find the quiet of upper Virginia Canyon to their liking, and anglers wanting a variety of lake and stream fishing for rainbow and eastern brook will pronounce this trip ideal.

DESCRIPTION (Moderate trip)

1st Hiking Day: Follow Trip 41 to East Lake, 4 miles.

2nd Hiking Day (East Lake to Lower Virginia Canyon, 9 miles): From the outlet of East Lake (9458′) the trail ascends above the lake's waters as it rounds the east shore, affording superlative views of Gabbro, Page and Epidote peaks foregrounded by the deep blue of East Lake. The trail drops briefly across the gentle ridge separating East Lake from the tiny lakelets to the east, and then veers away from East Lake on an ascending traverse before descending gently to the meadow-fringed shores of Nutter Lake. Through a sparse forest cover of lodgepole and hemlock, the trail then climbs above the west shore of beautiful Gilman Lake (9486'), passing a lateral trail down to it. Flanked by the steep west face of Dunderberg Peak, and foregrounded by a meadow and timber cover, this lake is a favorite of photographers. Anglers may also wish to linger—the better to sample the good fishing for rainbow.

From the Gilman Lake lateral our trail ascends past several small tarns, fords the stream joining Gilman and Hoover Lakes, and then rises steeply to the bench holding Hoover Lakes (9819'). These two alpine lakes are set between the dark rock of Epidote Peak and the burgundy-red rock of the magnificent unnamed mountain to the southeast. They are considerably colder than the lakes below, and they have been planted with eastern brook trout. The trail skirts the southeast side of the first, fords the stream between them, and passes along the northwest side of the second. After fording the inlet of upper Hoover Lake, it ascends steeply along the stream joining Hoover Lakes with Summit Lake. This rocky ascent through a thinning forest cover of lodgepole and occasional hemlock and whitebark pine meets the Virginia Lakes Trail on a small bench, where our route turns right (northwest). This moderate ascent fords the aforementioned stream and arrives at aptly named Summit Lake (10,183'). Like Peeler Lake to the north, Summit Lake contributes water to both sides of the Sierra. It sits atop the crest in a **V**'d notch between the dark rock of Camiaca Peak and a lighter ridge extending north from Excelsior Mountain.

The trail skirts the north side of Summit Lake to the Sierra crest, enters Yosemite National Park, and then switchbacks steeply down the west slope. Looking back toward Summit Lake, we can see clearly that the glaciers that had their beginnings below Camiaca Peak on both the east and the west sides met at the present site of Summit Lake. Across the cirque basin of upper Virginia Canyon, the rounded eminence of Grey Butte and the sharply nippled tops of Virginia Peak and Stanton Peak dominate the views to the west. The trail levels out before it fords Return Creek and continues down-canyon. There is excellent camping here at the ford and also downstream. Recent avalanches have made obvious incursions into the sparse forest cover of lodgepole, aspen and occasional red fir and hemlock, and have left broken stubs on every hand.

The trail then fords several tributary streams as it keeps to the west side of Return Creek on a long, moderate descent to a junction with the Pacific Crest Trail. At this junction our route turns left, fords Return Creek, and arrives at some good campsites (8600') in the granite ledge system on the east side of the creek. Fishing for eastern brook and rainbow is fair to good, and the wonderful pools in the vigorous stream invite you to swim, bathe, and play.

3rd Hiking Day (Lower Virginia Canyon to Glen Aulin, 8 miles): The trail from the campsites near the ford continues southwest along the banks of Return Creek and fords McCabe Creek before beginning the steep ascent of the canyon wall. This gentle descent along Return Creek passes the stream's beautiful bedrock-granite cascades. Dropping into deep, clear potholes, the creek has carved and sculpted the bedrock into smooth, mollescent lines that invite you to run your hands across them. Columbine clustered amid lupine and whorled penstemon add color to the green mats of swamp onion and gooseberry near the ford. (In late season fill your canteen at McCabe Creek, for there is usually no more water until Glen Aulin.)

Beyond this ford the trail begins a steep 600-foot ascent on long switchbacks across a slope moderately forested with fine specimens of western white pine, lodgepole and occasional red fir. These rocky switchbacks terminate at the McCabe Lake Trail junction, where our route turns right and descends gently over a duff surface. Birdlife abounds through the moderate-to-dense forest cover of red fir, lodgepole and western white pine, and the hiker is very likely to see chickadees, juncos, warblers, flycatchers, woodpeckers, bluebirds, robins and evening grosbeaks in these precincts.

A short ¾ mile beyond the last junction, close under Point 9182, you may find water even in late season. Then your route declines gently through cool, moist forest to a fairly large meadow east of Elbow Hill. After threading a course through a few stands of pines, you emerge in an even larger meadow—about 2 miles long, although the trail does not trace all 2 miles of it. At a stream fork shortly beyond a *very* large boulder to your west, you may find water even in late season. Then the trail climbs over a saddle in a low, forested ridge and gently descends for about ½ mile. Over the next mile, always near Cold Canyon Creek, the level, rutted path passes many possible campsites in pleasant meadowy areas studded with small lodgepole pines.

From this camping region a series of easy switchbacks accomplish about half the descent to the Tuolumne River, and where the trail re-reaches the creek there is another good campsite. On the final rocky downhill mile to the river, you catch glimpses of Tuolumne Falls and White Cascade, and their roar carries all the way across the canyon.

Finally, you reach "civilization" at the Glen Aulin High Sierra Camp (7880'). Within sight of the camp you pass the Tuolumne River Trail westbound, and in 15 yards come to the little spur trail that crosses Conness Creek on a bridge to the camp. Very meager supplies are sometimes available here. The backpacker campsites just upstream from the "lodge" are very popular with bears, and you would be less likely to have ursine visitors at one of the campsites a mile or two before you reach Glen Aulin—though it would be no guarantee.

4th Hiking Day (Glen Aulin to Tuolumne Meadows, 5.7 miles): From Glen Aulin the trail crosses the Tuolumne River on a low steel bridge, from which one has excellent views of White Cascade and the deep green pool below it. In a few minutes we pass the May Lake Trail, ascending west, and continue our steep climb to gain the height of White Cascade and Tuolumne Falls. The trail passes a fine viewpoint below the falls, and if the light is right, you'll get a great photograph. Above the falls, the river flows down a series of sparkling rapids separated by large pools and wide sheets of clear water spread out over slightly inclined granite slopes.

Soon the trail crosses the river for the last time, on a boulders-and-steel bridge, and then climbs a little way above the gorge the river has cut here. Across the stream one can easily make out basaltic "Little Devils Postpile," the only volcanic formation anywhere around here. Then we descend to larger, polished slabs near the river, and follow a somewhat ducked route across them for about a mile beside the beckoning waters. When trail tread resumes, you soon cross the three branches of Dingley Creek, which may be dry in late season, and stroll along a "levee" built to raise the trailbed above the flood level here. About ½ mile of almost level walking in cool forest brings you to the Young Lakes Trail junction, and then you touch the northwest edge of your destination, Tuolumne Meadows. Soon after, you cross three branches of Delaney Creek, the last being the only one of consequence. Just beyond this ford, a trail veers left, bound for the Tuolumne Meadows Stables. You instead veer right and ascend a long, dry, sandy ridge. From the tiny reeded lakes on top of this ridge, the trail drops gently down through meadowed pockets and stands of lodgepole pine to Soda Springs, once a drive-in and then a walk-in campground, but since 1976 closed to camping.

From the effervescent springs, in their dilapidated enclosure, the trail follows a closed-off dirt road east above the north edge of Tuolumne Meadows, the largest subalpine meadow in the Sierra Nevada. The spiring summits of the Cathedral Range across the meadow provide challenging vistas as we stroll the last, level ¾ mile to a parking lot beside State Highway 120, the Tioga Road—unless our car is waiting a few hundred yards short of the highway on the road to the stables.

Green Creek to Virginia Lakes **43**

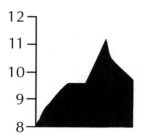

Distance	10 miles
Type	Shuttle trip
Best season	Mid or late
Topo maps	Dunderberg Peak

Grade (hiking days/recommended layover days)

Leisurely	2/1
Moderate	2/0
Strenuous	——

Trailhead   Green Creek Roadend (21), Virginia Lakes Roadend (22)

HIGHLIGHTS   This U-shaped trip circles around Kavanaugh Ridge and Dunderberg Peak, and in its passage touches 14 alpine and subalpine lakes. Scenery along this route is mostly of the open alpine variety, and the route is a fine sampling of the majestic Sierra crest. For the beginner or for the experienced back-country traveler, this trip is an excellent choice for a weekend excursion.

DESCRIPTION

1st Hiking Day: Follow Trip 41 to East Lake, 4.0 miles.

2nd Hiking Day (East Lake to Virginia Lakes Campground, 6.5 miles): Proceed to the Virginia Lakes Trail junction as described in the 2nd hiking day, Trip 42. At this junction our trail turns left (southeast) and climbs steeply up a series of switchbacks that overlook the Hoover Lakes in the valley of East Creek below. Beyond these zigzags we reach a sloping, willowed bowl surrounded by many snowbanks into late season. Then, under a small red cliff, the trail switchbacks up again, to cross the northern of the two streams in this two-headed canyon. Again the way steepens, and at frequent rest stops you can see the small white petals of Douglas phlox and the purple trumpetforms of Davidson's penstemon. There are even a few specimens of a yellow flower hardly ever found below 10,000 feet: alpine gold. Finally we cross the divide at 11,000 feet, where the red rocks of the crest on our right contrast with the somber dark grays of Black Mountain straight ahead.

The trail ahead has been altered slightly from that shown on the topo map, now being located farther south where it drops down the tundra steps of Frog Lakes. In Frog Lakes and in the willowed stream between them, anglers will find fair fishing for eastern brook and rainbow trout. Just north of Cooney Lake the new trail and that shown on the topo map once more coincide. This lake, with its willowed inlet and its precipitous outlet, contains thriving populations of eastern brook and rainbow.

Continuing the moderate descent over a rocky ledge system, the trail winds down through sparse clumps of whitebark pine past a mining claim, and then fords the willowed outlet stream of Moat Lake. In the wetter stretches here, wildflower fanciers will delight in the lush clumps of columbine, swamp onion and shooting star. Under the steep, avalanche-scarred south face of Dunderberg Peak, the second-highest peak in the North Boundary Country, the trail slopes down on a rocky traverse to the outlet of Blue Lake. The broken talus and scree to the north are a haven for marmots and conies, whose scats and hay harvests can be found on and between the rocks next to the trail. Like Cooney Lake, Blue Lake has a fishery of eastern brook and rainbow trout. Past Blue Lake the descending trail is within sight of one more tiny, unnamed lake. Soon the trail splits and ramifies, and even some roads appear, but route-finding is not a problem, because following any of them will in about ¼ mile bring you to Virginia Lakes Campground (9760′).

Hetch Hetchy to Rancheria Creek

44

Distance	13 miles
Type	Out and back trip
Best season	Early
Topo maps	**Hetch Hetchy Reservoir**, Lake Eleanor, Hetch Hetchy Reservoir
Grade (hiking days/recommended layover days)	
Leisurely	2/0
Moderate	Day
Strenuous	——
Trailhead	O'Shaughnessy Dam (17)

HIGHLIGHTS   Early season is the ideal time to view the falls along this route, and eager opening-day anglers will find the good fishing along Rancheria Creek a satisfying culmination to a fine trip.

DESCRIPTION

1st Hiking Day (O'Shaughnessy Dam to Rancheria Creek, 6.5 miles): From the trailhead at the south end of the dam, the thunder from the discharge pipe accompanies travelers as they cross this 600-foot-long piece of concrete. Although 8 miles of the Grand Canyon of the Tuolumne River were put under a reservoir for the sake of San Francisco's water supply, the actual intake for the aqueduct is 17 miles downstream in a relatively ordinary part of the canyon.

The first 0.7 mile of our route is on the service road (no longer used by vehicles, and badly deteriorated) to Lake Eleanor (part of San Francisco's water project). Once across the dam, the road passes through a long tunnel, beyond which it winds along the hillside above Hetch Hetchy's high-water mark. Views across the water include, from the left, Tueeulala Falls (seasonal), Wapama Falls, Hetch Hetchy Dome and Kolana Rock. Soon the road begins a gentle, shaded ascent through canyon live oak, incense-cedar, Douglas-fir, California bay, California grape, big-leaf maple and poison oak. As our route swings east and achieves a more southerly and drier position, trees become scarce. After we turn right onto the signed trail to Rancheria Creek, there are Digger pines and live oaks for shade. The trail winds along a sunny bench where glacial polish and glacial erratics remind us that at times during the Pleistocene Epoch glaciers up to 60 miles long—the longest in the Sierra—flowed down this canyon.

After crossing seasonal Tueeulala Falls creek, we descend to the bridges over Falls Creek. During high runoff this creek can be impassable, as the bridges may be under water or washed out. In early season Wapama Falls will cover these bridges with spray. Beyond the creek our fly-infested trail climbs onto a meadowy ledge system where we have an airy view of the water below. In spring, wildflowers dot the meadows here and you can see monkeyflower, paintbrush and Sierra onion. This hike usually boasts a great variety of wildlife, and commonly seen animals include alligator lizard, Steller jay and California ground squirrel.

Beyond the ledges our trail makes a long descent to cascading Tiltill Creek, which we cross on a bridge. From here we climb onto the low ridge separating Tiltill Creek and Rancheria Creek. About ¾ mile beyond the bridge, the trail enters a shaded flat where a spur trail (right) leads to streamside campsites ¼ mile below Rancheria Falls. Please be careful here as the area is heavily used and bears are persistent. Fishing in Rancheria Creek is poor-to-good for rainbow trout (to 10").

2nd Hiking Day: Retrace your steps (6.5 miles).

Hikers near O'Shaughnessy Dam

Hetch Hetchy to Tiltill Valley   **45**

Distance	18.6 miles
Type	Out and back trip
Best season	Early
Topo maps	**Hetch Hetchy Reservoir**, Lake Eleanor, Hetch Hetchy Reservoir

Grade (hiking days/recommended layover days)
Leisurely	4/0
Moderate	3/0
Strenuous	2/0
Trailhead	O'Shaughnessy Dam (17)

HIGHLIGHTS   Like the previous trip, this route tours the northern edge of Hetch Hetchy Reservoir. Across the lake the views of Kolana Rock and the sheer granite walls of the Grand Canyon of the Tuolumne provide a majestic accompaniment. The contrasting intimate serenity of Tiltill Valley is a pleasant terminus to this early-season trek.

DESCRIPTION (Leisurely trip)

1st Hiking Day: Follow Trip 44 to Rancheria Creek, 6.5 miles.
2nd Hiking Day (Rancheria Creek to Tiltill Valley, 2.8 miles): From the junction of the Pate Valley/Tiltill Valley trails above the campsites, the trail to Tiltill Valley climbs steeply for a full 1200 feet up to a timber-bottomed saddle. As the trail descends on the north side of the saddle, it traverses a pine forest with a sprinkling of incense-cedar and black oak. When this duff trail emerges at the east end of Tiltill Valley, it meets a trail to Tilden Canyon and Benson Lake. The valley is a long meadow which in early spring is usually quite wet and boggy at the east end. Lodgepole pine fringes the meadow, and the valley is flanked by polished outcroppings of granite and by brush-covered slopes. The trail crosses to the north side of the meadow and winds west to the excellent campsites just south of the Tiltill Creek ford (5600'). These camping places, located in an isolated stand of lodgepole and sugar pine, afford excellent views in both directions down the meadows. Campers have an

uninterrupted vantage point from which to watch the large variety of wildlife that make this meadow their home. Fishing on Tiltill Creek for rainbow (to 10″) is excellent in early season.

3rd and 4th Hiking Days: Retrace your steps, 9.3 miles.

Rancheria Falls

20 Lakes Basin Loop   **46**

Distance	8.5 miles
Type	Loop trip, part cross-country
Best seaso:	Mid or late
Topo maps	**WP Tuolumne Meadows**, Tioga Pass, Dunderberg Peak

Grade (hiking days/recommended layover days)

Leisurely	2/1
Moderate	2/0
Strenuous	Day
Trailhead	Saddlebag Lake (23)

HIGHLIGHTS   20 Lakes Basin is set among majestic peaks and is full of pretty lakes. Yet, in spite of its rugged setting, the trail through it is mostly gentle to moderate. Most of the basin lacks acceptable campsites, but a short cross-country jaunt brings hikers to scenic if Spartan campsites in a granite sub-basin. Timber is scarce; stoves are a must.

DESCRIPTION (Moderate trip)

1st Hiking Day (Saddlebag Lake to Cascade Lake, via Saddlebag's west side, 3 miles): In season, Saddlebag Lake Resort provides ferry service across Saddlebag Lake for a moderate fee, cutting your trip by as much as 3 miles if you take the ferry both ways.

Those preferring to walk will find the trailhead a few steps past the summer ranger station south of Saddlebag's dam, where the trail begins as an old road that dips below the face of the dam. (Crossing on the dam isn't recommended.) Climbing up on the other side, the road becomes a footpath north-northwest along Saddlebag Lake's west side, over shattered rocks in rust, brown, gray, and cream colors, and through a surprising array of flowers. The splendid peaks around the head of 20 Lakes Basin come into view, with North Peak and Mt. Scowden particularly striking. To the east are the gently rounded, metamorphic summits of the Tioga Crest. This region is full of ruins left by mostly unsuccessful mining ventures. To support one such venture, the Tioga (or Great Sierra) Mine's plans in the winter of 1882 called for men and mules to use huge sleds to haul 16,000 pounds of mining machinery up Mill Creek from the east, through Lake Canyon, over the Tioga Crest, down to Saddlebag Lake, and presumably from there to the mine, a few miles southwest of Saddlebag!

The trail fades out as you approach the stream that's the outlet of Greenstone Lake (10,120′) at 1¼ miles. Avoiding a spur trail around Greenstone's southwest side, you cross the stream to pick up the trail coming up from the ferry landing at Saddlebag's head and then bear west above Greenstone Lake to enter Hoover Wilderness at just over 1⅓ miles. Beginning a gradual-to-moderate climb on this wide, dusty trail that was once a road to a now-defunct mine deep in the basin, you traverse above skinny, rock-rimmed Wasco Lake, crossing a divide: behind you, streams drain southeast through Saddlebag Lake and Lee Vining Creek; ahead, streams drain north into Mill Creek and through Lundy Canyon. The trail descends a bit, passing Wasco's head and the ponds on its outlet, to reach lovely Steelhead Lake (10,270′) at a little over 2⅓ miles. The stream from higher, unseen Cascade Lake spills noisily into Steelhead's southwest side, and a use trail branches west (left) at Steelhead's south end.

Pick up that use trail to cross Steelhead's inlet and head west for about half a mile—the exact distance will depend on the route you take when the use trail fades out. You wander up ledges along the headwaters of Mill Creek, passing unnamed lakes west of Steelhead, into a handsome granite sub-basin around beautiful Cascade Lake (10,315′) at about 3 miles. Viewful though exposed campsites are scattered here and there in this sub-basin, whose south and west edges are defined by the east- and west-trending ridges of North Peak on the Sierra crest. A layover day here offers fine opportunities for cross-country exploring.

2nd Hiking Day (Cascade Lake to Saddlebag Lake via Saddlebag's east side, 5½ miles): Return to the main trail near Steelhead Lake and turn north on it, along the lake's east shore. There are no acceptable campsites along this day's route.

As the trail approaches Steelhead's north end, it swings east, descends a little past some lakelets, and crosses Steelhead's outlet to reach a signed trail junction: right (northeast) to Lake Helen and Lundy Canyon, left (north) to defunct Hess Mine. Go right, climbing steeply but briefly on a trail that's well-beaten but not yet on the 7½′ topo. You reach islet-filled Shamrock Lake (10,250′) at just over 4 miles, climb up and over a talus slope on Shamrock's north side, and then ascend a knob. Atop the knob, the trail may be indistinct—rows of rocks and ducks help—as it leads to an overlook of beautiful Lake Helen, Lundy Canyon, and some Great Basin peaks far to the east.

From this overlook, the trail curves right (northeast) and descends the knob's north face. You pass some lovely cascades and ponds southwest of Lake Helen and skirt the lake's northwest bay, touching down at last at Lake Helen's rocky outlet (10,107'). Ford the outlet to find a junction: left (northeast) to Lundy Canyon, right (south) to Odell Lake and back to Saddlebag Lake. There are lovely views over Lundy Canyon and its waterfalls about five minutes down the lefthand fork; however, the trail down into Lundy Canyon is extremely steep as well as easily and often washed out, and Lundy Canyon itself offers almost no acceptable campsites.

In any case, your route for this trip lies on the righthand fork, which begins with a short, steep climb to circumvent a low cliff. You trace the east shore of Lake Helen on a rocky path before climbing moderately southeast up a rocky draw through which Odell Lake's outlet flows into Lake Helen. The trail tops out briefly above Odell (10,267'), then climbs gradually to a high point, unsigned Lundy Pass (10,320'). Now you begin a gradual descent to Saddlebag Lake, crossing the outlet of little Hummingbird Lake, and soon leave Hoover Wilderness. Not long after, you reach a junction: right (west) on a spur that meets the main trail near Greenstone Lake; ahead (south) on a use trail to the ferry landing; and left (east) to begin traversing Saddlebag Lake's east side.

For this trip, turn left into forest cover and pass a cabin. On an old road above the lakeshore, you stroll through an open lodgepole forest, climbing a little on a gradual grade. The forest vanishes as you cross above the peninsula that juts south into the lake. Runoff on the steep slopes above the lake supports long, narrow, flowery meadows, and there are fine over-the-shoulder views back into 20 Lakes Basin. Trees reappear as you near the south end of Saddlebag Lake, and signs warn you out of the meadow below the trail: WILDLIFE HABITAT AREA. . .CLOSED TO FOOT TRAFFIC. The old road curves around the meadow, rising slightly to a gate that separates the trail from the parking lot where you close the loop and find your car.

47   Saddlebag Lake to McCabe Lakes

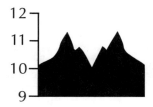

Distance	11 miles
Type	Out and back trip; part cross-country
Best season	Mid or late
Topo maps	**Tuolumne Meadows**, Tioga Pass, Dunderberg Peak
Grade (hiking days/recommended layover days)	
Leisurely	3/0
Moderate	2/1
Strenuous	Day
Trailhead	Saddlebag Lake (23)

HIGHLIGHTS   Alpine from beginning to end, this trip crosses the Sierra crest between the east end of Shepherd Crest and North Peak. High tundra meadows, sparkling clear-water lakes and weathered whitebark pines are hallmarks of this loftily routed excursion. Although the route is not marked as a trail on the topo map, there is sometimes a well-worn trace and sometimes adequate duck-on-the rock markings to delineate the route. This is a trip for intermediate and advanced backpackers.

DESCRIPTION (Moderate trip)

1st Hiking Day (Saddlebag Lake to Lower McCabe Lake, 5.5 miles): First, follow Trip 46 to Cascade Lake, 3 miles. At this point, anglers may wish to sample the golden trout fishing at Cascade Lake before going on. The steep ascent of the crest begins as our route turns northwest beside a flower-lined inlet stream. The course of this tiny rill bends northward, and our route follows it to the small, unnamed lake it drains, locally called Secret Lake.

Pausing at Secret Lake to survey your route up the headwall, you have three choices. Adept mountaineers can attack the wall directly, preferably keeping just to the right of the black, lichen-stained vertical streak on the headwall. Once on top, they will walk to the low point on the divide, from where a route descends the west side of the ridge. Hikers who want to put out some extra effort to achieve certainty and lack of steep exposure can arduously pick their way up the scree north of Secret Lake to the lip of what looks like—but isn't—a lake basin. From there, they will traverse slightly upward to their left, under the solid face of the east end of Shepherd Crest, to the low point on the headwall divide. Probably most people choose the third way: From the south side of Secret Lake walk directly up the increasingly steep headwall until, about halfway up, you come to a long ledge that slopes slightly up to the south. About 200 yards south up this ledge, you leave it and climb almost directly up to the ridgecrest. Once on it, follow it north to the low point of the divide to find a route descending on the west side of the ridgecrest.

> *NOTE:* Many hikers have reported to us an inability to find a route over the ridge that contains no Class-3 segments. Such routes exist, as we have written, but it's possible you'll end up crossing some very steep places.

Excellent views northwest from the ridgecrest include Tower Peak and Saurian Crest. Descending from this ridge, a steep, eroded trail follows the gully northeast of upper McCabe Lake. This section levels out near some small tarns, and our route continues to the north shore of upper McCabe Lake. (One could camp here in a small stand of whitebark pines.) Turning west along the shore, we ford the outlet and then strike out for the low, rock-cairned saddle due west of the outlet. Beyond this saddle, the best route drops past snowmelt tarns not shown on the topo map and then winds down through a dense forest cover of lodgepole and whitebark pine and hemlock to the east shore of beautiful lower McCabe Lake (9850'). The best campsites on the lake are near the outlet. Fishing for eastern brook (to 12") is excellent.

2nd Hiking Day: Retrace your steps, 5.5 miles.

48   Saddlebag Lake to Tuolumne Meadows

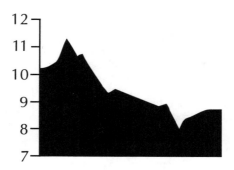

Distance	20.4 miles
Type	Shuttle trip; part cross-country
Best season	Mid or late
Topo maps	**Tuolumne Meadows**, Tioga Pass, Dunderberg Peak, Falls Ridge

Grade (hiking days/recommended layover days)

Leisurely	4/1
Moderate	3/1
Strenuous	3/0

Trailhead   Saddlebag Lake (23), Lembert Dome Trailhead (24)

HIGHLIGHTS   Some hikers may choose this trip for its easy shuttle, but the country that this route tours should be adequate reason in itself. The variety of a trip that is part cross country, part on trail and part over water should appeal to the most jaded mountaineer's appetite. This route does that and more. Crossing the Sierra crest above upper McCabe Lake, the trip traverses the long meadows of Cold Canyon, and finishes by touring the splashing cascades and roaring falls of the Tuolumne River.

DESCRIPTION (Moderate trip)

1st Hiking Day: Follow Trips 46 and 47 to Lower McCabe Lake, 5.5 miles.

2nd Hiking Day (Lower McCabe Lake to Glen Aulin, 9.2 miles): From the campsites at the outlet of lower McCabe Lake the trail descends along the west side of the stream through a moderate-to-dense forest cover of hemlock, lodgepole, whitebark and western white pine and occasional red fir. The trail between lower McCabe Lake and the place where it veers west is usually very wet and swampy, a soggy condition hospitable to the fields of corn lily that line the way. As the trail veers west it becomes drier, and most of the timber near the trail is lodgepole pine. Flowers indigenous to better-drained soils are found along this section of trail, including wall-flower, Douglas phlox, lupine, buckwheat, aster and pussy paws. The descent becomes gentle as the trail passes through a "ghost forest" caused by the needleminer moth and crosses an unnamed tributary of McCabe Creek before reaching the junction with the Virginia Canyon Trail. At this junction our route turns left (west) and continues to Glen Aulin as described in the third hiking day, Trip 42.

3rd Hiking Day: Follow the 4th hiking day, Trip 42, 5.7 miles.

White Cascade near Glen Aulin National Park Service

49   Tuolumne Meadows to Young Lakes

Distance	15.1 miles
Type	Semiloop trip
Best season	Mid or late
Topo maps	**Tuolumne Meadows**, Tioga Pass, Falls Ridge

Grade (hiking days/recommended layover days)

Leisurely	——
Moderate	2/1
Strenuous	2/0
Trailhead	Lembert Dome Trailhead (24)

HIGHLIGHTS   The three Young Lakes, cupped under soaring Ragged Peak, offer a large selection of campsites, some in heavy woods and some at timberline. These camps provide a base for exciting excursions into the headwaters of Conness Creek and for climbing Mt. Conness itself.

DESCRIPTION

1st Hiking Day (Lembert Dome Trailhead to Young Lakes, 8.2 miles): The first part of this trip follows the Glen Aulin "highway," a heavily traveled path from Tuolumne Meadows to the High Sierra Camp down the Tuolumne River. From the parking area west of State Highway 120 we stroll down a dirt road, pass a locked gate that bars autos, and continue west along the lodgepole-dotted flank of Tuolumne Meadows, with fine views south across the meadows of Unicorn Peak, Cathedral Peak and some of the Echo Peaks. Approaching a boulder-rimmed old parking loop, we veer right and climb slightly to the now-closed Soda Springs Campground. Once this campground was the private holding of John Lembert, namesake of Lembert Dome. His brothers, who survived him, sold it to the Sierra Club in 1912, and for 60 years Club members enjoyed a private campground in this marvelous subalpine meadow. But in 1972 the Club deeded the property to the National Park Service so that everyone could use it.

From the Soda Springs the sandy trail undulates through a forest of sparse, small lodgepole pines, and then descends to a boulder ford of Delaney Creek. Immediately beyond the ford we hop a branch of Delaney Creek, then hop another in 300 yards. Soon our trail almost touches the southwest arm of Tuolumne Meadows before ascending to the signed Young Lakes Trail. From the junction we ascend slightly and cross a broad expanse of boulder-strewn, grass-pocketed sheet granite. An open spot affords a look south across broad Tuolumne Meadows to the line of peaks from Fairview Dome to the steeplelike spires of the Cathedral Range.

After crossing the open granite, our trail climbs a tree-clothed slope to a ridge and turns up the ridge for several hundred yards before veering down into the meadowy, bouldery, shallow valley of Dingley Creek, an easy ford except in early season. In the first mile beyond this small creek, we jump across its north fork and wind gently upward in shady pine forest carpeted with a fine flower display even into late season. Groundsel, daisies, lupine, squawroot and gooseberries all are colorful, but one's admiration for floral beauty concentrates on the delicate cream flower cups of Mariposa lily, with one rich brown spot in the throat of each petal. Near the ridgetop, breaks in the lodgepole forest allow us glimpses of the whole Cathedral Range.

On the other side of the ridge a new panoply of peaks appears in the north—majestic Tower Peak, Doghead and Quarry peaks, the Finger Peaks, Matterhorn Peak, Sheep Peak, Mt. Conness, and the Shepherd Crest. From this viewpoint a moderate descent leads to a ford of a tributary of Conness Creek, where more varieties of flowers decorate the green banks of this icy, dashing stream. Soon our downwinding trail reaches the Dog Lake Trail junction, where we veer left and descend into thickening hemlock forest. On a level stretch of trail we cross another branch of Conness Creek, and then switchback ¼ mile up to a plateau from where the view is fine of the steep north face of Ragged Peak.

After passing a meadow which was the fourth Young Lake before it filled in with stream sediments, we descend to the west shore of lower Young Lake (9850'). There are both primitive and well-developed campsites along the north shore of this lake. More secluded campsites may be found on middle Young Lake by following the trail east from the ford of the lower lake, and forking right at a junction 400 yards beyond. From the middle lake you can go up the inlet to the upper lake (10,200'), which is the most attractive but also the most exposed. Fishing on the Young Lakes is fair-to-good for brook trout (to 12").

2nd Hiking Day (Young Lakes to Lembert Dome Trailhead, 6.9 miles): After retracing our steps to the Dog Lake Trail junction, we turn left onto the southwest spur of Ragged Peak and ascend a sandy, boulder-scattered slope under a moderate lodgepole-and-hemlock forest cover. From the shoulder of Ragged Peak the trail descends through a very large, gently sloping meadow. This broad, well-watered expanse is a wildflower garden in season, laced with meandering brooks. Paintbrush, lupine and monkey flower in the foreground set off the great views of the entire Cathedral Range, strung out on the southern horizon.

Near the lower edge of the meadow we cross the headwaters of Dingley Creek, and then descend, steeply at times, some 300 feet through a moderately dense forest of lodgepoles and a few hemlocks. Then the trail levels off and veers east on a gently rolling course through more lodgepole forest where the sandy soil sprouts thousands of prostrate little lupine plants. Beyond is a very large level meadow where the reddish peaks of Mts. Dana and Gibbs loom in the east, Delaney Creek meanders lazily through the grass, and Belding ground squirrels pipe away. The Delaney Creek ford is difficult in early season; shallower fords may be found upstream. Beyond the creek, you will find the trail about 20 yards upstream from the main ford.

After crossing a little ridge, our route drops once more toward Tuolumne Meadows. Lembert Dome, the "first ascent" of so many visitors to Tuolumne Meadows, can be glimpsed through the trees along this stretch of trail. The trail levels slightly before it meets the 0.1 mile lateral to Dog Lake. Then it passes a junction with a trail that leads east along the north side of Lembert Dome, and fords Dog Lake's outlet. The 560-foot descent from here is terribly dusty as it switchbacks down close under the steep west face of Lembert Dome. At the bottom of the deep dust, the trail splits into three paths. The right one leads to the stables, the left one to the parking area where we started.

Horse Meadow to Gibbs Lake **50**

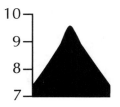

Distance	8 miles
Type	Out and back trip
Best season	Mid or late
Topo maps	Mt. Dana

Grade (hiking days/recommended layover days)
Leisurely	2/0
Moderate	Day
Strenuous	——

Trailhead   Gibbs Lake Trailhead (25)

HIGHLIGHTS   The destination of this trip is a little-known lake in Ansel Adams Wilderness on the dramatic east slope of the Sierra east of Yosemite Park. It's a great place to find peace and quiet, and for serious anglers there is a chance to catch some beautiful golden trout.

DESCRIPTION

1st Hiking Day (Horse Meadow to Gibbs Lake, 4 miles): Ordinary cars will have to park 2.1 miles up the dirt road from U.S. 395 in a little meadow that has a grove of aspen trees and a stream that runs until August. More mountain-worthy cars can ascend another mile to upper Horse Meadow.

We leave the lower meadow on the dusty road and climb steeply, leveling off at a fork where we go right. Soon we pass upper Horse Meadow on our right, which is bounded on the north by the gigantic right lateral moraine of Lee Vining Canyon.

Past the upper meadow the road forks, and 0.1 mile up the left fork is a small parking area below a locked USFS gate. Beyond the gate we climb steeply up an old road on a north-trending ridge, to a gentle dip with a view of Mono Lake. Continuing the steep climb, we walk through mixed forest eligible for cutting and pass a road leading left (east). Just beyond a level spot with campsites, a steel waterpipe crosses the road, and one hundred feet beyond it the road forks. You bear left. From here the road ascends gently for ¼ mile and then mercifully ends. From the roadend, a trail takes off up a dry ravine that lies over a little ridge east from Gibbs Canyon creek. Then it crosses the ridge and dips down near the stream, where blazes mark the trail. We ascend through a cool forest of lodgepole, whitebark and western white pine, with an occasional mountain hemlock and with much Labrador tea along the creek, to the signed border of Ansel Adams Wilderness. Here, perhaps, one will feel a distinct relief that autos and the rest of civilization are locked out beyond the invisible gate Congress erected here in 1964.

The remaining gentle climb to Gibbs Lake proceeds through moderate-to-dense forest near Gibbs Canyon creek, as we catch glimpses through the trees of the majestic Sierra crest dead ahead. There are fair-to-good campsites south of the outlet and west of the inlet of emerald-green Gibbs Lake (9530'). For the adventurous camper, an easy if steep route to Kidney Lake goes up the forested south side of the stream, and the expansive views of Mono Lake and the mountains around it are worth the climb. Most of the shore of this lake is barren, but some whitebark pines at the east end provide shelter for a primitive camp.

2nd Hiking Day: Retrace your steps, 4 miles.

Gibbs and Kidney lakes from Dana Plateau

Tenaya Lake to Sunrise Camp **51**

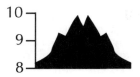

Distance	11.4 miles
Type	Out and back trip
Best season	Mid or late
Topo maps	**Tuolumne Meadows**, Tenaya Lake

Grade (hiking days/recommended layover days)

Leisurely	2/1
Moderate	2/0
Strenuous	Day
Trailhead	Tenaya Lake (29)

HIGHLIGHTS   Although this route is very popular, being within the Yosemite High Sierra Camp network, the superb, unusual scenery of the high country makes this trip a must. The spectacular topography of the Tenaya Canyon and of the serrated northwestern end of the Cathedral Range combine to overcome the most strident objections of the solitude-seeker.

DESCRIPTION

1st Hiking Day (Tenaya Lake to Sunrise High Sierra Camp, 5.7 miles): From the tiny parking lot south of Tenaya Lake (8150') the trail crosses the lake's outlet and skirts the meadowy edge of the closed walk-in campground. For a mile the trail winds south through moderate forest cover interrupted by small meadows where the quiet early-morning hiker will probably see browsing mule deer. The first part of this trail is lush with wildflowers as late as July, and one can expect to see blooming lupine, aster, larkspur, brodiaea and buttercup. Just past the stream from Lower Sunrise Lake the ascent begins to steepen, and soon it becomes a long series of rocky switchbacks up a slope clothed with pine and hemlock. From these switchbacks one can see the highway and can hear passing autos, but these are infinitesimal compared to the polished granite expanses of Tenaya Canyon. The Indian name for Tenaya Creek, Py-wi-ack ("Stream of the Shining Rocks"), was quite apt, for this canyon exhibits the largest exposed granite area in Yosemite, and its shining surfaces are barren except for sporadic clumps of hardy conifers that have found root in broken talus pockets.

Where the trail begins to rise, the long, gradual slope falling from the promontory called Clouds Rest comes into view in the south. This slope is a 4500-foot drop, one of the largest continuous rock slopes in the world. Travelers who feel sated by the panorama will find a different world to wonder at, right at their own boot-clad feet, for these slopes grow dozens of wildflower species, among them pussy paws, penstemon, paintbrush, lupine, streptanthus, aster, larkspur, brodiaea and buttercup. Finally the switchbacks end and the trail levels as it arrives at a junction with the trail to Sunrise camp. Turning left (east), we stroll on a nearly level path under a sparse forest cover of pine and fir until the trail dips for about ¼ mile to the first Sunrise Lake.

After passing the west side of the lake on a trail fringed with red mountain heather, we cross the outlet and ascend gradually northeast. Then the trail levels off and wanders roughly north through a sparse lodgepole forest. The second Sunrise Lake comes into view on the left, but we veer east and climb away from it, paralleling its inlet some distance from the cascading water. The few trees here are not enough to block our views of granite domes all around. Then our trail skirts the south side of the meadow-fringed highest Sunrise Lake and begins a gradual ascent by crossing the lake's inlet stream.

Continuing southeast, we cross a little saddle and descend gradually almost straight south from the upper lake. After passing most of the hogback lying east of us, we swing northeast and switchback down to a bench overlooking spacious Long Meadow (may be dry late in the year). There are fair campsites or, if advance reservations have been made, one may enjoy the luxury of a hot shower, a hot meal and a made-up bed at the High Sierra Camp (9320') nearby.

2nd Hiking Day: Retrace your steps, 5.7 miles. Alternatively, you could retrace the steps of Trip 53, 8.4 miles.

Tioga Road to Upper Cathedral Lake

52

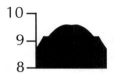

Distance	7.4 miles
Type	Out and back trip
Best season	Mid or late
Topo maps	**Tuolumne Meadows**, Tenaya Lake
Grade (hiking days/recommended layover days)	
Leisurely	2/0
Moderate	Day
Strenuous	Day
Trailhead	Cathedral Lakes Trailhead (28)

HIGHLIGHTS   Used since the time of the Indians, this trail takes you past two of Tuolumne Meadows' famed granite domes, Fairview and Medlicott, to a charming lake below the area's foremost landmark, Cathedral Peak. The short mileage, gentle terrain, and excellent scenery make this an ideal trip for beginners. Fires are not permitted in Cathedral Basin.

DESCRIPTION

1st Hiking Day (Cathedral Lakes Trailhead to Upper Cathedral Lake, 3.7 miles): From the parking area (8560′) on the Tioga Road, we follow a gently ascending trail that is very dusty except after rain. This area is very popular with dayhikers as well as backpackers and is consequently overused. A few steps from the trailhead our route joins the John Muir Trail and then begins to climb more steeply. After ¾ mile of ascent under a welcome forest cover, the trail levels off and descends to a small meadow that is boggy in early season. From here we can see the dramatically shaped tops of Unicorn Peak and the Cockscomb, and the apparent granite dome in the south is in reality the north ridge of Cathedral Peak, whose steeples are out of sight over the "dome's" horizon.

The trail cruises gently up and down through more little meadows set in hemlock forest and then dips near a tinkling stream whose source, we discover after further walking, is a robust spring on a shady set of switchbacks. Beyond this climb our tread levels off on the west slope of Cathedral Peak and makes a long, gentle, sparsely forested descent on sandy underfooting to a junction with the spur trail to lower Cathedral Lake: left (ahead, southeast) to upper Cathedral Lake, right (south) to lower Cathedral Lake. Lower Cathedral Lake is closed to camping, so we continue ahead, soon entering Cathedral Basin, throughout which fires are prohibited.

After an easy, mile-long climb we dip slightly into the shallow bowl that holds upper Cathedral Lake (9585'), where the sandy trail stays above and east of the lake. Rugged Tressider Peak lies southwest of the lake, while the delicate "steeples" of Cathedral Peak rise to the northeast. One of the unforgettable sights here is that of Cathedral Peak mirrored in the lake's still waters. The rounded, polished tops of the domes seen earlier prove that the domes were completely covered by ice, while the jagged summits of Cathedral and Tressider peaks prove that they stood a few hundred feet above the grinding ice and hence were not rounded and smoothed by it. Look for campsites well away from the water, on the gentle, forested slopes of this pretty bowl.

2nd Hiking Day: Retrace your steps, 3.7 miles.

Upper Cathedral Lake and Cathedral Peak

Tioga Road to Sunrise Camp   **53**

Distance	16.8 miles
Type	Out and back trip
Best season	Mid or late
Topo maps	**Tuolumne Meadows**, Tenaya Lake

Grade (hiking days/recommended layover days)

Leisurely	4/1
Moderate	2/1
Strenuous	2/0
Trailhead	Cathedral Lakes Trailhead (28)

HIGHLIGHTS   This leg of the John Muir Trail is also known as the Sunrise Trail and is a justly famous and popular route on its own. Superlative views confront the traveler at every summit and oftentimes in between—views of whole subranges in the distance as well as spectacular peaks nearby.

DESCRIPTION (Leisurely trip)

1st Hiking Day: Follow Trip 53 to Upper Cathedral Lake, 3.7 miles.

2nd Hiking Day (Upper Cathedral Lake to Sunrise High Sierra Camp, 4.7 miles): Regain the John Muir Trail and follow it southward, up to Cathedral Pass, where the excellent views include Cathedral Peak, Tressider Peak, Echo Peaks, Matthes Crest, the Clark Range farther south, and Matterhorn Peak far to the north. Beyond the pass is a long, beautiful swale, the headwaters of Echo Creek, where the midseason flower show is alone worth the trip.

Alas, our Muir/Sunrise Trail doesn't descend into that swale but instead continues climbing gradually along Tressider Peak's east flank to the actual high point of this trail, at a marvelous viewpoint overlooking most of southern Yosemite National Park. The inspiring panorama includes the peaks around Vogelsang High Sierra Camp in the southeast, the whole Clark Range in the south, and the peaks on the Park border in both directions farther away. Then our high trail switchbacks quickly down to the head of the upper lobe of Long

Meadow, levels off, and leads down a gradually sloping valley dotted with little lodgepole pines to the head of the second, lower lobe of l-o-n-g Long Meadow (may be dry by late season). Passing a junction with the trail down Echo Creek, this route continues its meadowy descent to the fair campsites along the stream at the south end of the meadow, past Sunrise High Sierra Camp, which is near the south end of the meadow, almost out of sight on a bench above and west of the trail. There are other well-used campsites south of the High Sierra Camp on the bench west of the meadow. The view east across Long Meadow toward rugged peaks hints at wonders as yet unseen.

3rd and 4th Hiking Days: Retrace your steps, 8.4 miles. Alternatively, you could retrace the steps of Trip 51, 5.7 miles.

Lower Cathedral Lake, Columbia Finger

National Park Service

Tioga Road to Merced Lake   **54**

Distance	34 miles
Type	Shuttle trip
Best season	Mid or late
Topo maps	**Tuolumne Meadows, Merced Peak**, Tenaya Lake, Merced Peak, Vogelsang Peak

Grade (hiking days/recommended layover days)

Leisurely	6/1
Moderate	5/1
Strenuous	3/1
Trailhead	Cathedral Lakes Trailhead (28), Tuolumne Lodge (27)

HIGHLIGHTS   This looping excursion out of Tuolumne Meadows samples everything the Cathedral Range has to offer, from sweeping vistas at 10,000-foot passes to the deeply glaciated Merced River canyon to forested side streams with secluded campsites. For anglers there are lakes large and small, meadowed creeks, and huge river pools.

DESCRIPTION (Moderate trip)

1st Hiking Day: Follow Trip 52 to Upper Cathedral Lake, 3.7 miles.

2nd Hiking Day (Upper Cathedral Lake to Echo Creek Crossing, 9 miles): First, follow Trip 53 to the trail junction in Long Meadow. Here we turn left (east) on the signed Echo Creek Trail and ford the Long Meadow stream on boulders. The trail quickly switchbacks up to the top of the ridge that separates this stream from

Echo Creek and then descends through dense hemlock-and-lodge-pole forest toward the Cathedral Fork of Echo Creek. Where our route approaches this stream, we have fine views of the creek's water gliding down a series of granite slabs, and then the trail veers away from the creek and descends gently above it for more than a mile. Even in late season this shady hillside is watered by numerous rills that are bordered by still-blooming flowers. On this downgrade the trail crosses the Long Meadow stream, which has found an escape from that meadow through a gap between two large domes high above our trail.

Then our route levels out in a mile-long flat section of this valley where the wet ground yields a plus of wildflowers all summer but a minus of many mosquitoes in early season. Beyond this flat "park," the trail descends a more open hillside, and where it passes the confluence of the two forks of Echo Creek, we can see across the valley the steep course of the east fork plunging down to its rendezvous with the west fork. Finally the trail levels off and reaches the good campsites just before a metal bridge over Echo Creek (8100'). Fishing in the creek is good for rainbow and golden trout (to 10").

3rd Hiking Day (Echo Creek Crossing to Merced Lake, 4.9 miles): After crossing the bridge over Echo Creek, our trail leads down the forested valley and easily fords a tributary stream, staying well above the main creek. This pleasant, shaded descent encounters fibrous-barked juniper trees and then tall, brittle red firs as it drops to another metal bridge 1 mile from the last one. Beyond this sturdy span, the trail rises slightly and the creek drops precipitously, so that we are soon far above it. Then our sandy tread swings west away from Echo Creek and traverses down a hillside where views are excellent of Echo Valley, a wide place in the great Merced River canyon below. Our trail passes a junction with the High Trail, which leads west to the Sunrise Trail, and then descends south to a green-floored forest of mixed conifers threaded by a tinkling all-year stream.

Then a last series of switchbacks span the descent to the floor of Echo Valley, where we meet and turn left (east) on the Merced River Trail. After crossing several forks of Echo Creek on wooden bridges, we pass a burn area where a 1966 fire killed most of the mature trees. But new, small lodgepoles grow by the hundreds, and the grassy valley floor is extensively decorated with the blue flowers of lupine and the white blossoms of yarrow and yampah. Leaving Echo Valley, the trail leads up immense granite slabs.

At the hairpin angle of a set of switchbacks, the trail comes very close to the cascading Merced River, and a breather stop here will allow the traveler to drink in the sights and sounds of this dramatic part of the river—a long series of chutes, cascades, falls, cataracts and pools that are all due to the glacier that roughened up the formerly smooth bed of the Merced River. Above this turbulent stretch, the trail levels off beside the now-quiet river and arrives at the outlet of Merced Lake (7212'). This large lake has a High Sierra Camp at its east end, where the only presently legal campsites are. You can buy a few provisions at the small store, or even rent a rowboat to try your luck for rainbow and brown trout to (9″). Be sure to bearproof your food.

4th Hiking Day (Merced Lake to Emeric Lake, 5.6 miles): The first short mile of this day's hike follows an almost level, wide, sandy path under a green forest canopy of fir and pine, juniper and aspen. Immediately beyond a bridge over roaring Lewis Creek we arrive at the Merced Lake Ranger Station (emergency services available in summer) and beside it find the Lewis Creek Trail, leading north. Quickly the ascent up this cobbled trail becomes steep, and it remains so for a panting half-mile-plus. Fortunately, Sierra junipers and Jeffrey pines cast plenty of morning shade. The trail levels momentarily as we pass a fine viewpoint for taking pictures of Merced Lake, far below, and Half Dome, due west. One more cobbled, steep climb leads to a junction with the Fletcher Creek Trail, and we turn left onto this path.

Several switchbacks then descend to a wooden bridge over Lewis Creek. There is ample, hardened camping near the bridge. From here the trail begins an initial 400-foot ascent, at times moderate, often steep, over unevenly cobbled, exposed trail—a grunt on a hot day. The path is bordered by proliferating bushes of mountain whitethorn and huckleberry oak. Just past a tributary ½ mile from Lewis Creek, we have fine views of cataracts and waterfalls on Fletcher Creek where it rushes down open granite slopes dotted with lodgepole pines. The trail then passes very close to the creek before veering south and climbing, steeply at times, on the now-familiar cobbling placed by trail crews. Here one has more good views of Fletcher Creek chuting and cascading down from the notch at the base of a granite dome before it leaps off a ledge in free fall. The few solitary pine trees on this otherwise blank dome testify to nature's extraordinary persistence.

At the notch, our trail levels off near some nice but illegal campsites, and then soon passes a side trail to small Babcock Lake. From this junction the sandy trail ascends steadily through a moderate forest cover just east of Fletcher Creek. After a mile, the trail rises steeply via rocky switchbacks from which one can see nearby in the north the outlet stream of Emeric Lake—though not the lake itself, which is behind a dome just to the right of the outlet's notch. For an adventurous shortcut to Emeric Lake, follow this outlet up to the lake. First, leave the trail and wade across granite-bottomed Fletcher Creek as best you can—there is no natural place to do so, and in a wet year you may get very wet yourself. Then follow up this outlet and stroll along the northwest shore of Emeric Lake (9338') to the excellent campsites midway along this shore. Fishing is often good for rainbow trout (to 12"). Sometimes windy, this lake was nevertheless so still one night that one author saw the Milky Way clearly reflected in it.

5th Hiking Day (Emeric Lake to Tuolumne Lodge, 10.8 miles): This is the longest hiking day on this trip, but the ascent is not severe and it comes at the beginning: from Tuolumne Pass at the crest of the Cathedral Range, the rest is downhill.

Circle the head of Emeric Lake; stay near the lake to protect the meadow to the north and northeast of the lake, which is carpeted with delicate wildflowers. Cross the inlet stream and find a trail at the northeast corner of the lake, at the base of a granite knoll. This trail leads east-northeast for 0.6 mile to an **X** junction in the valley of Fletcher Creek. (This junction is not shown on the topo map.) Taking the left branch up the valley, we follow a rocky-dusty trail through the forest fringe of the long meadow that straddles Fletcher Creek. This trail climbs farther from the meadow and passes northwest of a bald prominence that sits in the center of the upper valley of Fletcher and Emeric creeks, separating the two. Topping a minor summit, the trail descends slightly and then winds levelly past a long series of lovely ponds that are interconnected in early season. The Park Service is attempting to restore the meadows surrounding the ponds; numerous signs ask you to stay on the main trail. You soon pass a trail of use to the south end of Boothe Lake (9845'). There is excellent camping all around the lake, as the bears well know. At the top of a little swale, the trail reaches an overlook above Boothe Lake, then contours along this meadowy hillside about 50 vertical feet above the lake, passing a junction with another use trail down to the lake. About ¼ mile farther we reach west Tuolumne Pass and a junction with the trail to Vogelsang High Sierra Camp. From here we retrace most of the steps of Trip 60.

Tioga Road to Tenaya Lake **55**

Distance	25.6 miles
Type	Shuttle trip
Best season	Mid or late
Topo maps	**Tuolumne Meadows, Merced Peak**, Tenaya Lake, Merced Peak

Grade (hiking days/recommended layover days)
Leisurely	4/1
Moderate	4/0
Strenuous	3/0
Trailhead	Cathedral Lakes Trailhead (28), Tenaya Lake (29)

HIGHLIGHTS   The first and last parts of this trip are along favorite and well-used trails, but in the middle we follow a little-used stretch of trail in the heart of Yosemite's spectacular glaciated highlands. Views of the immense domes and deep-cut canyons will impress the traveler's eye forever.

DESCRIPTION (Leisurely trip)

1st and 2nd Hiking Days: Follow Trip 54 to the Echo Creek Crossing, 12.9 miles.

3rd Hiking Day (Echo Creek Crossing to Sunrise Creek, 5.1 miles): First follow the third hiking day, Trip 54, to the junction of the Echo Creek and High trails above the Merced River. Here our route turns right (west) and climbs rockily several hundred feet before leveling off above the immense Merced River canyon. This trail segment was part of the route from Yosemite Valley to Merced Lake until a path up the canyon was constructed in 1931. Before that, the steep canyon walls coming right down to the river near Bunnell Point, the great dome to our southwest, had made passage impossible. Finally a trail was built that bypasses the narrowest part of the canyon by climbing high on the south wall, and the trail we are now on fell into relative disuse.

With fine views of obelisk-like Mt. Clark in the south, we descend gradually for ½ mile over open granite in a setting that is sure to give you a feeling of being above almost everything. Then the trail passes a stagnant lakelet and ascends to even better viewpoints for appreciating the grandeur of the glaciated granitic wonder of nature spread out before you. It takes time to grasp the immensity of Mt. Clark, Clouds Rest, Half Dome, Mt. Starr King, Bunnell Point, and the great unnamed dome across the canyon west of it. Our continuing ascent then rounds a ridge and veers north into a forest of handsome Jeffrey pines. Here the trail levels off, and it remains level for a mile of exhilarating walking through Jeffreys, lodgepoles and red firs which shade patch after patch of vivid green ferns and a complement of multihued floral displays. Still in forest, we descend slightly to meet the John Muir Trail, go right on it for 150 yards to the Forsyth Trail, and then go left up it 200 yards to the fair campsites on Sunrise Creek (8080'). Fishing in this enticing stream for small rainbow and brook trout is fair at best.

4th Hiking Day (Sunrise Creek to Tenaya Lake, 7.6 miles): Begin by reversing the latter part of the 1st hiking day of Trip 57, up Sunrise Creek and over Sunrise Mountain's west flank to the junction with the lateral to Sunrise Lakes and Sunrise High Sierra Camp. From here, reverse the first part of the 1st hiking day of Trip 51, down to the trailhead near Tenaya Lake.

Tuolumne Meadows and their guardians   *National Park Service*

Tioga Road to Yosemite Valley **56**

Distance	21 miles
Type	Shuttle trip
Best season	Mid or late
Topo maps	**Tuolumne Meadows, Merced Peak, Yosemite,**
	Tenaya Lake, Merced Peak, Half Dome

Grade (hiking days/recommended layover days)

Leisurely	4/0
Moderate	3/0
Strenuous	2/0

Trailhead Cathedral Lakes Trailhead (28), Happy Isles (31)

HIGHLIGHTS The John Muir Trail route, also called the Sunrise Trail, from Tuolumne Meadows to Yosemite Valley is one of the Park's most famous and most used backpack routes. Its reputation is an honest one, for these miles contain a magnificent range of flora and fauna, and the trail surveys some of the Park's best-known landmarks. This is a fine trip for the beginning backpacker who has a couple of shorter trips under his or her belt, and wants more.

Description (Leisurely trip)

1st and 2nd Hiking Days: Follow Trip 52 and then Trip 53 to Sunrise High Sierra Camp, 8.4 miles.

3rd Hiking Day (Sunrise High Sierra Camp to Sunrise Creek, 5.1 miles): The trail from Sunrise High Sierra Camp continues south through Long Meadow, undulating gently below the eastern crest of

Sunrise Mountain. After climbing to a forested saddle over a mile past the meadows, the trail parallels the headwaters of Sunrise Creek, descending steeply by switchbacks down a rocky moraine.

This moraine is the largest of a series of ridgelike glacial deposits in this area, and the gigantic granite boulders along their sides testify to the power of the mer-de-glace that once filled Little Yosemite Valley and its tributaries. One such "erratic," about the size of a compact car, was found poised on the side of Moraine Dome to the southwest, and geologists have determined that it came from the slopes of the peaks at the northwest end of the Cathedral Range. At the foot of the morainal descent, the trail crosses Sunrise Creek, and then descends on a westward course to the fair campsites on Sunrise Creek (8080') 200 yards up the Forsyth Trail from our trail's junction with it. Fishing on Sunrise Creek is poor-to-fair for rainbow and brook (fry).

4th Hiking Day (Sunrise Creek to Yosemite Valley, 7.5 miles): First retrace your steps 200 yards south to the last junction. Back on the John Muir Trail, our route continues southwest on a gradual descent, passing the High Trail to Merced Lake. Our trail is bounded on the north by the Pinnacles (the south face of the Clouds Rest eminence) and on the south by Moraine Dome. François Matthes, in an interesting "detective story" written in the form of a geological essay (Professional Paper 160), discusses Moraine Dome extensively. He deduced, using three examples (one was the "erratic" cited above), that the moraines around the dome were the product of at least two glacial ages—a notion contrary to the thinking of the time. The morainal till of the last glacial age characterizes the underfooting of our descent into Little Yosemite Valley. A mile from the last junction is a ford of Sunrise Creek in a red-fir forest whose stillness is broken by the creek's gurgling and by the occasional screams of Steller jays. In another mile we ford Sunrise Creek again (campsites), shortly ford a tributary (campsites), and then pass the trail to Clouds Rest (campsites). Broad, well-worn use trails to the campsites here may temporarily be mistaken for the main trail. About ½ mile from there is the lateral to Half Dome (about 4 miles round trip). From this junction our shady path switchbacks down through a changing forest cover.

There are improved campsites on Sunrise Creek at the foot of the descent, and more numerous ones along the Merced River south of the river trail. A summer ranger is on duty near the trail junction. This is prime bear territory, so be sure to secure your food.

From here, reverse the steps of the 1st hiking day, Trip 66, to Yosemite Valley.

Tenaya Lake to Yosemite Valley 57

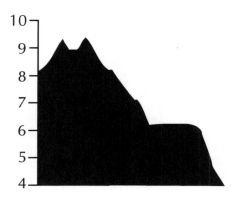

Distance	15.1 miles
Type	Shuttle trip
Best season	Mid or late
Topo maps	**Tuolumne Meadows, Merced Peak, Yosemite**, Tenaya Lake, Merced Peak, Half Dome

Grade (hiking days/recommended layover days)

Leisurely	2/1
Moderate	2/0
Strenuous	Day
Trailhead	Tenaya Lake (29), Happy Isles (31)

HIGHLIGHTS Through an elevation change of over 5000 feet (mostly downhill) this route covers most of Yosemite's spectrum of life zones. Views from various points above Tenaya Canyon are breath-taking in their panoramic scope. By contrast, a different kind of appreciation is evoked when walking alongside the serene waters of the Merced River as it serpentines across the floor of Little Yosemite Valley. The ever-changing nature of a river is a high point of this trip—slides, cascades, and earth-shaking waterfalls add exclamation points.

DESCRIPTION

1st Hiking Day (Tenaya Lake to Sunrise Creek, 7.6 miles): First, follow Trip 51 to the junction of the trail going east to Sunrise Camp. From the junction, our trail makes a 320-foot descent on switchbacks, rises over a talus-swollen little ridge, and drops beside a pleasant-looking lakelet. The lightly forested hillside ahead leads up to three unnamed streams that we cross in quick succession. This watery slope is boggy till midseason, and the plentiful groundwater nourishes rank gardens of wildflowers throughout the summer. Leveling off beyond the streams, our trail meets the 2-mile trail to the summit of Clouds Rest. Hikers with plenty of energy may take this short lateral to this lofty prominence. Views from Clouds Rest are among the most spectacular in the Sierra, including a 4500-foot continuous granite slope stretching all the way down to Tenaya Creek and rising on the other side—the largest exposed granite area in the Park.

From the Clouds Rest junction, the trail meanders over sandy, level terrain for ½ mile, detouring around many fallen trees, before it starts its plunge down toward Sunrise Creek. This switchbacking descent is a little tough on the knees but in repayment the green fir-and-pine forest is a classic of its kind, and occasional views down into the Merced River Canyon are sweeping in their range. Finally our trail approaches a stream, parallels it for almost ½ mile, fords it and then fords Sunrise Creek to the fair campsites on the creek (8080'). Fishing for rainbow and brook (fry) is poor-to-fair.

2nd Hiking Day: Follow the 4th hiking day, Trip 56, 7.5 miles.

Looking up the Merced River Canyon

Tuolumne Meadows to Nelson Lake 58

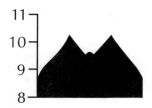

Distance	11.8 miles
Type	Out and back trip
Best season	Mid or late
Topo maps	**Tuolumne Meadows**, Vogelsang Peak
Grade (hiking days/recommended layover days)	
Leisurely	——
Moderate	2/1
Strenuous	Day
Trailhead	Tuolumne Meadows Campground (26)

HIGHLIGHTS   This interesting and varied route visits the scenic Elizabeth Lake basin and then crosses the serrated Cathedral Range to Nelson Lake. No trail route offers finer views of those geologic wonders called Unicorn Peak and the Cockscomb. Open, meadow-fringed Nelson Lake makes a pleasantly fitting end to this exciting trip, and anglers can look forward to good brook-trout fishing on the placid waters of this subalpine gem.

DESCRIPTION

1st Hiking Day (Tuolumne Meadows Campground to Nelson Lake, 5.9 miles): To reach the trailhead, walk to the Group Camping Section of the Tuolumne Meadows campground, where the trail begins across from a masonry building. In a few hundred feet we cross the Tenaya Lake/Lyell Canyon Trail and then continue a steady southward ascent. The shade-giving forest cover is almost entirely lodgepole pine as the trail crosses several runoff streams that dry up by late summer. More than a mile from the start, our route veers close to Unicorn Creek, and the music of this dashing, gurgling, cold-water stream makes the climb easier. When the ascent finally ends, the hiker emerges at the foot of a long meadow containing Elizabeth

Lake, at the foot of striking Unicorn Peak.

Past Elizabeth Lake, the meadow gives way to a moderately dense forest cover of lodgepole interspersed with mountain hemlock, and the trail climbs, steeply, then moderately, and steeply again. A few hundred feet before you reach the ridgecrest, you come to a late-lingering snowbank where the trail splits. If you go left, you will pass through a narrow gully between granite walls. If you go right, you will walk up a bare granite-sand slope. We recommend that if you have a full pack, you take the right trail going to Nelson Lake and the left one returning, because of some steep places on the left trail just beyond the crest.

Because of the close proximity of the Cockscomb, about 1 mile due west, the hiker has excellent views of that knifelike spire from just beyond the left pass. Well-named by François Matthes, this slender crest bears clear marks of the highest level reached by the ice of the last glacial episode. Its lower shoulders reveal the rounded, well-polished surfaces that betray glacial action, while its jagged, sharply etched crest shows no such markings. Further evidence of glacial action may be clearly seen on the steep descent into the head of long, typically U-shaped Echo Creek valley. The shearing and polishing action of the ice mass that shaped this rounded valley is evident on the cliffs on the west side.

About ⅓ mile from where the trail split, and several hundred yards beyond the crest, the forks come together again on a steep, tree-dotted, ravined hillside. As our route descends along winding, clear, meadowed Echo Creek for about 2 miles, the valley floor is lush with wildflower growth. During midseason the passerby can expect to see Davidson's penstemon, Douglas phlox, groundsel, red heather, lupine and swamp whiteheads. At the end of the second large meadow in this canyon, our trail leaves Echo Creek and veers east up a low, rocky ridge, undulating through sparse forest. We are almost at Nelson Lake (9605′) before we can see our destination, meadow-fringed at the foot of imposing granite Peak 11357. Good campsites may be found on the southeast and southwest sides. Anglers will find the lake's waters good fishing for brook trout (7–11″).

2nd Hiking Day: Retrace your steps, 5.9 miles.

Tuolumne Meadows to Lyell Canyon   **59**

Distance	18 miles
Type	Out and back trip
Best season	Early, mid or late
Topo maps	**Tuolumne Meadows**, Vogelsang Peak, Tioga Pass
Grade (hiking days/recommended layover days)	
Leisurely	2/1
Moderate	2/0
Strenuous	——
Trailhead	Tuolumne Lodge (27)

HIGHLIGHTS   Alpine meadows have a fascination that claims the trail traveler, whether he be novice or hoariest veteran. Campers' descriptions of favorite camping places invariably favor the forested western fringe of a remote meadow (your camp gets the first warming sunlight there). The meadows of Lyell Canyon are the stuff of which such memories are built. Idyllic from beginning to end, this long, gentle grassland with its serpentining river is a delight to travel. Bears are a very serious problem throughout Lyell Canyon; bear-resistant food canisters are highly recommended.

DESCRIPTION

1st Hiking Day (Tuolumne Meadows Lodge to Lyell Base Camp, 9 miles): The trailhead is beside the Tuolumne Meadows Lodge parking lot, southwest of the office-dining room. The route goes about 100 yards to the Dana Fork of the river, crosses it on a bridge, passes a trail up the canyon, and heads south. Then this segment of the Pacific Crest Trail leads over a slight rise and in a half mile descends to the Lyell Fork, where there is a substantial double bridge. The meadows above this bridge are among the most delightful in all the Sierra, and anytime you happen to be staying all night at the lodge or nearby, they are a wonderful place to spend the last hour before dinner. Mts. Dana and Gibbs fill the eastern horizon, catching the late sun, and the river has good fishing for brown trout.

About 50 yards past the bridge we meet the trail that comes up the river from the campground, turn left (east) onto it, and skirt a long, lovely section of the meadow. This re-routed trail was established because of extensive trail wear and subsequent erosion of the old route. Re-routing is one of several far-sighted Park Service policies that have been adopted to allow areas in the wilderness a "breather"— a chance to recover from overuse. In a dense forest cover of lodgepole pine, our route passes the trail that ascends south to Tuolumne Pass and Vogelsang High Sierra Camp, and then crosses Rafferty Creek on a sturdy bridge.

From this point on, the trail traverses alternating meadowed and forested sections as it veers southward, and the silent walker may come upon grazing deer in the meadows and an occasional marmot that has ventured from the rocky hillside on the right. In this heavily used area, backcountry camping is prohibited within 4 miles of Tioga Road (Highway 120). Hikers ready to stop for the night can begin looking for campsites after the river curves south-southeast into Lyell Canyon. Fields of wildflowers color the grasslands from early to late season, but the best time of the year for seeing this color is generally early-to-mid season. From the more open parts of the trail, one has excellent views of the Kuna Crest as it slopes up to the southeast and the river itself has delighted generations of mountain photographers.

Our route then passes a trail branching southwest to Ireland and Evelyn lakes, Vogelsang High Sierra Camp, and Tuolumne Pass. There are fair campsites around this junction. Beyond this junction the trail fords Ireland Creek (difficult in early season), passes below Potter Point, and ascends gently for almost 3 miles to the fair campsites at Lyell Base Camp (9040'). Fishing is fair for brook trout. This base camp, surrounded on three sides by steep canyon walls, marks the end of the meadowed sections of Lyell Canyon, and is the traditional first-night stopping place for those touring the John Muir Trail beginning at Tuolumne Meadows.

2nd Hiking Day: Retrace your steps, 9 miles.

Tuolumne Meadows to Vogelsang

60

Distance	15.4 miles
Type	Out and back trip
Best season	Mid or late
Topo maps	**Tuolumne Meadows**, Vogelsang Peak

Grade (hiking days/recommended layover days)

Leisurely	2/1
Moderate	2/0
Strenuous	——
Trailhead	Tuolumne Lodge (27)

HIGHLIGHTS   Vogelsang Camp has the most dramatic setting of all the famous High Sierra Camps. Located right under the somber north face of Fletcher Peak, it offers eagle views of valleys, granite domes, and lakes below. Many nearby lakes offer exciting side-trip possibilities for anglers, swimmers, and picnickers, and Fletcher Peak, a class-2 scramble, invites the climber.

DESCRIPTION

1st Hiking Day (Tuolumne Lodge to Vogelsang High Sierra Camp, 7.7 miles): From the well marked trailhead at about 8600 feet, located southwest of the office-dining room of Tuolumne Meadows Lodge, go about 100 yards to the Dana Fork of the Tuolumne River, cross it on a bridge, pass a track up the canyon, and head south. Now we ascend a slight rise and descend to the beautiful Lyell Fork, over which there is a substantial double bridge. Just past the bridge at a signed **T**-junction, you turn left (east). Soon, in dense lodgepole-pine forest, we encounter our signed trail to Tuolumne Pass and the Vogelsang High Sierra Camp. Turn right onto this trail and immediately begin one of the toughest climbs of this entire trip—about 400 feet on trail ravaged by stock. Even so, the grade is moderate as often as it is steep, the trail is fairly well shaded by lodgepole pines, and the length of the climb is well under a mile. Then, as the ascent decreases to a gentle grade, we pass through high, boulder-strewn meadows that offer good views eastward of reddish-brown Mts. Dana and Gibbs, and gray-white Mammoth Peak. Soon the trail dips close to Rafferty Creek, and since this stream flows all year you can count on refreshment here. Then the nearly level trail passes above an orange snowcourse marker in a large meadow below and continues its long, gentle ascent through a sparse forest of lodgepole pines unmixed with a single tree of any other species. The lodgepoles have suffered heavily from drought and pollution. Although a few seedlings give hope that the forest may regenerate, there are thousands of dead trees. The dead spires haunt a starkly beautiful terrain with huge, lichened boulders and meadows bounded by polished granite walls. About ⅓ mile beyond a stream that dries up in late summer, we ford another that also does in some years. Much of this trail has been recently constructed and relocated to allow the damaged meadow below to recover from the pounding of too many feet.

As you begin the gentle ascent to Tuolumne Pass, nearby Rafferty Creek invites you to pause and examine dense, varied wildflower displays. Finally the exclusive lodgepole pines allow a few whitebark pines to join their company, and these trees diminish the force of the winds that often sweep through Tuolumne Pass (9992'). In the pass a signed trail junction indicates the right fork to Boothe, Emeric, Babcock, and Merced lakes, and the left fork, your route, to Vogelsang High Sierra Camp. Through breaks in this forest one has intermittent views of cliff-bound, dark-banded Fletcher Peak and Peak 11799 in the south. Then our path leaves the green-floored forest and leads out into an area of bouldery granite outcroppings dotted with a few trees. Now on the west side of saucer-shaped Tuolumne Pass, a major gap in the Cathedral Range, we follow a rocky-dusty path up a moderately steep hillside below which Boothe Lake and its surrounding meadows lie serene. Finally, our trail reaches the top of this climb, and suddenly we see the tents of Vogelsang High Sierra Camp (10,157') spread out before us. A few snacks may be bought here, or dinner or breakfast if you make a reservation. There are good campsites along Fletcher Creek just beyond the camp, but remember the bears that live here are always interested in your food. Even if you are not planning to camp here, walk the several hundred feet east to see Fletcher Lake, nestled at the foot of Fletcher Peak (11,410').

2nd Hiking Day: Retrace your steps, 7.7 miles.

Tuolumne Meadows to Emeric Lake   **61**

Distance	28.8 miles
Type	Semiloop trip
Best season	Mid or late
Topo maps	**Tuolumne Meadows, Merced Peak**, Vogelsang Peak, Mt. Lyell, Merced Peak, Tenaya Lake

Grade (hiking days/recommended layover days)

Leisurely	5/1
Moderate	4/0
Strenuous	3/0
Trailhead	Tuolumne Lodge (27)

HIGHLIGHTS   With Tuolumne Pass as the neck of the "noose," this trip "lassos" Vogelsang Peak by dashing down the valley of Lewis Creek and then cruising back up the valley of Fletcher Creek. In addition to the spectrum of views of this fine peak, the traveler will constantly have good vistas of many parts of the Cathedral Range, and anglers will find good fishing in both creeks and at Emeric Lake.

DESCRIPTION (Moderate trip)

1st Hiking Day: Follow Trip 60 to Vogelsang High Sierra Camp, 7.7 miles.

2nd Hiking Day (Vogelsang High Sierra Camp to Florence Creek, 4.3 miles): Taking the Vogelsang Pass Trail from the camp, we descend slightly to ford Fletcher Creek on boulders and then begin a 550-foot moderate ascent with occasional steep sections to the pass. New trailwork has placed the dramatic trail on exposed granite. The panting hiker is rewarded, as always in the Sierra, with increasingly good views. Fletcher Peak rises grandly on the left, far north stands Mt. Conness, and Clouds Rest and then Half Dome come into view in the west-southwest. The trail skirts above the west shore of Vogelsang Lake. Windswept camping occurs among the whitebarks bordering this timberline lake. Nearer the pass, views to the north are occluded somewhat, but expansive new views appear in the south: from left to right are Parsons Peak, Simmons Peak, Mt. Maclure, the tip of Mt. Lyell behind Maclure, Mt. Florence and, in the south, the entire Clark Range, from Triple Divide Peak on the left to Mt. Clark on the right.

From the windswept pass (10,650') we look down to the east onto Gallison and Bernice lakes. The trail rises briefly northeast before it follows murderously steep switchbacks down into sparse lodgepole forest where many small streams provide moisture for thousands of giant lupine plants, with flowers both dark velvet and light blue in color. The singing of the unnamed outlet stream from Gallison Lake becomes clear as the trail begins to level off, and then we reach a flat meadow through which the stream slowly meanders. There is a fine campsite beside this meadow, though wood fires are illegal here. There are many excellent camping sites from here to Florence Creek.

Proceeding down a rutted, grassy trail for several hundred yards, we come to a brief, steep descent on a rocky path that swoops down to the meadowed valley of multi-braided Lewis Creek. In this little valley in quick succession we boulderhop the Gallison Lake outlet and then cross Lewis Creek on a log. In a few minutes we pass the steep ½ mile lateral to Bernice Lake (incorrectly indicated as 1 mile on the sign). The shady trail winds gently down east of the creek under a moderate overhead canopy of lodgepole pine mixed with some hemlock, crossing a little stream about ½ mile from the last ford. Then, after almost touching the creek opposite a steep, rusty west canyon wall, the trail veers away and crosses another small tributary stream. Here the trail crosses the scars of invading avalanches, first one from the north side, then second a much larger one that demolished the forest to the south, as it winds through dense hemlock forest to the good campsites beside Florence Creek (9200'). This year-round creek cascades dramatically down to the camping area over steep granite sheets, and the water sounds are a fine sleeping potion at bedtime. Fishing in Florence and Lewis creeks is good for brook trout (to 12").

3rd Hiking Day (Florence Creek to Emeric Lake, 6.0 miles): Leaving the densely shaded hemlock forest floor, our trail descends a series of lodgepole-dotted granite slabs, and Lewis Creek makes pleasant noises in a string of chutes not far away on the right. Then, where the creek's channel narrows, we find on our left a lesson in exfoliation: granite layers peeling like an onion. This kind of peeling is typically seen on Yosemite's domes, but this fine example is located on a canyon slope. As the bed of Lewis Creek steepens to deliver the stream's water to the Merced River far below, so does the trail steepen, and our descent reaches the zone of red firs and western white pines. After dipping beside the creek, the trail climbs away from it. At about 8700 feet you pass the signed Isberg Trail, which leads south along the rim of the Merced River canyon.

From this junction the Lewis Creek Trail, now out of earshot of the creek, switchbacks down moderately, sometimes steeply, under a sparse cover of red fir, juniper, and lodgepole and western white pine for 1 mile to a signed junction with the Fletcher Creek Trail. We turn right onto this trail and follow the latter part of the 4th hiking day, Trip 54 ("Several switchbacks then descend to a wooden bridge over Lewis Creek. . . ."), to Emeric Lake.

4th Hiking Day: Follow the 5th hiking day, Trip 54, to Tuolumne Lodge, 10.8 miles.

Mt. Clark above Emeric Lake

62 Tuolumne Meadows to Lyell Fork

Distance	40.3 miles
Type	Semiloop trip
Best season	Mid or late
Topo maps	**Tuolumne Meadows, Merced Peak**, Vogelsang
	Peak, Mt. Lyell, Merced Peak, Tenaya Lake

Grade (hiking days/recommended layover days)

Leisurely	7/1
Moderate	6/1
Strenuous	4/0
Trailhead	Tuolumne Lodge (27)

HIGHLIGHTS   Beginning backpackers sooner or later want to try their newfound skills on a challenging trip of some length. This excursion in Yosemite Park is made to order for them: long mileage but not too long; tough but manageable climbs; lonely stretches, but two popular campsites in between. And it encompasses some of the best scenery in Yosemite National Park.

DESCRIPTION (Moderate trip)

1st and 2nd Hiking Days: Follow Trip 61 to Florence Creek, 12.0 miles.

3rd Hiking Day (Florence Creek to Lyell Fork, 7.4 miles): First, follow the 3rd hiking day, Trip 61, to the junction of the Isberg Trail and the Lewis Creek Trail, and turn left. The ascent from here is a tough, unrelieved 1000 vertical feet, but fortunately most of it is in shady forest of red fir and western white and lodgepole pine. Near the top, where the grade is a little less steep, the panting hiker is also shaded by altitude-preferring whitebark pines. At about 9000 feet, views to the west and north grow expansive, and one can make out Half Dome, Clouds Rest, the Cockscomb and Unicorn Peak. After crossing a ridge, our sandy path descends into a meadow long since invaded by lodgepole trees and reaches an all-year stream where you can refill your body's cooling system depleted by the long climb.

Beyond this easy ford the High Trail traverses a broad bench about 10,000 feet above sea level. A second all-year stream, larger than the last, can present slight fording problems in early season. Then the trail climbs again, away from the lip of the main canyon, until it veers south back to the lip at a spectacular viewpoint for studying the headwaters of the Lyell Fork (in the east) and the Merced Peak Fork (in the south) of the Merced River. One could spend many days in these vast, trailless headwaters without seeing another human being.

From this overlook the trail descends a bit steeply in places to a third all-year stream, an easy boulderhop, and then continues down to the cascading, chuting Lyell Fork (9080′). The last segment of trail before the stream, over granite slabs, is a little hard to follow, but the route leads where you would expect it to. The campsites at the ford are poor, but good ones lie 150 yards downstream, where the chutes and rapids flowing over the sculpted granite bedrock are fine visual attractions and provide good music to sleep by. There are also good campsites ½ mile upstream, a better base if you are going to explore the remote lake basins at the headwaters of the Lyell Fork. Fishing in the Lyell Fork is good for brook trout (to 11″).

4th Hiking Day (Lyell Fork to Babcock Lake, 9.1 miles): First, retrace your steps to the Lewis Creek Trail and turn left (south). From this junction the Lewis Creek Trail, now out of earshot of the creek, switchbacks down moderately, sometimes steeply, under a sparse cover of red fir, juniper, and lodgepole and western white pine for 1 mile to a signed junction with a trail that comes steeply up from the main canyon floor. We turn right on this trail and follow several switchbacks down to a bridge over tree-shaded Lewis Creek. From here the rocky trail enters more open hillside as it climbs moderately on a cobbled path bordered by clumps of mountain whitethorn and huckleberry oak. Just past a tributary ½ mile from Lewis Creek we have fine views of cataracts and waterfalls on Fletcher Creek where it rushes down open granite slopes dotted with lodgepole pines. The trail then passes very close to the splashing creek before veering northeast and climbing, steeply at times, on the now-familiar cobbling placed by trail crews. Here one has more good views of Fletcher Creek chuting and cascading down from the notch at the base of a granite dome before it leaps off a ledge in free fall. The few solitary pine trees on this otherwise blank dome are mute testimony to nature's extraordinary persistence.

At the notch our trail levels off near some nice but illegal campsites and soon we arrive at the trail to Babcock Lake. Turning left (north) we ford Fletcher Creek (difficult in early season) and follow a winding trail ⅓ mile west to narrow, granite-bound Babcock Lake (8885'). There are fine campsites all around this forested lake, and fishing is good for brook trout (to 10").

5th Hiking Day (Babcock Lake to Boothe Lake, 4.4 miles): After retracing our steps to the Fletcher Creek Trail, we turn left (north). From this junction the sandy trail ascends steadily through a moderate forest cover just east of the verdant banks of rollicking Fletcher Creek. After a mile, the trail breaks out into the open and begins to rise more steeply via rocky but shaded switchbacks. These zigzags lead to another notch between two granite domes, and upon reaching this notch the slogging traveler suddenly achieves a wonderful panorama. A long, barely sloping, lush meadow stretches several miles ahead, and it is flanked on both sides by soaring, snow-streaked peaks. Down this meadow flows Fletcher Creek, meandering from pool to trout-holding pool. Here one has the feeling of being in truly high country, and the distance passes easily as we stroll to an **X** junction (not shown on the topo) with trails to Emeric Lake and Vogelsang. From this junction (". . .an **X** junction in the valley of Fletcher Creek" in Trip 54's words) follow part of the 5th hiking day, Trip 54, to the overlook of Boothe Lake (9845') and then leave the trail to find the good campsites on the south side of the lake.

6th Hiking Day (Boothe Lake to Tuolumne Lodge, 7.4 miles): First, hike briefly cross country back to the trail you left at the end of the previous hiking day. From that point, near broad Tuolumne Pass, hike up to the junction in the pass, and then retrace most of the steps of Trip 60.

Tuolumne Meadows to Triple Peak Fork

63

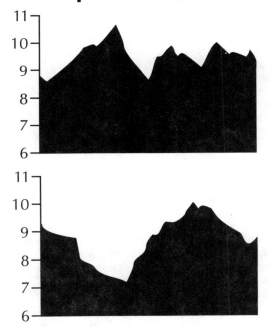

Distance	51.3 miles
Type	Semiloop trip
Best season	Mid or late
Topo maps	**Tuolumne Meadows, Merced Peak**, Vogelsang
	Peak, Mt. Lyell, Merced Peak, Tenaya Lake

Grade (hiking days/recommended layover days)

Leisurely	8/1
Moderate	7/0
Strenuous	5/0
Trailhead	Tuolumne Lodge (27)

HIGHLIGHTS The headwaters of the Triple Peak Fork of the Merced River are about as far as one can get from civilization, so this is a trip for those who feel they encounter too many people on most of their hikes. Their opportunity to view most of the High Sierra from the southern border of Yosemite is won by a long walk through grand high country.

DESCRIPTION (Moderate trip)

1st, 2nd and 3rd Hiking Days: Follow Trip 62 to the Lyell Fork of the Merced River, 19.4 miles.

4th Hiking Day (Lyell Fork to Triple Peak Fork Meadows, 6.9 miles): This day's hike starts off strenuously up switchbacks on the south wall of the Lyell Fork canyon. As we progress slowly up the rocky path, views open up to reward us for our struggle. In the northeast, on the Sierra crest, are Mt. Maclure and Mt. Lyell, highest point in Yosemite Park. After Lyell passes from view, Rodgers Peak, second highest in the Park, appears as the dark triangle beyond the right flank of Peak 12113. Other towering peaks in view this side of the crest don't even have names, but in the company of lesser summits they surely would have. Where our trail extends close to the lip of the Merced River canyon, we can step off the path to an overlook for viewing most of the Clark Range in the southwest, and Clouds Rest in the northwest.

Beyond the top of the ascent, the route winds among large boulders on "grus"—granite sand—which is the result of the breakup of just such boulders by the fierce erosional forces at work in these alpine climates. After crossing a seasonal stream, the trail ascends to a second broad ridge, from which views through the whitebark-pine trees continue to be excellent. About ½ mile beyond this ridge a trail to Foerster Lake (not named on the topo map) veers off to the left. This unsigned trail is indicated by parallel rock borders and occasional flame-shaped blazes on trees. Secluded Foerster Lake has no fish, but swimming and camping there are excellent.

From this spur trail our route makes a long descent, paralleling Foerster Lake's outlet part of the way, to a boulder ford of Foerster Creek. The well-shaded trail then undulates past a number of pocket meadows to another small stream, and yet another not shown on the map. A gentle traverse downward extends almost a mile to a small creek that winds through a flat area densely forested with hemlock and lodgepole pine. From this flat the High Trail begins a climb that doesn't end until it reaches the Yosemite border at Isberg Pass. Very soon the trail fords the outlet of the unnamed lake north of Isberg Peak, and in another 200 yards it reaches a large cairn which marks the junction with a trail down to the Triple Peak Fork. All hikers who arrive here with any surplus energy will greatly enjoy a 4-mile round trip to Isberg Pass before heading down to camp on the Triple Peak Fork.

The trail to Isberg Pass first climbs moderately for ¼ mile up a beautiful hillside covered with whitish broken granite in whose cracks a dozen species of alpine wildflowers grow. Looking west and north from this slope, one can see all the peaks of the Clark Range and most of the peaks of the Cathedral Range. Using your **Tuolumne Meadows** map, you can probably make out Tenaya Peak, Tressider Peak, Cathedral Peak, Echo Peaks, Matthes Crest and the Cockscomb. At the top of this little climb a truly marvelous sight comes into view, for here we enter a large, high bowl nearly encircled by great peaks which has in it an enormous meadow and two sparkling lakes. Here and there, clumps of whitebark and lodgepole pines help give scale to the vast amphitheater, and the delicateness of the meadow flowers is a perfect counterpoint to the massiveness of the encircling summits. The setting is absolutely euphoric.

On the far side of the bowl, the trail begins to rise toward the crest and soon comes to a junction where the right fork leads to Post Peak Pass and the left to Isberg Pass, ¾ mile away. The left fork ascends moderately a short way to reach the height of the pass, and then contours over to it. The best views—other than those we have already been enjoying for the last several miles—are to be had from a point on the ridgeline a few hundred yards beyond the sign-marked pass. You can see most of the High Sierra, from the Ritter Range close in the east, to peaks around Mt. Goddard southwest of Bishop. Back at the cairned junction, our route turns west and starts straight downhill, then veers southwest and switchbacks down into deep hemlock forest, turning north for the last ¾ mile down to the river. There are good campsites around the junction of our trail and the trail to Red Peak Pass, which begins just across the placid Triple Peak Fork (9100'). Fishing is good for brook and rainbow trout (to 9").

5th hiking Day (Triple Peak Fork Meadow to Washburn Lake, 6.9 miles): Reverse the 4th and part of the 3rd hiking day, Trip 72, to the good campsites at the head of Washburn Lake.

6th Hiking Day (Washburn Lake to Emeric Lake, 7.3 miles): The sandy trail along the east side of Washburn Lake leads over slopes dotted with white fir, aspen, juniper, lodgepole pine and Jeffrey pine, and from these slopes on a typical morning, the still water makes a fine mirror for the soaring granite cliffs across the lake. Beyond this lake, our descending trail stays near the singing river in open forest, fording a small stream every quarter mile or so as it descends on a moderate grade. Then the canyon floor begins to widen, and the trail proceeds levelly under a canopy of imposing Jeffrey pines and other tall conifers to a junction with the Lewis Creek Trail beside the Merced Lake Ranger Station. Here we turn right and follow the latter part of the 4th hiking day, Trip 55, to Emeric Lake.

7th Hiking Day (Emeric Lake to Tuolumne Lodge, 10.8 miles): Follow the 5th hiking day, Trip 54.

64 White Wolf to Morrison Creek

Distance	11 miles
Type	Out and back trip
Best season	Early, mid or late
Topo maps	**Hetch Hetchy**, Tamarack Flat
Grade (hiking days/recommended layover days)	
Leisurely	2/0
Moderate	Day
Strenuous	Day
Trailhead	White Wolf (30)

HIGHLIGHTS Of all the major canyons in the Sierra, only one is named the Grand Canyon: the Grand Canyon of the Tuolumne. This easy trip brings one to the brink of this geologic wonder for an overview of its awesome grandeur.

DESCRIPTION (Leisurely trip)

1st Hiking Day (White Wolf to Morrison Creek, 5.5 miles): Just opposite White Wolf Lodge, our trail begins by skirting the south side of White Wolf campground and then heads east for a level mile through a forest of lodgepole pine. After crossing seasonal Middle Fork Tuolumne River, we soon reach a signed junction with a trail to Lukens Lake. Turning left, we continue through an almost level forest to eventually cross a nearly imperceptible ridge. Now descending, our trail follows a lush creek to a beautiful, forest-fringed meadow. After skirting this meadow, our route climbs gently for an easy mile to a more open, distinctive ridgetop. Here, we stand on the crest of a moraine that was deposited by a glacier that once flowed down the Grand Canyon of the Tuolumne. From here we begin descending a slope that eventually leads to the bottom of the canyon. At first we cannot see the canyon, as our trail crosses several more lateral moraine crests. As we lose altitude, the forest cover changes rapidly; lodgepole pine and red fir soon give way to western white pine, Sierra juniper and Jeffrey pine.

As the grade steepens and the forest cover thins, we get our first views across the canyon, and where the trail crosses some glacially polished bedrock we can take a vista break and consider that ice once filled this canyon to this height—and more—during the Ice Ages of the Pleistocene Epoch. Continuing into denser forest again, we meet incense cedar, white fir, and quaking aspen, which indicates a locally high water table. After many switchbacks our route meets a signed junction with a trail to Harden Lake. We turn right and continue descending along a forested slope where we catch views of broad Rancheria Mountain across the canyon to the north. Along this section we meet more lower-elevation trees including black oak, sugar pine and, near an unmarked creek, some alder. Soon we can hear Morrison Creek to our right as we cross a densely forested bench, where a plank bridge helps keeps our feet dry. A little beyond, the forest cover opens, and just south of a bedrock granite ridge there are good campsites near the creek. If you start heading down steep switchbacks, you've gone too far. A few minutes climb to the north of the campsites, and east of the ridge's high point, you can find a breathtaking view of the canyon. You could even carry water up and camp out near several majestic ponderosa pines. You could wake early to behold the broad chasm of Piute Creek to the northeast and watch the shadowy depths of the Grand Canyon become illuminated in the early morning light.

2nd Hiking Day: Retrace your steps, 5.5 miles.

65   Grand Canyon of the Tuolumne: The Big Loop

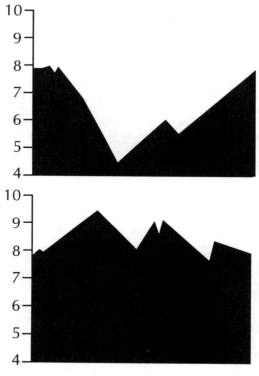

Distance	46 miles
Type	Loop trip
Best season	Early or late
Topo maps	**Hetch Hetchy**, **Tuolumne Meadows**, Tamarack Flat, Hetch Hetchy Reservoir, 10 Lakes, Falls Ridge, Tenaya Lake

Grade (Hiking days/recommended layover days)

Leisurely	8/0
Moderate	6/1
Strenuous	4/0
Trailhead	White Wolf (30)

HIGHLIGHTS   The lowest and highest trails in and around the
                   Grand Canyon of the Tuolumne are only a few
miles apart—as the crow flies—but it takes days to hike from the
bottom in Pate Valley to the top beside Ten Lakes, a vertical distance
of over 5000 feet. This trip offers a memorable experience of the full
range of what the mighty Tuolumne River has created over tens of
millions of years.

DESCRIPTION (Moderate trip)

1st Hiking Day (White Wolf to Pate Valley, 9.5 miles): First,
follow the first day of Trip 64 to Morrison Creek, 5.5 miles. Leaving
the Morrison Creek campsites, we soon begin the final plunge to the
bottom of the Grand Canyon, still over 2000 feet below. At first, our
trail steepens into a series of switchbacks beside Morrison Creek
through a forest of white fir, incense-cedar, sugar pine and dogwood.
After dropping about 500 feet, the trail veers north, and views open
up dramatically. At 5700 feet we cross a bench where one can stop
for serious views of this phenomenal canyon, including the incon-
gruous reservoir of Hetch Hetchy. You could camp here on this
bench, and Morrison Creek isn't too far for water, which usually
flows down to this elevation through midsummer. As we descend,
the environment continues to change rapidly; already, canyon live
oak has made its first appearance, and where we cross now-seasonal
Morrison Creek are large incense cedars and black oaks.

The last 1500 feet to the bottom are mostly across exposed slopes
where the expertly built and very steep trail is often "riprap"—
wedge-shaped rocks intricately fitted together to form a staircase of
various-sized steps. Along this breathtaking descent we can see and
hear the Tuolumne River, far below, and on a hot summer's day
anticipate a cool dip. At 5000 feet the trail crosses a seasonal creek
channel which is also an avalanche chute in the winter. Five hundred
feet lower we cross another seasonal creek (this one on the topo
map). Both of these creeks can be dangerous torrents in very high
runoff times, such as late afternoon in late spring of a heavy snow
year. At 4400 feet the grade levels briefly and we pass a moraine-
dammed pond before entering tall forest again.

Another 200-foot descent brings us to the canyon floor, and we
find our first—and perhaps long-awaited—campsite near the river.
If you'd like to camp in grander forest away from the burned area,
continue upcanyon and in 1 to 1½ gentle miles you'll find several
excellent campsites in a cathedral forest of tall incense-cedars, white
firs and ponderosa pines. If you get to the first bridge over the river
you've passed these campsites. This idyllic sanctuary of Pate Valley

is a rare gem, as there are very few low-elevation wilderness valleys left in the Sierra. Here, we can appreciate why it is said that John Muir died of a broken heart after Hetch Hetchy Valley was dammed. In what turned out to be the final campaign of his life, John Muir worked passionately to save Hetch Hetchy. But, alas, big money prevailed and the City of San Francisco built O'Shaughnessy Dam. Bears are plentiful here in Pate Valley, so diligent food protection is advised.

2nd Hiking Day (Pate Valley up Tuolumne Canyon, 7 miles): Today's journey takes us deep into the inner sanctum of the Grand Canyon of the Tuolumne—the less-traveled stretch from Pate Valley to Waterwheel Falls. Not only is this the least-traveled section upriver, it's also through the narrowest and deepest part of the canyon.

Continuing briefly upriver, our level trail crosses one and then another channel of the river via bridges; the short section between these two bridges can flood in a very wet year. Once on the north side of the river—which we'll stay on until Glen Aulin—we enter another burned area and come to a junction with the Pleasant Valley Trail. Turning right onto the trail leading upriver, we pass through a brief, narrow part of the valley where perhaps bedrock, acting like an underground dam, has forced groundwater near the surface to produce a lush, muddy area. Though too wet for trees to grow, many species of water-loving flowers and shrubs thrive here, including cow parsnip and rushes. Beyond, the trail returns to riverside for a while and we cross a short section of riprap that is set in cement in order to withstand flooding. Wading may be required here. Though it's very unlikely that any one would be here during flood time in the spring of an exceptionally wet year, if you find yourself unsure of your safety here (or anywhere else), please turn back rather than risk drowning.

More gentle ascent brings us to another, older, burned area where the fire was hot enough to burn large trees as well as the ground cover. Just beyond this area we come to some fantastically large and deep pools in the bedrock—a fine swimming and fishing spot. From here the canyon narrows and the trail stays close to the river for a mile, where again there are a few spots where we might get our feet wet during high water. This beautiful, shady stretch of canyon gives way to a wider, sunnier valley that is very deep. Part way through this valley the trail climbs away from the river up an open slope; nearby is a stately campsite just downstream of a large pool that sits at the base of some wide slabs that the river runs down. In these drier areas especially, you may encounter many reptiles, usually blue-bellied lizards, though there are a variety of snakes here in the canyon, including a few rattlesnakes. After nearly 2 miles through this lightly- visited Yosemite, the canyon again narrows as we approach Muir Gorge. Named after a man who eagerly sought out inaccessible places, Muir Gorge is the only part of the canyon whose walls are too steep for a trail, so we're obliged to climb around it. Beyond two live-oak-shaded campsites the trail begins climbing well above the river, and at one point we can look straight up the dark chasm of Muir Gorge. First the trail crosses Rodgers Canyon creek on a bridge, and then bridges adjacent Register Creek. Our route then briefly heads up the side canyon of Register Creek before climbing south over a low, shady ridge. After a short descent we switchback steeply up for 500 feet to a granite ridge It is well worth the short hike to peer down into mysterious Muir Gorge—a real eagle's view, as long as you stay on the ground.

The descent back to the river is mostly shady, and the canyon again widens above Muir Gorge. Where granite slabs come down to the river the trail can be wet in early season, though climbing above high water is easy. In another ¼ mile we come to a seasonal stream channel in white gravel. Between the trail and the river is an excellent campsite, and you are unlikely to meet many people here, as it is about the same long distance to a road in either direction. Savor your time this far into wilderness.

3rd Hiking Day (Tuolumne Canyon to McGee Lake, 9.5 miles): Like the first day, this day is a long one, and if you break it up into two days you could take more time to be near the waterfalls upriver. Our ascent is gentle for about a mile until the canyon again narrows and we approach close under the looming south wall above. Nearing the base of this cliff we pass some seasonally flooded campsites before beginning a steeper section of the canyon. The last Douglas fir and bay laurel fall behind as we climb alongside the river for about a mile. When the canyon again widens we find ourselves in a dense forest on a flat away from the river. Another ½ mile brings us into the open close to the river and we pass some low falls that can barely hint at the awesome features to come. Soon we bridge Return Creek and quickly begin climbing again. Waterwheel Falls loom above, and in early season these falls are at their best: thunderous and spectacular as protrusions in the granite throw wheeling sprays of water far out into the air. Don't be in a hurry because these falls are best viewed from below. And on a hot day cooling spray from the falls provides a soothing respite before we climb the steep switchbacks that take us up and around the falls. Our brilliantly routed trail returns to the river just above the brink of the falls, beyond which is a small lake.

Continuing, we climb behind a low bedrock ridge for about ¼ mile to an open, juniper-dotted slope where there is a unsigned trail of use down to a broad, forested flat near the river. On this flat there are several excellent campsites beneath a cathedral forest of towering Jeffrey pines, white firs and incense cedars. This is a wonderful place to stay overnight if you want to take it easier today and linger by the river.

Above this flat, our trail again steepens as we climb past a short lateral trail to LeConte Falls, which are well worth getting close (but not too close) to. Leaving behind the last cedars and sugar pines, the trail becomes increasingly steep and sunny until we come close under the massive south buttress of Wildcat Point. Again we find a trail tread of riprap—an appropriate building material in this land of granite. The grade eases before we reach California Falls. A relatively short climb brings us near the top of these, the third and lowest of the three major falls below Glen Aulin. Much of Glen Aulin experienced fire recently, and many of the former camping areas are now undesirable, and due to potential tree fall they may be dangerous. Where the trail swings close to the river there is one unburned area. Nature continues her cycles here, as fire is a regular player in the ecology of Sierra forests, and we see the timely succession of plant and animal species. Aspen is quick to grow back because, unlike conifers, it can resprout from the crown of its roots; therefore, aspen is an early-successional plant species, while firs, which need shade to grow, are late-successional trees. After more than a mile of level ground we leave Glen Aulin proper and make a short climb to a junction with the Pacific Crest Trail. Glen Aulin High Sierra Camp is just beyond, across Conness Creek. There is a backpackers' camp behind the compound that has bear-proof poles for hanging food, and limited supplies are sold at the office during the summer.

After a rest break, we cross the Tuolumne River via a bridge. White Cascade plummets into a large pool and occasionally the trail just beyond the bridge is flooded but easily negotiable. Leaving the river, we make a short climb to a junction where we leave the Tuolumne Canyon Trail and turn right onto the May Lake Trail. Now in forest, the grade is easy and soon we come to the north shore of peaceful McGee Lake. The more secluded campsites at this lake are found on the south side of the outlets at either end of the lake; surprisingly, McGee Lake drains into both the Tuolumne River and Cathedral Creek.

4th Hiking Day (McGee Lake to Tuolumne Peak Ridge, 6.5 miles): From the northwest side of McGee Lake our trail descends southwest to cross the west outlet of McGee Lake and then Cathedral Creek. Though a seasonal stream, Cathedral Creek can be a wet ford in early season. From the creek we begin climbing, steeply at first and then more gently as we cross a low ridge. Continuing southwest, the mostly shady trail ascends gently for over a mile to a junction with the Murphy Creek Trail, reached 2.5 miles beyond Cathedral Creek. Turning right, we stay on the High Sierra Camps loop for another level ½ mile to a junction with the Ten Lakes trail, where we again turn right. After heading southwest for another ¼ mile, our route bends north and begins climbing the lower eastern slopes of Tuolumne Peak. At first our ascent is gentle and the views are minimal, but as we gain altitude both the grade and the views increase until we reach the northeast ridge of Tuolumne Peak at one, and then a second, high point. This ridgetop marks the highest point of the trip, at about 9,900 feet above sea level. To the east beyond Tuolumne Meadows rises the Sierra crest; to the south of the Meadows stands the ice-sculpted Cathedral Range; to the north the Grand Canyon of the Tuolumne lies hidden behind Falls Ridge; and to the northeast is the massive, white southwest face of Mt. Conness. Just below to the west is a small pond, and a short descent brings us to the sparsely populated environs of this highly perched body of water. Even more impressive views can be found by climbing part way up Tuolumne Peak. Being centrally located in almost the middle of Yosemite National Park, and being higher than any other point around except Mt. Hoffman, Tuolumne Peak sports some of the most comprehensive views in the entire park.

  5th Hiking Day (Tuolumne Peak Ridge to Ten Lakes, 6.5 miles): This hiking day is as short as the previous, and allows time to linger here in the area north of Tuolumne Peak, which is probably the least-traveled portion of this loop. First heading west and then northwest, our winding trail climbs up and down for over a mile to an overlook above South Fork Cathedral Creek canyon. The trail then switchbacks down to the west, contours south, and switchbacks west again to reach the South Fork. Turning north, we descend along the east side of the creek for 2 miles to a seasonally wet ford and continue heading north briefly before turning west to climb out of the canyon of the South Fork. As we switchback up this open slope we can see down into the deep canyon of Cathedral Creek and beyond to the north side of the much deeper Grand Canyon. As the slope eases we find ourselves in forest again. After a mile the trail begins heading down, and soon we reach the northeast shore of the eastern-most and largest of the Ten Lakes. Good campsites can be found on the north and west sides of the lake.

  6th Hiking Day (Ten Lakes to White Wolf, 11 miles): Today, our last day, is a long one, but it's mostly downhill and by now we are likely to be in pretty good condition, even if we didn't start the trip that way. Heading northwest from the lake our route is nearly level for ½ mile before turning southwest to descend to the south shore of the large western Ten Lake. The Ten Lakes basin is a popular area—and no wonder, as these lakes are both pleasant and beautiful. Just west of this lake the trail meets a trail to the higher, southwestern Ten Lakes and then crosses their outlet. Soon we begin climbing the 600 feet to the broad ridge on the west side of Ten Lakes Basin. As we cross over the top of this gently-sloping upland we have extensive vistas in most directions, providing us with a final overview of the Tuolumne River drainage. Descending southwest the grade is at first gentle as we pass the Grant Lakes Trail on our left. Soon, however, the trail becomes steep until we reach the north side of Half Moon Meadow. The trail skirts the meadow's north side before continuing to descend southwest. The grade eases briefly and the trail makes a short northwest jog and then returns to a generally downcanyon focus for another 1½ miles. Just beyond a small creek we leave the Ten Lakes Trail and turn right toward White Wolf. Ascending gently-to-moderately, our trail climbs 1½ miles to a forested ridge. Here we enter the drainage of the Middle Tuolumne and begin the last hill—down. Heading down through a quiet forest of lodgepole pine and red fir, the trail soon crosses the headwaters of the Middle Tuolumne, and then follows its direction southwest along a very gentle slope. After 2 miles near the creek we meet the more popular Lukens Lake Trail coming in on our left. Continuing west for a level mile we meet the trail to Pate Valley, thereby completing our big loop-tour of the Grand Canyon of the Tuolumne and adjacent uplands. It's now just a level mile back to the road and civilization, and we can walk in reflection of how the place called "The Grand Canyon of the Tuolumne" has affected us deeply, just as it did John Muir over one hundred years ago.

Yosemite Valley to Merced Lake **66**

Distance	27.8 miles
Type	Out and back trip
Best season	Early
Topo maps	**Yosemite, Merced Peak**, Half Dome, Merced Peak
Grade (hiking days/recommended layover days)	
Leisurely	4/1
Moderate	3/1
Strenuous	2/1
Trailhead	Happy Isles (31)

HIGHLIGHTS   An early-season trip (low altitude, early snow-melt), this route offers all the scenic grandeur of the Valley attractions, plus the intimate knowledge of the back country that only the backpacker can have. Fishing is good during early season on the Merced River and at Merced Lake. Swimming is poor during the early season, owing to the chilly waters, but photographers and naturalists will find an exciting area of geologic spectacle and history.

DESCRIPTION (Leisurely trip)

1st Hiking Day (Yosemite Valley to Little Yosemite Valley, 4.7 miles): Though this trip is graded "leisurely," the first hiking day is rigorous, with over 2000 feet of hot, steady climbing. But the route is so spectacular that hikers can easily forget their aches and pains. This trip starts at the beginning of the John Muir Trail, across the Merced River from Happy Isles.

The John Muir Trail—which is paved and more like a road here—climbs steeply southward above the Happy Isles, two islets in the river, under canyon live oak, maple, and California bay. As we round Sierra Point in early season, a glance across the river and up Illilouette Gorge reveals Illilouette Fall.

A brief descent brings us to a footbridge from which there is a fine view upstream to Vernal Fall. We cross the footbridge, on the other side of which are a drinking fountain, restrooms, and an emergency telephone. Then the Muir Trail curves east to a junction with the Mist Trail: left (ahead, east) along the river on the extremely steep, seasonally-soaking-wet Mist Trail; right (south, then east) on the higher, more gradual Muir Trail. The Muir Trail, which we recommend for backpackers, is easier, safer, drier, and less crowded than the Mist Trail. We suggest you save the Mist Trail for a dayhike. Both routes will be described below.

If you ascend the Mist Trail from here to Nevada Fall, you and your pack will get soaking wet in season unless you put on your rain gear and cover your pack. The steep, slick, crowded trail offers poor footing. Climbing toward Vernal Fall, the trail soon becomes extremely steep as it ascends large, rocky steps where the mist can be a driving rainstorm in spring. As we rise above the base of the 320-foot fall, we pass through a hole, and then reach the base of a large, dripping overhang. Then we turn left on a ledge that exits onto slabs above Vernal Fall. From the railing by the fall proceed up past Emerald Pool to a junction with a lateral, the Clark Trail, leading to the right to the Muir Trail. Here we turn left, then cross the river and ascend to a level area below Nevada Fall. Then the last section of the Mist Trail switchbacks up a steep, rocky gully several hundred yards north of Nevada Fall.

If you ascend the John Muir Trail from here to Nevada Fall, you start by bypassing a marked horse trail that comes in on the right. Then you begin ascending a long series of switchbacks. At Clark Point we have our first, excellent view of Nevada Fall and reach a junction with the Clark Trail down to the Mist Trail near Vernal Fall: left (ahead) is the Clark Trail, right leads around a switchback turn on the Muir Trail. Staying on the Muir Trail, we climb more switchbacks and get very good views of Half Dome, Mt. Broderick and Liberty Cap. These last two, though rounded like Half Dome, were overridden by glaciers while Half Dome was not. Our trail then passes a couple of junctions with the Panorama Trail and arrives at the top of Nevada Fall. While admiring the view of Glacier Point you may notice patches of shiny, smooth bedrock at your feet—glacial polish—indicating that a glacier has been here recently. There is very little glacial polish below this point, which marks the farthest extent of a glacier that was here about 13,000 years ago.

The John Muir Trail meets the Mist Trail several hundred yards northwest of Nevada Fall. From the junction it is a short ascent and then a gentle descent into Little Yosemite Valley. Our trail passes a cutoff that later rejoins the Muir Trail, and ½ mile farther we leave the Muir Trail at a junction near the well-used camping area by the summer ranger station.

2nd Hiking Day (Little Yosemite Valley to Merced Lake, 9.2 miles): From the well-used, misused and abused camping area, our shaded route heads toward the east end of Little Yosemite Valley. The trail—40 feet wide in places—swings away from the complacent river and stretches along the flat valley floor under Jeffrey pines and white firs. As an indication of how thick glaciers were here, look up at Moraine Dome to the east: ice filled the valley almost to its summit 750,000 years ago. Since then glaciers have repeatedly entered this valley, but none that thick.

At the east end of Little Yosemite Valley the trail swings close to the river again. Here the lofty canyon walls converge and the grade steepens as we pass another camping area. The next section of our route is through a short, narrow gorge leading to Lost Valley. In this section of canyon, glaciers did very little to modify the pre-existing V-shaped, stream-cut canyon.

Soon we arrive in wide, level Lost Valley, where the vertical walls reflect the vertical jointing in the bedrock. At the east end of Lost Valley we enter yet another short, narrow section of canyon, which leads to yet a smaller valley, on the north side of exfoliating Bunnell Point. Before the canyon narrows again, the trail crosses one branch of the river via an island, and a second branch on a wood bridge. The lumber for this bridge was hewn in 1984 from a 175-year-old sugar pine that stood just below the trail.

From the bridge our rocky trail stays near the river until we begin the steep stretch up to Echo Valley. The trail avoids the gorge bottom by climbing 400 feet south and traversing over open slabs where glacial erratics have been rearranged to mark the trail. Our route then descends to cross the river on a bridge at the west end of Echo Valley. Following the river, then turning north, the trail arrives at a junction and a multibridged crossing of Echo Creek. We continue east through a very dense young forest of lodgepole pines.

Soon our route winds up slabs, and where the river is confined in yet another gorge we walk right above the fast-moving water. The grade eases once again as we arrive at yet another wide, flat valley, this one containing Merced Lake. Following the north shore, the trail passes a drift fence and arrives at the camping area at the lake's east end. Bears are plentiful. The lake contains a population of brook and rainbow trout. A High Sierra camp with tents, showers and meals—if you have a reservation—is here.

3rd and 4th Hiking Days: Retrace your steps, 13.9 miles.

67 Bridalveil Creek to Royal Arch Lake

Distance	26 miles
Type	Out and back trip
Best season	Early or mid
Topo maps	**Yosemite**, Half Dome, Mariposa Grove

Grade (hiking days/recommended layover days)

Leisurely	4/1
Moderate	3/0
Strenuous	2/0
Trailhead	Bridalveil Creek (33)

HIGHLIGHTS   In early season this trip route is lush with wild flowers of every variety, and color film is a must for the photographer. Anglers will find few lakes within the Park to rival the fishing at Royal Arch Lake. The easy grade of the topography makes this an excellent early-season choice.

DESCRIPTION (Leisurely trip)

1st Hiking Day (Bridalveil Campground to Turner Meadows, 6.3 miles): From the trailhead at the southeast end of the campground, the trail begins winding southeastward along meandering Bridalveil Creek. The grade is gentle as the trail winds through the dense lodgepole forest. Periodically, the thick undergrowth gives way to intimate, mountain-bluebell-filled meadows. Beyond a left-leading trail to the Glacier Point Road, near Lost Bear Meadow, the trail veers south beside one of the larger tributaries of Bridalveil Creek. It crosses this tributary, passes a lateral to the Ostrander Lake trail, and in ½ mile crosses the tributary again, and each fording is heralded by banks covered with lavender shooting stars.

The second crossing marks the beginning of an easy 400-foot climb over the ridge that separates the Bridalveil Creek and Alder Creek watersheds. In early and mid season this ridge is colorfully decked out in lush pink and white fields of pussy paws, brodiaea, mat lupine and Douglas phlox. From the top of this ridge, the trail drops to the Deer Camp Trail junction, climbs over Turner Ridge and then offers a short walk to Turner Meadows and the campsites at the northern end. The cabin site at the head of the meadows (indicated by the rock fireplace) is all that remains of Bill Turner's pioneer abode. He occupied these grasslands while running cattle around the turn of the 20th century. There is stream water except in late season.

2nd Hiking Day (Turner Meadows to Royal Arch Lake, 6.7 miles): Before leaving Turner Meadows, one should take the opportunity to study the wildlife that frequents the meadows, particularly in the early morning. On the trail you will pass many little rills supporting colorful wildflower gardens before you reach, in ½ mile, the Wawona Trail, which branches south, and ¾ mile farther, the Chilnualna Lakes Trail, branching east. These trails were used by U.S. Cavalry patrols at the turn of the 20th Century. Their purpose was to facilitate administration of the Park.

Just after the last junction you ford swirling Chilnualna Creek (difficult in early season), and then climb on switchbacks over an eastward-rising ridge to a junction with a second lateral trail to Wawona, leading right. South of the ridgecrest, where views to the south open up, we turn east up the valley of Grouse Lake's little outlet stream and ascend gently for 2 miles. You can leave the trail where it veers a bit northward away from the creek and follow that stream to Grouse Lake, should that be your goal, or you can stay on the trail for another ¼ mile to find a spur trail leading to the right to the lake.

From the spur-trail junction your trail provides an easy, shaded walk over a small rise and thence down to cross the inlet of shallow Crescent Lake, just out of sight in the south. Another mile of level walking into increasing mosquito-infested forest brings us to Johnson Lake, with its good fishing for brook and rainbow (9–13″). Johnson Lake and its perimeter were one of the last acquisitions of private property within the Park's boundaries, and two crumbling cabins remain to remind us of our homesteading era.

The next ¾ mile, to a junction with the Royal Arch Lake Trail, is a 250-foot ascent up a lodgepole-covered slope. Here our route leaves the Buck Camp Trail and turns north for a small climb through dense forest that gives way to open hillside as we approach dramatic Royal Arch Lake (8685′). This lake is small but it is deep, and it supports an excellent, self-sustaining fishery of brook and rainbow (8–14″). Its regal name derives from the blackened granite streaks that rainbow across the steep eastern face of the lake basin. There are numerous good campsites not far from a seasonal lakelet beside the west shore, which is perfect for bathing when it has warmed up by mid-season.

3rd and 4th Hiking Days: Retrace your steps, 13 miles.

68 Bridalveil Creek to Glacier Point

Distance	29.1 miles
Type	Shuttle trip
Best season	Early or mid
Topo maps	**Yosemite**, Half Dome, Mariposa Grove

Grade (hiking days/recommended layover days)

Leisurely	5/1
Moderate	4/1
Strenuous	3/0
Trailhead	Bridalveil Creek (33), Glacier Point (32)

HIGHLIGHTS   On this trip, early- and mid-season travelers will find splendid forests, lush meadows, delightful wildflower displays, beautiful creeks, and excellent angling, all topped off with thrilling vistas of Yosemite's most famous scenery.

DESCRIPTION (Moderate trip)

1st and 2nd Hiking Days: Follow Trip 67 to Royal Arch Lake, 13 miles.

3rd Hiking Day (Royal Arch Lake to Buena Vista Creek Tributary, 11 miles): Today's hike is long but it's mostly downhill. It's also unusual as it crosses several areas that are in the early stages of fire succession. We gain most of our elevation today by climbing 2 miles from Royal Arch Lake to Buena Vista summit. This easy ascent winds past delightful meadows that are drained by a small creek. From the pass (9300') it is an easy ¾-mile climb to the top of aptly named Buena Vista Peak (9709'). Being the highest point for miles around, this peak offers some of the most expansive views in the Sierra.

After a short descent past the north shore of Buena Vista Lake, we meet the signed Chilnualna Lakes Trail on a ridge. Turning right, we descend steeply past two ponds into Buena Vista Creek canyon. After crossing the creek several times and then the outlet from Hart Lakes, we climb over a large moraine. Beyond, our descent is steady for 2 miles through dry forest until we cross the seasonal outlet from Edson Lake between two wet meadows. Turning northeast, the grade soon steepens and we descend over indistinct glacial moraines. Presently, the forest of white fir and Jeffrey pine shows sign of a fire that occurred in 1981.

As we near some-years-seasonal Buena Vista Creek, we see many living trees whose trunks were barely touched by flames, indicating that the fire here was not very hot and burned slowly along the ground. This type of low-intensity fire is a normal event of natural coniferous forests. Such fires prevent a large buildup of dead wood, which in turn prevents fires from reaching severe intensity. But always, there are variations in nature, and after we climb over a low ridge we descend to cross two small creeks where stands of lodgepole pine have been completely killed. Lodgepoles, like most pines, burn easily, and having thin bark also, they often die in a fire. The logical counterpart to this property is that lodgepole pines produce a dense crop of fast-growing seedlings. The new generation thrives in bright light and dry soil, and out-competes other trees in newly opened parts of a forest.

After crossing another low ridge we descend along the margins of a flowery meadow to ford a larger creek, beside which we find a good campsite in a stand of unburned pine and fir.

4th Hiking Day (Buena Vista Creek Tributary to Glacier Point, 5.1 miles): Descending northwest, we see more signs of fire, as well as massive Mt. Starr King looming in the northeast. Our route passes several giant sugar pines, survivors of many fires over the centuries. After 1⅓ miles we reach a signed junction near Illilouette Creek, on the right. (A short distance toward the creek is an overused campsite, but there are better ones upstream). We go left and in 50 yards reach a signed junction with a trail west to Mono Meadow. Our trail veers right and soon steepens, and in ⅓ mile we cross the creek from Mono Meadow on rocks or logs.

From here, we descend parallel to Illilouette Creek as it winds through a gorge for almost a mile. Beyond the gorge we begin the challenging 1200-foot ascent to Glacier Point. Soon we leave the shade of huge white firs and enter an area that burned in 1987. The ascent here is gentle, and we see fire succession in the form of black oaks that have regrown from the crown of their roots. A small creek provides a lush rest stop before we meet the Panorama Trail, coming up from Illilouette Fall.

On this famous trail, on a clear day, one can look across the vast chasm of the Merced River canyon and with the aid of binoculars see hikers on the summit of Half Dome. Nearer at hand, we can see the work of avalanches that have thundered down from the heights, carrying rocks, trees and soil across the trail. The fine views from just below Washburn Point include Nevada Fall, Vernal Fall, Half Dome, Mt. Starr King, and many high peaks of eastern Yosemite, marching off to the southeast horizon. The last half mile to Glacier Point (7214') is accomplished by switchbacks that rise to the parking area near this famous overlook.

Half Dome, Vernal Fall and Nevada Fall from Glacier Point

Bridalveil Creek to Yosemite Valley

69

Distance	32.7 miles
Type	Shuttle trip
Best season	Early or mid
Topo maps	**Yosemite, Merced Peak**, Half Dome, Mariposa Grove

Grade (hiking days/recommended layover days)

Leisurely	5/1
Moderate	4/1
Strenuous	3/0
Trailhead	Bridalveil Creek (33), Happy Isles (31)

HIGHLIGHTS   This route traverses some of the finer forest stands in Yosemite, crosses the Buena Vista Crest, and concludes via the famous Panorama and Nevada Fall trails into the Valley. On this trip you get close-up views of many world-famous Yosemite landmarks.

DESCRIPTION (Leisurely trip)

1st and 2nd Hiking Days: Follow Trip 67 to Royal Arch Lake, 13 miles.

3rd Hiking Day: Follow the 3rd hiking day of Trip 68 to Buena Vista Creek Tributary, 11.0 miles.

4th Hiking Day (Buena Vista Creek tributary to Yosemite Valley, 8.7 miles via the John Muir Trail, or 8.0 miles via the Mist Trail): From the unburned area by the creek we reenter recently burned forest. Descending northwest, we pass several centuries-old sugar pines, the survivors of more than one fire. In 1.3 miles we reach a signed junction with the trail up Illilouette Creek. We turn right on it and descend past an overused campsite. A short ascent then brings us to a small clearing on red ground. Ford Illilouette Creek here, toward a leaning Jeffrey pine on the north bank (difficult in high runoff). A short ascent on deeply weathered glacial deposits brings us to a dry flat and a signed junction with the Merced Pass Trail. Here we go left and descend through trees to cross a lovely little creek. There is a good campsite shortly before the creek.

Ascending steeply now, and then moderately through Jeffrey pine, white fir and bracken fern, we come to a seasonal creek. Here the soil thins, as does the forest cover, and the grade steepens. This sunny slope gets hot and we can rest while taking in the view of the burn across the canyon. There we can see one reason forests vary in both tree age and species composition. This typical mosaic pattern results when a fire kills some trees entirely while barely touching others nearby.

From this slope we climb through more shady environs and reach a signed junction where we turn left and cross a low ridge to join the aptly named Panorama Trail. Turning right, we begin a paved descent into the immense, glacially polished canyon of the Merced River. Half Dome falls behind Liberty Cap as we drop 600 to the John Muir Trail. To descend this famous trail to the Valley, reverse most of the 1st hiking day, Trip 66.

Nevada Fall from above

Dick Beach

Bridalveil Creek to Royal Arch Lake

70

Distance	27.7 miles
Type	Semiloop trip
Best season	Early or mid
Topo maps	**Yosemite**, Half Dome, Mariposa Grove

Grade (hiking days/recommended layover days)

Leisurely	5/1
Moderate	4/1
Strenuous	3/0
Trailhead	Bridalveil Creek (33)

HIGHLIGHTS   For the first-timer, exploring Yosemite's South Boundary Country is a memorable experience, and this loop trip provides an exciting route. Angling on the many lakes around Buena Vista Peak is excellent, particularly in early season, and the easy access and return recommend this trip as an early-season "warm up."

DESCRIPTION (Leisurely trip)

1st Hiking Day: Follow Trip 67 to Turner Meadows, 6.3 miles.
2nd Hiking Day: (Turner Meadows to Upper Chilnualna Lake, 4.9 miles): From Turner Meadows the trail continues southeast. One half mile from the campsites at the south end of the meadow our route passes the Wawona Trail, and ¾ mile later, at a junction, it turns east along Chilnualna Creek. This junction marks the beginning of a long, easy ascent that is pleasantly accompanied by the creek. Fishing along this cascading stream is fair (small brook and rainbow); most anglers will keep their lines dry until they reach Chilnualna Lakes (8480'). Here, all except the lowest lake provide excellent fishing for brook and rainbow (7–12"). Small (7-acre) upper Chilnualna Lake, alongside the trail, has several good campsites on its north side, but the best and most secluded Chilnualna Lake is the southernmost one.

3rd Hiking Day (Upper Chilnualna Lake to Royal Arch Lake, 3.5 miles): From the north side of the lake, the trail climbs steeply up the 480-foot, densely forested slope to a junction with the Buena Vista Trail. Our route turns right (southeast) and climbs the ridge to beautiful Buena Vista Lake (9077'). On this high lake fishing is good for rainbow and brook (9–13") and anglers may wish to tarry. It is a 300-foot hike up to the pass (and another 400 feet east up Buena Vista Peak, if you choose). The remaining 2 miles to Royal Arch Lake are an easy descent past lovely patches of meadow between granite slabs.

Royal Arch Lake (8685') is a fine fishing lake (excellent angling for brook and rainbow to 14"), and there are numerous good-to-excellent campsites on the west shore. The lake's name is well-suited, deriving from the blackened granite streaks that rainbow across the sheer eastern facade of the lake basin.

4th and 5th Hiking Days: Reverse the steps of the 1st two hiking days, Trip 67, 13 miles.

The arches at Royal Arch Lake

Glacier Point to Merced Lake 71

Distance	31.8 miles
Type	Out and back trip
Best season	Early
Topo maps	**Yosemite, Merced Peak**, Half Dome, Merced Peak
Grade (hiking days/recommended layover days)	
Leisurely	4/1
Moderate	4/0
Strenuous	2/1
Trailhead	Glacier Point (32)

HIGHLIGHTS   This early-season excursion has all the scenic advantages of the Yosemite-Valley-to-Merced-Lake trip (Trip 66) without the 2000-foot climb from Happy Isles to Nevada Fall. Beginning high above the Merced River canyon, one gets an airy view that provides a better feeling for the glacial history of the area. Mild elevation change and solid mileage make this route a fine choice for the hiker who wants to shake winter's kinks out of early-season muscles.

DESCRIPTION (Leisurely trip)

1st Hiking Day (Glacier Point to Little Yosemite Valley, 6.7 miles): This trip begins near the snack bar east of the parking-lot restrooms. If you haven't seen the views from the actual point, you should walk 200 yards north to the fenced-in-overlook. Views are very impressive of the east end of Yosemite Valley, Half Dome, Vernal and Nevada falls, and domelike Mt. Starr King in the southeast. From the picnic area by the snack bar our route climbs a short distance south to a signed junction where we turn left onto the big, wide Panorama Trail. The trail begins a moderate-to-steep descent, and makes one switchback before angling south toward Illilouette Creek. Views of Half Dome and the sound of the falls filter through a forest cover that includes white fir, sugar pine, Jeffrey pine and black oak. Under them, manzanita, huckleberry oak and deer brush form most of the ground cover.

After 1⅔ miles we find a junction with the Buena Vista Trail, leading up-canyon. We turn left here and switchback down to seasonally raging Illilouette Creek. Just before the bridge a short spur trail leads down to an airy overlook of Illilouette Fall. Beyond the large steel, rock and concrete bridge, the here-less-used trail begins an 800-foot ascent to the top of Panorama Cliff. On this ascent, at about 6500 feet, we see some Douglas-firs. This is an unusually high elevation for this species. Warm air flowing up the Merced River canyon rises up Panorama Cliff, creating an unusually warm and favorable microclimate here.

Our route traverses along the top of aptly named Panorama Cliff to a junction with the Mono Meadow Trail (leading right), and then our now-paved trail begins the 800-foot descent to Nevada Fall. Via a long series of switchbacks the trail descends through a dense forest of tall, water-loving Douglas-firs and incense-cedars. Then our route joins the John Muir Trail and soon arrives at the slabs above Nevada Fall. On these slabs you may notice large patches of smooth, shiny rock—glacial polish. All these slabs were polished by glaciers of the Tioga glaciation—the last time glaciers were here—at the end of the Pleistocene epoch, about 12,000 years ago. There is much, much less glacial polish below this point, indicating that no glaciers may have entered the Yosemite Valley from the Merced River canyon during the late Pleistocene. In fact, the last time glaciers flowed through the Valley was probably 750,000 years ago.

Beyond Nevada Fall the trail ascends past a junction with the Mist Trail and switchbacks over a low bedrock ridge under Liberty Cap. After ½ mile we pass a John Muir Trail cutoff and soon reach a junction where the John Muir Trail itself turns left (north). Here is the main, heavily used camping area, where there are outhouses, a ranger station and bear boxes. If this area doesn't suit you, you could continue for about 2 level miles to the less crowded sites at the east end of Little Yosemite Valley.

2nd Hiking Day: Follow the 2nd hiking day, Trip 66, to Merced Lake, 9.2 miles.

3rd and 4th Hiking Days: Retrace your steps, 15.4 miles.

Glacier Point to Rutherford Lake

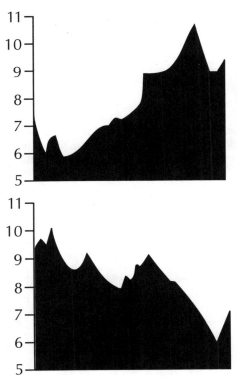

Distance	71.5 miles
Type	Loop trip
Best season	Mid or late
Topo maps	**Yosemite, Merced Peak**, Half Dome, Merced Peak, Mt. Lyell, Timber Knob, Sing Peak, Mariposa Grove

Grade (hiking days/recommended layover days)

Leisurely	12/2
Moderate	10/1
Strenuous	6/0
Trailhead	Glacier Point (32)

HIGHLIGHTS   Designed for the experienced backpacker, this trip offers a combination of excellent fishing and superlative vistas. Almost a dozen angling lakes, most of them in high-country settings, also provide swimming to alleviate the trail dust. Three major passes challenge the most ambitious hiker, and the wide variations in plants and wildlife will satisfy the most discriminating naturalist.

DESCRIPTION (Moderate trip)

1st Hiking Day: Follow Trip 71 to Little Yosemite Valley, 6.7 miles.

2nd Hiking Day: Follow the 2nd hiking day, Trip 66, to Merced Lake, 9.2 miles.

3rd Hiking Day: (Merced Lake to Lyell Fork, Merced River, 5.8 miles): From Merced Lake High Sierra Camp the trail ascends slabs to a drift fence and enters an area much used by livestock. A shaded ¾-mile stroll brings us to an engineered ford of multibranched Lewis Creek, a junction with the Lewis Creek Trail, and the Merced Lake Ranger Station. From the station we continue our level stroll to a riverside drift fence. Staying closer to the river now, our trail soon begins a moderate ascent along the east canyon wall, crossing several small creeks before traversing above the outlet of Washburn Lake (7600').

The outlets of Merced and Washburn lakes are similar, as both lakes are dammed by similar bedrock ribs. Skirting the east shore of the lake, we cross a small creek and pass the shaded campsites at the head of the lake, near a fine sandy beach for swimming. Beyond the lake our trail ascends a dry slope and then swings over to riverside by a lovely waterfall. The gentle ascent continues as the trail passes through very large stands of bracken fern under a beautiful, tall forest of huge white firs and Jeffrey pines, with smaller lodgepole pines and aspens. An emerald-green, placid Merced River flows near the trail in places along this idyllic setting. Where the Lyell Fork comes down on the left we meet the main river, and good campsites can be found in the vicinity of the bridge. Fishing in the river is fair-to-good for rainbow trout (to 9").

4th Hiking Day (Lyell Fork, Merced River, to Triple Peak Fork Meadow, 4.2 miles): Beyond the sturdy wood bridge spanning the Merced River, our trail soon begins to climb south into the great granite **V** carved by the lower stretches of the Merced Peak Fork of the river. This ascent steepens as it enters the zone of red fir and juniper, and then the path levels momentarily where it crosses the Merced Peak Fork on another wooden bridge, which spans a short section of quiet water between roaring cascades above and below.

Our trail leaves the riverside and climbs by long switchbacks up the north side of the bowl, leading to excellent viewpoints for visual enjoyment of the huge granite slabs, the aspen grove and the pockets of conifers below.

Another overlook at a switchback turn is close beneath a cascade and a waterfall on the Triple Peak Fork, whose upper reaches our trail is searching out. It was in these upper reaches of the river that the Merced glacier began, and the polished granite on every hand is a constant reminder of its presence. Above the switchbacks our trail ascends gently to a verdant flat where the green Triple Peak Fork slowly winds among the tall trees. After one more steep—but short—climb, the trail ascends gradually near the river under a moderate forest cover of lodgepoles for 2 miles to the foot of long Triple Peak Fork Meadow. The river curves in a lovely fashion through this mile-long grassland, past many campsites made illegal by the prohibition against camping within 100 feet of streams. Side pools out of the main current warm up enough to provide pleasant swimming in midsummer. The best campsites are at the south end of the meadow, near the junction with the Red Peak Pass Trail (9100'). Fishing is good for brook and rainbow trout (to 9").

5th Hiking Day (Triple Peak Fork Meadow to Post Creek, 7.2 miles): This hiking day begins with a gradually increasing climb for a long mile southward away from the Triple Peak Fork, out of lodgepole forest into dense hemlock. Then the duff trail turns northeast and climbs almost a mile on a traverse interrupted by two short switchbacks, to arrive at the rock monument at the junction with the high trail that goes along the top of the east wall of the Merced River canyon.

Here our route turns right (south) and quickly ascends a beautiful hillside with broken, light-colored granite close on the left and the soaring Clark Range across the canyon on the right. The trail then levels off in a spectacular high bowl, encircled by Triple Divide Peak, Isberg Peak and some unnamed peaks between. The feeling of spaciousness here is worth the four days' hike to get to this Shangri-la, and in midseason the green grass and many-hued flowers add enough stimulation to surfeit the senses. After fording the un-mapped, unnamed outlet of the unnamed but mapped lakes in this bowl, our trail dips into a bowl-within-the-bowl and there crosses another clear stream.

Finally we ascend out of the huge meadow and cross another stream before arriving at a hillside junction with the Isberg Pass Trail, where we turn right (south). Our Post Peak Pass Trail climbs to the ridgeline north of Post Peak, then follows this ridge south to the actual pass (10,700'). This ascent is not without compensation, for the views from the trail are among the most outstanding in the South Boundary Country. From this divide between the Merced and the San Joaquin rivers the traveler has views of the Clark Range to the west, the Cathedral Range to the north and the tops of Banner Peak, Mt. Ritter and the Minarets to the east.

At this point our route leaves Yosemite, later to recross the boundary at Fernandez Pass—6 miles away. The trail descends 600 feet to little Porphyry Lake (10,100'), where fishing is fair for brook and rainbow. Below the lake, the trail improves slightly in the stretch to Isberg Meadow, then becomes fairly good. Conies and marmots may appear on the rocky parts of this trail, and deer, grouse and quail in the meadowy parts. After going almost level for ½ mile through several meadows, we enter lodgepole forest and descend moderately to the good campsites at Post Creek (9040'). Fishing along the creek is good for brook trout (to 8").

6th Hiking Day (Post Creek to Rutherford Lake, 3.9 miles): From Post Creek the trail crosses a small rise, passes two small, unnamed lakelets (no fish), and fords West Fork Granite Creek. Shortly beyond, the trail fords Fernandez Creek and strikes the Fernandez Pass Trail. Here our route turns right (west) along a gently ascending, densely timbered stretch that offers fine views across Fernandez Creek. After a long ½ mile the trail switchbacks moderately up a morainal slope, trending northwest, to a junction with the Rutherford Lake lateral. Here our route turns right (north) and climbs steeply to the cirque nestling 28-acre Rutherford Lake (9800'). There are fair-to-good campsites on the west side of the lake south of the outlet. Views from these sites are excellent, and fishing is fair for brook and golden (to 16").

7th Hiking Day: Reverse the steps of the 2nd hiking day, Trip 83, to Middle Chain Lake, 9.4 miles.

8th Hiking Day: Follow the 2nd hiking day, Trip 84, to Royal Arch Lake, 9 miles.

9th and 10th Hiking Days: Follow the 3rd and 4th hiking days, Trip 68, 16.1 miles.

Glacier Point to Granite Creek 73

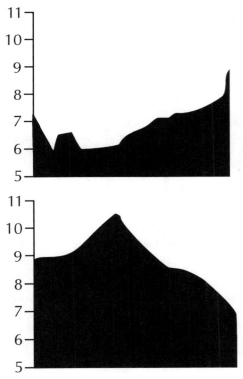

Distance	41.5 miles
Type	Shuttle trip
Best season	Mid or late
Topo maps	**Yosemite, Merced Peak**, Half Dome, Merced Peak,
	Mt. Lyell, Timber Knob, Sing Peak

Grade (hiking days/recommended layover days)

Leisurely	7/1
Moderate	5/1
Strenuous	3/1
Trailhead	Glacier Point (32), Granite Creek Campground (35)

HIGHLIGHTS   This route traverses the very heart of Yosemite's South Boundary Country, and crosses the divide of the Merced and San Joaquin River watersheds at Isberg Pass.

Fishing on the lakes and streams is fair-to-excellent, and the life zones range from Canadian to Arctic-Alpine. Remoteness and panoramic vistas beckon the traveler to choose this trip.

DESCRIPTION (Leisurely trip)

1st Hiking Day: Follow Trip 71 to Little Yosemite Valley, 6.7 miles.

2nd Hiking Day: Follow the 2nd hiking day, Trip 66, to Merced Lake, 9.2 miles.

3rd and 4th Hiking Days: Follow the 3rd and 4th hiking days, Trip 72, to Triple Peak Fork Meadow, 10 miles.

5th Hiking Day (Triple Peak Fork Meadow to Isberg Lakes, 4.9 miles): First, follow the 5th hiking day, Trip 72, to the junction of the Post Peak Pass and Isberg Pass trails. From this junction at timberline, our route turns left (northeast) and climbs steadily among large blocks of talus. The views north and west, which already have been excellent, become even better as our route switchbacks farther up the ridge, as high as the pass we are approaching. Then the tread goes more or less level to signed Isberg Pass (10,500′) and beyond it continues to weave sinuously along the crest. Finally it passes through a tiny defile between two stunted whitebark pines which frame a very dramatic view of the Ritter Range a few miles east. In the distance to the right of this dark range, most of the High Sierra is visible, and hikers who have rambled among its summits will spy some of their favorite monuments. From this pass between the Merced River and the San Joaquin River watersheds, the trail descends by switchbacks to rocky upper Isberg Lake, and then more gradually to lower Isberg Lake (9800′). Fishing in these lakes is fair-to-good for brook and some rainbow (to 8″). There are a few fair campsites at lower Isberg.

6th and 7th Hiking Days: Follow the steps of the 4th and 5th hiking days, Trip 86, 10.3 miles.

Devils Postpile

This area of *Sierra North* hikes is reached through the popular winter-summer resort of Mammoth Lakes. From the town, one drives west over Minaret Summit, which is on the Sierra Nevada crest. The road to Devils Postpile is the only eastside road that surmounts the Sierra crest, and you could be misled into thinking you were still east of the crest because the Ritter Range, west of this summit and of the Postpile, is so imposing.

If you want to acclimate overnight before hiking, there are many places to stay in Mammoth Lakes, and a few cabins at Reds Meadow Resort at the end of the Postpile road.

In recent years no cars have been allowed beyond Minaret Summit during daytime hours unless the driver had a reservation at a campground up ahead or at Reds Meadow Resort. To find out the status of this requirement, write Mammoth Ranger District, Mammoth Lakes, CA 93546, or phone (760) 924-5500.

This is the gateway to 228,669-acre Ansel Adams Wilderness, created in 1984 by Congress when it enlarged the formerly named Minarets Wilderness.

One trailhead—Rush Creek—not reached via the Postpile road is included in this chapter because the destination of the trip from there is shared with trips from the Postpile road.

74 Silver Lake to Thousand Island Lake

Distance	21 miles
Type	Semiloop trip
Best season	Early or mid
Topo maps	**Devils Postpile**, Koip Peak, Mt. Ritter
Grade (hiking days/recommended layover days)	
Leisurely	4/1
Moderate	3/0
Strenuous	2/0
Trailhead	Rush Creek (37)

HIGHLIGHTS   This trip visits many lakes, forested and alpine, manmade and natural. After joining the John Muir Trail, the route crosses a gently inclined pass amid several lakelets surrounded by wildflowers to reach Thousand Island Lake. The spectacular return descent looks out over Mono Lake more than 3000 feet below.

DESCRIPTION (Moderate trip)

1st Hiking Day (Rush Creek Trailhead to Waugh Lake, 7 miles): This excellent trail begins at the Rush Creek trailhead parking lot (7220'). Leaving the aspen cover along Alger Creek, you ascend somewhat steeply, and relentlessly, for 1300 feet. The first half of this climb is very exposed and hot, but affords glorious views of Silver Lake and the abstract marsh patterns at its south end. Colorful wildflowers abound: paintbrush and Bridges penstemon, stonecrop and wild buckwheat, blazing star and pennyroyal. Ahead, Rush Creek forms a several-hundred-foot-long waterfall ribbon, very full in early season. Giant, windshaped cedars provide patches of welcome shade. The trail switchbacks steeply to cross and then recross an active Southern Cal Edison funicular track, ascending stairs blasted out of the rock toward the dam at the outlet of Agnew Lake (8508'). If you wish to camp here, descend to and cross the outlet below the dam: campsites are very sparse but good.

To continue toward Gem Lake stay high and to the right of Agnew Lake: you quickly climb the 500 feet of switchbacks to Gem Lake (9052'). On the opposite side of Agnew Lake, you can see the steep trail to the Clark Lakes, your return route. Gem Lake richly deserves its name, despite the stark evidence of man's handiwork in the dam at its east end. As you skirt the lake's north side, the beauty of the lake, the surrounding peaks, the stalwart lodgepoles and the breath-taking giant junipers compensate for the dusty, stock-used trail, which perversely reaches the top of every ridge and the bottom of every gully. About halfway around the north side of the lake there are several attractive campsites with privacy and superlative views, but they require a hike down for water.

At the northwest end of Gem Lake, you cross Crest Creek and immediately encounter the signed trail to Alger Lakes. There is extensive camping here—also intensive mosquitoes and extensive evidence of stock. Continuing around Gem Lake, the trail converges with an old mine road and, passing a cabin, ascends westward. A quick southward descent brings you past two lovely tiny lakes (the first is called Billy Lake; the second is unnamed) and beautiful Rush Meadow. The trail junction to Waugh Lake is very well marked, though it is hard to see on the maps, being at the border of two topo maps. Just beyond this junction, you can see the bridge over Rush Creek on the trail to Clark Lakes, but your route turns right (west) toward Waugh Lake. There are ample excellent campsites here. An easy 300-foot climb (the route still coincides with an old road) brings you to the dam at the outlet of Waugh Lake (9424'). There are only a few poor campsites at the outlet. To your left, a signed trail leads south to Weber Lakes. Your route ascends the rounded granite to your right and skirts the north side of Waugh Lake. In about ½ mile beyond the outlet you will find excellent campsites upslope from the trail, and there are many more toward the west end of the lake. Mt. Ritter and Banner Peak own the sky beyond the west end of the lake. A layover day here would permit you to visit Weber and Sullivan lakes.

2nd Hiking Day (Waugh Lake to Thousand Island Lake, 6.5 miles): The trail along the northwest shore of Waugh Lake passes through beautiful lodgepole pines to an unmarked junction at the west end of the lake. The left fork leads to campsites; you keep right, climbing through large pines and over granite slabs. The indicated crossing over Rush Creek is underwater; fifty feet upstream is a considerably drier log. Shortly you reach a signed trail junction with the John Muir and Pacific Crest trails, which coincide from here to Thousand Island Lake: left (southeast) to Island Pass and Thousand Island Lake; right (northwest) to Rush Creek's headwaters and Donohue Pass. Turn left here and begin a steady ascent under a continuing forest cover of lodgepole and mountain hemlock. Beyond a junction with a trail to Davis Lakes, we climb southeast to the low saddle known as Island Pass (10,200'). Just south of this pass the trail passes two small lakes (locally called "Ham and Eggs Lakes"; campsites) and then veers eastward.

The trail emerges from the lodgepole-and-hemlock ground cover to a metamorphic slope above the outlet at the east end of Thousand Island Lake. Views from this rocky slope are sweeping, and the hiker immediately notices the difference between the predominantly darker rock of the Ritter Range and the lighter granite of the Sierra crest's alpine peaks. Geologically, the Ritter Range is made up of somewhat older rocks originally volcanic in nature, and the spectacularly jagged skyline from Banner Peak southward attests to the strength of this rock, which resisted the massive glaciers that gnawed at the range. As the trail switchbacks down to the outlet of Thousand Island Lake, there are classic views across the island-studded waters to the imposing east facades of Banner Peak and Mt. Ritter.

Shortly before the outlet, we reach the junction where the Pacific Crest and John Muir trails diverge. A few steps more on the Muir Trail bring us to a trail that branches right through a no-camping zone to campsites on Thousand Island Lake's northwest shore. Take this trail along the lakeshore; the campsites get better the farther you go toward the head of the lake. There are almost no acceptable camp-sites along the lake's southeast shore. Bears are a serious problem here; fishing for rainbow and brook (7–13") is particularly good in early and late season.

A layover day here would permit an adventurous, part-cross-country loop trip to Garnet Lake via the obvious saddle that's the low point (10,100') on the ridge to the southeast; return on the Muir Trail, past Ruby and Emerald lakes.

3rd Hiking Day (Thousand Island Lake to Silver Lake, 7.5 miles): Return to the junction where the Pacific Crest and John Muir trails diverge and take the Pacific Crest Trail northeast. In this region, the Pacific Crest Trail is also known as "the High Trail" in contrast to the nearby, lower River Trail down in the canyon of the Middle Fork San Joaquin River.

At the next junction, where the Pacific Crest Trail goes left (ahead, east) and the River Trail turns right (southeast) toward the Middle Fork San Joaquin River, we go left and soon reach another junction. Here, the left fork goes ahead (northeast) toward the Clark Lakes, while the right branch—the Pacific Crest Trail—goes toward the Badger Lakes and Agnew Meadows. We take the left fork, ascending steeply through lodgepoles to cross the Sierra Crest at an unmarked pass. Looking back, you view the San Joaquin River canyon, with the Minarets crowning the far ridge, and Ritter and Banner closer on your right. Directly below you can see the Badger Lakes. Gently descending, you pass three small Clark Lakes, one of which is guarded by a sheer and beautiful rock wall. Your descent continues along the west side of the largest Clark Lake, where windswept grass and wild onion border the west end of this lake.

At the outflow is a three-way signed junction: the left branch descends to Gem Lake; the right one skirts the lake on its east and leads up over Agnew Pass to the High Trail and thence to Agnew Meadows. Your route is the middle branch, which ascends gently past a tarn and then descends through meadows full of senecio, lupine and shooting stars. Pause here to view Mono Lake nearly 20 miles away and 3000 feet below, before the trail switchbacks steeply down to Spooky Meadow. After descending along a stream garnished with monkeyflowers, you then switchback steeply down the 1000-foot south wall of Agnew Lake's basin. The trail, not maintained here and mostly over talus, has been obliterated by rockslides. At the west ends of the switchback legs you find solid turf and welcome shade under immense red firs. Crossing the outflow of Agnew Lake on a footbridge, you meet the funicular tracks and then the Rush Creek Trail. Now retrace the first part of the first hiking day.

75   Agnew Meadows to Shadow Creek

Distance	8.4 miles
Type	Out and back trip
Best season	Mid or late
Topo maps	**Devils Postpile**, Mammoth Mtn., Mt. Ritter
Grade (hiking days/recommended layover days)	
Leisurely	2/0
Moderate	Day
Strenuous	——
Trailhead	Agnew Meadows (38)

HIGHLIGHTS   Shadow Lake has been subject to very heavy use, and in consequence the Forest Service no longer allows camping there, but there are fine campsites up the inlet stream. This short trip is a good one for beginning backpackers.

DESCRIPTION

1st Hiking Day (Agnew Meadows to Shadow Creek, 4.2 miles): Look for a Pacific Crest Trail marker at the trailhead on the south side of the first of the two parking lots. The trail departs southbound, crossing two branches of a little creek, bobs over a low ridge, and skirts a lobe of Agnew Meadows; colorful San Joaquin Ridge rises steeply to the north. Cross the creek again, leaving the meadow behind, and follow the nearly level trail as it winds between rocky knobs under lodgepoles. You pass an unsigned track coming in on the right and presently reach a junction: left (southeast) on the Pacific Crest Trail to Reds Meadow; right (ahead, northwest) on the River Trail to Olaine and Shadow lakes.

Go right to descend into the canyon of the Middle Fork San Joaquin River on the open, scrub-dotted trail. Reaching the flats bracketing the river, you re-enter forest cover and not long after skirt the east side of shallow Olaine Lake. Just beyond is a **Y**-junction: left (west) to Shadow Lake; right (northwest) to continue on the River Trail.

Taking the left fork through aspens, you pass a packer campsite and cross the noisy river on a stout footbridge. The trail begins a series of hot, open, rocky, view-filled switchbacks that lead up nearly 700 feet to idyllic Shadow Lake, whose outlet cascades down steep cliffs just south of the trail. Camping is prohibited at Shadow Lake and severely restricted around its inlet, Shadow Creek, and the latest regulations are usually posted where our trail first touches Shadow Lake. (As of 1996, camping was prohibited at Shadow Lake. Camping was permitted along Shadow Creek only on its *south* side. North of the creek, camping was permitted only *north of the trail*. Camping was prohibited between the trail and the creek.)

After studying the regulations, skirt Shadow Lake's north shore and begin ascending Shadow Creek. At a junction above the lake, our trail meets the John Muir Trail by a handsome footbridge: left (southeast) across Shadow Creek to Rosalie and Gladys lakes and Reds Meadow; right (ahead, west) along Shadow Creek to Ediza and Garnet lakes. Depending on the regulations, either fork may lead to legal campsites in this Shadow Creek area, where bears are a serious problem. Another possible camping area is found on a flat along the Muir Trail shortly after it forks right (northwest) to climb the ridge separating Shadow Creek from Garnet Lake; the left fork here (ahead, generally west) leads to Ediza Lake, where camping is also restricted.

2nd Hiking Day: Retrace your steps, 4.2 miles.

Shadow Lake   Ron Felzer

Routes Between Agnew Meadows
and Thousand Island Lake

Three very different trails connect Agnew Meadows and Thousand Island Lake, offering the hiker a choice of several loop trips.

The River Trail (7.1 miles) is the shortest, most gradual and smoothest. This route descends to the San Joaquin River and follows it upward, often through forest. You are almost always within the sound of water, and the forest cover offers welcome shade on hot days. One wonderful section of this trail climbs polished rock slabs directly along the water, which falls in sheets over the smooth rock into deep pools. See the 1st hiking day of Trip 76.

The Pacific Crest Trail (9.1 miles), also shown as the High Trail on the topo map, ascends 500 feet of switchbacks, then contours up the side of San Joaquin Mountain before turning westward to intersect the River Trail about 1 mile from Thousand Island Lake. This is the return route of Trip 78. The trail is exposed much of the way to sun and wind (the latter very welcome during mosquito season). The route offers panoramic views of the glaciers and the jagged peaks of the Ritter Range; it also traverses innumerable tributaries of the San Joaquin, banked by spectacular gardens of head-high delphinium, lupine, and corn lilies.

The John Muir Trail (10.5 miles) is the longest and most strenuous route. Trips 76 and 77 use it. You descend to the San Joaquin on the River Trail, then climb upward 800 feet to Shadow Lake, to join the John Muir Trail. After turning northward and ascending 1100 dusty feet, the trail descends to round the eastern end of Garnet Lake. A brief 500-foot ascent and a stroll past Ruby and Emerald lakes are sufficient to reach Thousand Island Lake. Shadow and Garnet lakes are almost impossibly beautiful yet they differ greatly, being located in different life zones: Shadow Lake is surrounded by tall trees; in contrast, Garnet Lake, 942 feet higher, is stark and alpine. If you have the time and the fitness, this is the route of choice—better taken *from* Thousand Island Lake or Garnet Lake *to* Shadow Lake, rather than the reverse.

Agnew Meadows to Garnet Lake **76**

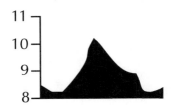

Distance   14.1 miles
Type   Semiloop trip, part cross-country
Best season   Mid or late
Topo maps   **Devils Postpile**, Mammoth Mtn., Mt. Ritter
Grade (hiking days/recommended layover days)
   Leisurely   3/1
   Moderate   3/0
   Strenuous   2/0
Trailhead   Agnew Meadows (38)

HIGHLIGHTS   Employing about a 4-mile stretch of the well-known John Muir Trail, this trip visits some of the northern Sierra's most dramatic country. In the region east of the jagged Ritter Range are some of the area's most vivid alpine lakes and spectacular landforms. A short, steep, trailless section on the 1st day calls for bouldering skills.

DESCRIPTION (Leisurely trip)

1st Hiking Day (Agnew Meadows to Garnet Lake via the River Trail, part cross-country, 5.6 miles): Follow Trip 75 past Olaine Lake to the Y-junction just beyond. Turn right to stay on the River Trail, which begins a gradual-to-moderate ascent along the Middle Fork San Joaquin River. The trail switchbacks up through fragrant scrub, then climbs gradually under patchy forest cover, crossing streams draining San Joaquin Ridge and passing potential campsites. Below the trail on your left, the river splashes along, occasionally forming inviting pools.

You skirt a meadow before reaching another Y-junction: right (northeast) on a spur to the Pacific Crest Trail—here also called the High Trail; left (northwest) on the River Trail to Garnet and Thousand Island lakes. Go left across a stream, ascend switchbacks, and curve west to yet another junction: right (west) to Thousand Island

Lake, left (southwest) to Garnet Lake. Go left to cross the Middle Fork again. The trail may be faint and muddled by multiple tracks as it climbs steeply away from the river to level out briefly at an overused campsite. From here, your route—wrongly shown as a trail on the topo—veers slightly right (southwest) into a trailless, boulder-choked slot. You'll need to use your hands for balance as you ascend. Fortunately, this section is brief, and you emerge in the meadow just below Garnet Lake. (Also from the overused campsite, a faint track heads left, reportedly to Altha Lake and a circuitous stock route to Garnet.)

From this meadow you can plainly see the rickety log bridge that carries the John Muir Trail over Garnet's outlet, but you'll have to scramble up a boulder to get to it. If the outlet's flow is low, it's easier to rock-hop across it. Either way, pick up the Muir Trail on the outlet's north side. Camping is prohibited around this end of Garnet (9678'), and the latest regulations are usually posted near here. The view across the lake is breathtaking.

After studying the regulations, take the northbound Muir Trail around Garnet's northeast shore. Where the Muir Trail rounds a promontory and then begins climbing the ridge separating Garnet and Thousand Island lakes, you find a rough use trail that branches left, southwest along the lakeshore. Follow this track beyond the no-camping zone to find legal campsites that get better the farther you go toward the head of the lake.

2nd Hiking Day (Garnet Lake to Shadow Creek, 4.3 miles): Return to the John Muir Trail and turn right toward the bridge over the outlet. Cross the bridge to reach the junction with the "trail" down the boulder-choked slot that you ascended on this trip's 1st hiking day. Go right (south), staying on the Muir Trail.

The trail traces Garnet's east shore before climbing some 500 feet to a saddle (10,105') with a little tarn. From here, the trail drops 1100 rocky-dusty feet, mostly in forest, to Shadow Creek. We pass potential campsites on this descent, but the area may be dry by late season. At Shadow Creek there's a junction: right (generally west) up Shadow Creek to Ediza Lake, left (northeast) on the Muir Trail down Shadow Creek to Shadow Lake. Camping is severely restricted in this overused area—see the end of the 1st hiking day, Trip 75—and the latest restrictions are posted here and there; be sure to look for them. Bears are a serious problem in this area. After studying the restrictions, find a legal campsite.

3rd Hiking Day (Shadow Creek to Agnew Meadows, 4.2 miles): Reverse the steps of the 1st hiking day of Trip 75 from Shadow Creek to Agnew Meadows.

Agnew Meadows to Thousand Island Lake   **77**

Distance	17.6 miles
Type	Semiloop trip
Best season	Mid or late
Topo maps	**Devils Postpile**, Mammoth Mtn., Mt. Ritter
Grade (hiking days/recommended layover days)	
Leisurely	3/1
Moderate	3/0
Strenuous	2/0
Trailhead	Agnew Meadows (38)

HIGHLIGHTS   Spectacular Garnet and Thousand Island lakes are the high points of this trip. Settings of alpine grandeur make these large lakes favorites of photographers and naturalists alike. Although this trip can be made in a weekend, the superlative scenery warrants a slower pace. Almost half of this route follows the scenic John Muir Trail.

DESCRIPTION (Leisurely trip)

1st Hiking Day (Agnew Meadows to Thousand Island Lake, 7.1 miles): Follow Trip 75 past Olaine Lake to the Y-junction just beyond. Then, as described in Trip 76, turn right and take the River Trail past the meadow, going left at the next Y-junction to stay on the River Trail. At the next junction, after the River Trail curves west, take the right fork uphill through dense lodgepole and fir to a signed junction with the Pacific Crest (High) Trail: left (west) toward Thousand Island Lake, right (east) toward the Badger Lakes and back to Agnew Meadows. Go left to curve northwest and then southwest, passing several snowmelt tarns, to the meadowy outlet of Thousand Island Lake and a junction with the John Muir Trail: right (northwest) to Island Pass, left (southeast) to cross the lake's outlet on a footbridge. Turn left for a few steps on the Muir Trail to another junction, this one a spur trail branching right around the northwest shore of Thousand Island Lake (9816′). Camping is prohibited at this end of the lake but, as described in the 2nd hiking day of Trip 74, you can take this spur trail to legal campsites farther west.

2nd Hiking Day (Thousand Island Lake to Shadow Creek, 6.3 miles): Return to the John Muir Trail; go right on the Muir Trail to cross the lake's outlet on a footbridge. Now climb gradually past Emerald Lake (campsites) and Ruby Lake (campsites) to a saddle from which the trail descends to big, windy Garnet Lake. Use trails lead right (west-southwest) through a no-camping zone to campsites along Garnet; the sites get better the farther you go toward the head of the lake.

Go left to stay on the Muir Trail, and follow the steps of the 2nd hiking day of Trip 76 from Garnet Lake to Shadow Creek.

3rd Hiking Day (Shadow Creek to Agnew Meadows, 4.2 miles): Turn northeast on the John Muir Trail, toward Shadow Lake, and reverse the steps of Trip 75 to Agnew Meadows.

Thousand Island Lake and Banner Peak

Agnew Meadows to Thousand Island Lake   **78**

Distance	19.6 miles
Type	Loop trip
Best season	Mid or late
Topo maps	**Devils Postpile**, Mammoth Mtn., Mt. Ritter

Grade (hiking days/recommended layover days)

Leisurely	2/1
Moderate	2/0
Strenuous	Day
Trailhead	Agnew Meadows (38)

HIGHLIGHTS   We enjoy a very different Thousand Island Lake trip from that of Trip 77 by taking the River Trail to the lake, as Trip 77 does, but then returning on the Pacific Crest Trail (here also called the High Trail). On this leg, instead of an up-and-down through the dense forests and past the lakes along the Ritter Range's east flank, we traverse the stream-blessed, flower-lined slopes of San Joaquin Ridge while savoring magnificent views of the Ritter Range country.

DESCRIPTION (Leisurely trip)

1st Hiking Day (Agnew Meadows to Thousand Island Lake, 7.1 miles via the River Trail): Follow Trip 75 past Olaine Lake to the Y-junction just beyond. Then, as described in Trip 76, turn right and take the River Trail past the meadow, going left at the next Y-junction to stay on the River Trail. At the next junction, after the River Trail curves west, take the right fork uphill through dense lodgepole and fir, following the rest of the directions of the 1st hiking day of Trip 77 to campsites at Thousand Island Lake.

2nd Hiking Day (Thousand Island Lake to Agnew Meadows, 10.5 miles via the High Trail): Return to the Muir Trail-Pacific Crest (High) Trail junction just north of the lake's outlet. Pick up the High

Trail and retrace your steps of the 1st hiking day to the junction where the High Trail meets the River Trail. Go left (ahead, east) on the High Trail and shortly reach the next junction: right (east, then southeast) on the High Trail to the Badger Lakes and Agnew Meadows; left (east-northeast) to the Clark Lakes and Rush Creek Trailhead. You go right on the High Trail, through lodgepoles and past mosquito-heaven Badger Lakes.

On this first slope the trail emerges from the dense forest cover, and then it winds up and down through a ground cover that, except for a few scattered stands of pine, is sagebrush, bitterbrush, willow, and some mountain alder. Passing three junctions in the mile beyond Badger Lakes, the trail then contours along the side of San Joaquin Mountain. The dry sage slopes are slashed by streams lined with wildflowers as far up as you can see: larkspur, lupine, shooting star, columbine, penstemon, monkey flower, scarlet gilia and tiger lily. For a while views are excellent of the Ritter Range to the west; particularly impressive is the **V**'d view of Shadow Lake directly across the San Joaquin River canyon about 2¾ miles from the trailhead. The trail then descends through a forest of pine and fir. Five hundred feet of well-graded switchbacks bring you to the parking lot north of the pack station. Turn right (west) on the road that runs by the pack station and follow it to the parking lot at your starting trailhead.

Agnew Meadows to Ediza Lake 79

Distance	14 miles
Type	Out and back trip
Best season	Mid or late
Topo maps	**Devils Postpile**, Mammoth Mtn., Mt. Ritter

Grade (hiking days/recommended layover days)

Leisurely	2/1
Moderate	2/0
Strenuous	——
Trailhead	Agnew Meadows (38)

HIGHLIGHTS   This is one of the finest routes in the Mammoth Lakes region for viewing the spectacular Ritter Range, including Banner Peak, Mt. Ritter and the Minarets. The alpine beauty of Ediza Lake is almost legendary. In the shadow of the breathtaking Minarets, one can appreciate the grand processes that formed this very striking landscape.

DESCRIPTION

1st Hiking Day (Agnew Meadows to Ediza Lake, 7.0 miles): First follow Trip 75 to Shadow Creek, 4.2 miles. The ascent from Shadow Creek to the outlet of Ediza Lake is gradual and beautiful but very dusty. Those seeking campsites must avoid sites that are now illegal and concentrate their search on the north side of the trail. Following the John Muir Trail for about ⅔ mile, we wind in and out of tall firs, some slashed down by 1986 avalanches, passing some lovely waterfalls and pools along the creek. At the next junction, the Muir Trail turns right (northwest) to scale the ridge separating Shadow Creek and Garnet Lake, while our route continues left (ahead, generally west) toward Ediza Lake. We cross several meadows, and then rock-hop or chance unstable logs to cross the lovely, shaded outlet from Nydiver Lakes. Continuing up Shadow Creek you will have several choices of trail but you should have no trouble getting to the outlet of Ediza Lake (9265′). To get to the legal campsites on the west end of the lake, you can go around the south side, but the north-side route is shorter. The delicate environs of this lake are heavily used, so please be careful. Ediza Lake makes a fine base for exploring the basin above.

2nd Hiking Day: Retrace your steps, 7.0 miles.

80   Agnew Meadows to Devils Postpile

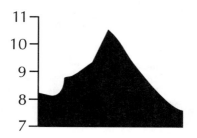

Distance	16.2 miles
Type	Shuttle trip, part cross-country
Best season	Mid or late
Topo maps	**Devils Postpile**, Mammoth Mtn., Mt. Ritter
Grade (hiking days/recommended layover days)	
Leisurely	——
Moderate	3/0
Strenuous	——
Trailhead	Agnew Meadows (38), Devils Postpile (39)

HIGHLIGHTS   For those travelers who enjoy spectacular alpine landscapes this trip is excellent. The route, however, is difficult, and is recommended for highly experienced backpackers only. Climbers use this route to reach the base of the jagged Minarets.

DESCRIPTION

1st Hiking Day: Follow Trip 79 to Ediza Lake, 7.0 miles.

2nd Hiking Day (Ediza Lake to Minaret Lake, 3.0 miles): From the south side of Ediza Lake the trail steeply and unevenly climbs the south wall over scree and through dense willows in streambeds. There are several routes: the best switches against the east wall (to your left). A beautiful meadow of red and white heather, penstemon and rockfringe leads to Iceberg Lake (9800'). There are a few campsites on the northeast side of the lake.

Looking up to the south one can see the outlet from Cecile Lake pouring over the lip of its basin. You want to climb to that point. The trail circles and gradually ascends on the east side of Iceberg Lake, then disappears in boulders on the big talus slope above the lake, where there is usually a large snowbank, which may be icy. The last 60 vertical feet are just east of the waterfall from Cecile—and just as precipitous. At the top of this 500-foot ascent is windswept Cecile Lake (10,280'), right at the base of towering Clyde Minaret. The trip around Cecile Lake is a boulderwalk on either side. The east side is shorter; the west a bit easier. There are several campsites in the whitebarks at the northwest end of the lake, and one wonderful site at the southeast end.

The route to Minaret Lake begins in the left end of the moraine that forms the southeast side of Cecile Lake. Cross this moraine and descend to a tarn. Then go to the whitebarks at the far end. The trail goes over the lip of a steep wall at the extreme left, against the mountainside. The first few steps demand both hands—they are difficult with a backpack. From here head south and pass between two rock outcrops. The trail descends steeply down a scree slope that offers few firm footholds. It then turns south and follows the contours of the rockface. After a few switchbacks it reaches an inlet of Minaret Lake, below. The trail then descends to the north shore of the lake, passes a small lake on the left and rounds the eastern lobe of Minaret Lake (9800') to the outlet. There are many lovely campsites around this lake (campfires illegal), and the trout-filled waters often reflect the Minarets at sunset.

3rd Hiking Day (Minaret Lake to Devils Postpile Campground, 6.2 miles): From the outlet of Minaret Lake one gets a last view of the spectacular Minarets over the lake before descending steeply to a forested flat along Minaret Creek. Our trail then crosses a tributary and steepens again to temporarily join the old road from Minaret Mine. We pass through a meadow along the creek with 6- to 10-foot stumps, trees that were decapitated by avalanches in 1986; the differing stump heights indicate how deep the snow was when an avalanche topped a particular tree. Now you descend an outcrop of red rock down which the creek cascades in a spray of white. After about two miles of gentle and then moderate descent in dense fir forest, we arrive at a junction with the John Muir Trail beside Johnston Meadow; you can see little Johnston Lake just past the junction, where the northbound Muir Trail heads left (north) upslope toward Gladys and Rosalie lakes, and the southbound Muir Trail goes right (ahead, southeast) toward Devils Postpile.

Go ahead on the southbound Muir Trail, leaving Ansel Adams Wilderness and soon reaching a ford of Minaret Creek. If the water is high, look for a log crossing upstream. On the other side of the ford, avoid an angler's trail upstream (right), back to Johnston Lake, and stay on the Muir Trail. You soon reach another junction: right (west) to the Beck Lakes; left (east) on the Muir Trail to the Postpile.

Go left for the Postpile and descend a dusty, loose, pumice slope to a confusing **X**-junction where the southbound Muir and Pacific Crest trails converge and their northbound counterparts temporarily diverge. For the sake of describing this junction, face south (you're actually facing southeast as you reach this junction). Behind you are the **X**'s lower right arm, which is the Muir Trail northwest to Johnston Meadow and Gladys and Rosalie lakes, and the **X**'s lower left arm, which is the Pacific Crest Trail, a little downslope and headed northeast for Minaret Falls and Agnew Meadows. In front of you is the **X**'s upper right arm, which is the joined Muir and Pacific Crest trails, which stay on the west side of the river southbound before descending to cross the river near Reds Meadow, on their way to Mt. Whitney. The **X**'s upper left arm descends southeast to cross the river near Devils Postpile; this is your route.

Taking the upper left arm of the **X**, you soon reach the river and cross it on a handsome footbridge.* A few steps beyond, there's a junction: left (north) to Devils Postpile ranger station and the parking lot where your shuttle car should be waiting; right (south) to the geological wonder called Devils Postpile. As the Postpile is only a few yards away, detour briefly to see it and to read the signs explaining its origin. Then head north to the parking lot.

Devils Postpile

Don Denison

*The Devils Postpile area was severely damaged by flooding in January 1997. Expect construction and detours for some time.

Agnew Meadows to Devils Postpile

81

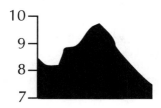

Distance	12.2 miles
Type	Shuttle trip
Best season	Mid or late
Topo maps	**Devils Postpile**, Mammoth Mtn., Mt. Ritter

Grade (hiking days/recommended layover days)

Leisurely	——
Moderate	2/0
Strenuous	——

Trailhead   Agnew Meadows (38), Devils Postpile (39)

HIGHLIGHTS   After crossing the Middle Fork San Joaquin, this route ascends to picturesque Shadow Lake. Then, doubling back, it traverses the long, narrow, lake-dotted bench that breaks the slope from Volcanic Ridge to the river. Dense fir forests, intimate lakes, and good fishing make this an excellent beginner's weekend trip.

DESCRIPTION

1st Hiking Day (Agnew Meadows to Rosalie Lake, 5.4 miles): Follow the 1st hiking day, Trip 75, to Shadow Lake. Just past a small rise, about 200 feet beyond the inlet to beautiful Shadow Lake, this route joins the John Muir Trail and crosses Shadow Creek on a large log bridge. The eastbound trail rounds the south side of the lake, and begins a long, long series of loose, dusty switchbacks up the densely forested ridge south of Shadow Lake. Breather stops along this 600-foot climb rarely afford views because of the forest cover. You crest the ridge on a saddle before descending to campsites near the outlet of Rosalie Lake (9350′). Fishing is good for rainbow and brook (to 9″). If Rosalie is crowded, Gladys Lake (see 2nd hiking day) offers campsites, too, and may be less crowded.

2nd Hiking Day (Rosalie Lake to Devils Postpile Campground,
6.8 miles): Continue around Rosalie Lake before climbing over the
next saddle to the south of Rosalie and dipping down to smaller
Gladys Lake. Campsites dot the slopes and benches around Gladys;
one on its east side offers an awe-inspiring view over the Middle
Fork San Joaquin to San Joaquin Ridge. The Muir Trail skirts
Gladys's west shore before descending 200 feet into the Trinity
Lakes basin, where a string of small, grass-fringed lakes offer water
for the occasional campsite. Access to Castle and Emily lakes is via
a short, steep foot trail that takes off from the west side of our trail,
and fishing at these lakes is fair-to-good for rainbow and brook (to
8″). From the lowest Trinity Lake, the trail descends on pumice
footing to a junction with the trail from Minaret Lake: left (southeast)
on the Muir Trail to Devils Postpile; right (northwest) to Minaret
Lake.

From this junction, turn left on the Muir Trail and follow the latter
half of the hiking directions of the 3rd hiking day of Trip 80 to the
parking lot at Devils Postpile.

Shadow Lake and the Minarets as seen from the High Trail

South of Yosemite

South of Yosemite's Tioga Road (State Highway 120), there are no roads all the way across the Sierra until one is well south of Mt. Whitney. Only one, the road from Mammoth Lakes down to Agnew Meadows and Devils Postpile, crosses the Sierra Crest. See the preceding chapter for trips out of the Agnew Meadows/Devils Postpile area.

Most of the trips in this chapter go into the 584,478-acre John Muir Wilderness, the largest in any California national forest, which stretches along the east Sierra slope from Mammoth Lakes south to beyond Mt. Whitney, and also curls around the northwest side of Kings Canyon National Park.

For acclimating the night before your hike, there are numerous hotels, motels, lodges, bed-and-breakfasts, and resorts in communities like Mammoth Lakes, Oakhurst, Fish Camp, and Crowley Lake. There are also resorts dotted along the access roads serving the trailheads out of the Mammoth Lakes basin, Lake Edison, and Rock Creek. In addition, there are numerous campgrounds serving all of these trailheads.

Two trailheads in this chapter—Rock Creek (Mosquito Flat) and Lake Edison—are also used for some trips in *Sierra South*, which you might like to consult.

Finally, five trips in this variegated chapter have trailheads along the Beasore Road, just south of Yosemite, and several of them actually enter the Park. There are no resorts along that road, but there are several campgrounds.

82   Chiquito Creek to Chain Lakes

Distance	14.6 miles
Type	Out and back trip
Best season	Mid
Topo maps	**Merced Peak**, Sing Peak

Grade (hiking days/recommended layover days)

Leisurely	2/1
Moderate	2/0
Strenuous	——
Trailhead	Chiquito Pass Trailhead (34)

HIGHLIGHTS   Chain Lakes are a traditional and attractive destination for a moderate weekend trip. Though not difficult, this hike is long enough and varied enough to provide the hiker with the feeling of a substantial trip. Fishing is often good at Chain Lakes.

DESCRIPTION

1st Hiking Day (Chiquito Creek Trailhead to Middle Chain Lake, 7.3 miles): From the trailhead parking lot (7235') the signed Chiquito Lake Trail heads northwest through mixed forest. Although it is designated a hiker trail only, horses use this trail, and even motor vehicles travel the first ¼ mile. After the first ¼ mile, the dusty trail steepens and climbs a hot, sunny hillside; then it levels off to pass the old trail coming in on the left. Soon we cross a small creek and climb another hot hillside before swinging into shade to come within earshot of Chiquito Creek.

The trail continues on a moderate ascent until it fords the creek just below Chiquito Lake. From the lake's south shore we head briefly west and then pass a junction with a trail to the Sky Ranch Road. Then we traverse north to the Yosemite Park boundary. Leaving the cows behind, we go through a barbed-wire fence to another junction. Turning right here, we stroll to a sharp-crested moraine, cross it, and descend gently for ½ mile to ford the seasonally wide outlet of Spotted Lakes. From the ford our trail ascends moderately through red fir up a large moraine to a small meadow. This meadow marks the top of the moraine, and the remainder of this 500-foot climb takes us past a few bedrock outcrops. Past the top of the ridge, we descend gently through mixed forest to ford Chain Lakes creek. On the other side of the creek is a junction; here we turn right (east) and then ascend steeply to lower Chain Lake, signed CHAIN LAKES. From here the trail swings around the north side of the lake, turns south, crosses a seasonal stream and makes a rocky, 150-foot ascent to the middle lake, also signed CHAIN LAKES. Camping is best on the south side of this lake.

Those wishing to visit the upper lake can reach it from the abused campsite near the middle lake's outlet. From here the trail to the upper lake climbs steeply above the north shore of the middle lake onto a rocky ridge. The trail then passes a tarn, turns left around a small lake and crosses the creek. From here a short ascent leads to the timbered west side of beautiful Upper Chain Lake. All three lakes contain rainbow or brook trout, or both.

2nd Hiking Day: Retrace your steps, 7.3 miles.

Fishing at Middle Chain Lake   National Park Service

83 Chiquito Creek to Rutherford Lake

Distance	25.4 miles
Type	Shuttle trip
Best season	Mid or late
Topo maps	**Merced Peak**, Sing Peak, Timber Knob

Grade (hiking days/recommended layover days)

Leisurely	4/1
Moderate	3/1
Strenuous	3/0
Trailhead	Chiquito Pass Trailhead (34), Fernandez Trailhead (36)

HIGHLIGHTS   On this trip the hiker will encounter a great variety of terrain and scenery, going from dense red-fir forests to alpine lakes and back again. Fishing on both sides of Fernandez Pass is good-to-excellent.

DESCRIPTION (Moderate trip)

1st Hiking Day: Follow Trip 82 to Middle Chain Lake, 7.3 miles).

2nd Hiking Day (Middle Chain Lake to Rutherford Lake, 9.4 miles): This hiking day takes one through a wide variety of land-scape features: forests, meadows, streams, lakes and passes. After we retrace our steps to the junction by the outlet of Chain Lakes, we turn right to continue the steep descent beside the creek. The grade soon eases where there is a newly formed clearing along the creek. Here are downed trees and a jumble of boulders—the remains of a debris flow. A debris flow is something like a combination flood and landslide—a thick, slow-moving, water-saturated mixture of rock, soil, trees and anything else lying around.

Turning north away from the creek, we soon pass a signed junction with a trail to Buck Camp. Continuing north, our trail winds among glacial erratics and over bedrock outcrops under a partial forest cover, climbs steeply over a low ridge, and passes a glacial tarn. The trail then descends along a small watercourse to a lodge-pole-pine-covered flat where a zealous CCC and Park Service crew has dug trenches in order to lower the water table. The excavated soil has been used to build a causeway nearby. From here a very short ascent brings us past a packer campsite on the left, and then to the Merced River in Moraine Meadows. Beyond the ford (wet in early season) the trail passes more campsites and arrives at a signed junction with another trail to Buck Camp.

Here we turn right and then ascend gently under lodgepole pine over a very maintained trail. After an easy mile the trail turns south and fords the flower-lined Merced River (wet in early season). The grade soon steepens as we begin a two-stage climb to Fernandez Pass. For 400 vertical feet the shaded trail winds up to a shallow, meadow-fringed lake, crossing a seasonal stream en route. Here the grade eases, and in another ¾ mile we reach a signed junction with the trail south to Breeze Lake. This trail leads past a small lake, then becomes faint, and the last stretch is a ducked route over slabs to the hemlock-lined north shore of large, scenic Breeze Lake.

From the junction we begin the second stage of the climb to Fernandez Pass, and immediately the trail becomes very steep and rocky. Our route ascends through lodgepole and western white pine over weathered granite for 600 feet to signed Fernandez Pass (10,175'). Here we leave the Park and then ascend a bit more before descending past another tree-dotted saddle. The trail now winds down ledges into the headwaters of Fernandez Creek, and we get good views of the Ritter Range to the east. The grade eases temporarily where we cross a small meadow, and steepens again before we arrive at a signed junction with a trail to Rutherford Lake (9800'). This eroded trail begins in a small forested flat and climbs very steeply for ¼ mile to the small dam at the south end of this well-used alpine lake. Campsites can be found on the lake's east side. Fishing is fair for brook and golden (to 16").

3rd Hiking Day (Rutherford Lake to Fernandez Trailhead, 8.7 miles): From the small dam at the south end of Rutherford Lake we descend the steep trail ¼ mile back to the Fernandez Trail and turn left onto it. This rocky trail switchbacks down the sunny canyon wall to the gentler descent under tall red firs. About 1½ miles from

Rutherford Lake we ford Fernandez Creek (wet in early season) and arrive at a junction with the Post Peak Pass Trail. Keeping to the right on the Fernandez Trail, we traverse past a low exfoliation dome. Soon we pass over a low ridge, descend a wooded gully, and arrive at the signed trail to Rainbow Lake. From here it is an easy 1½ miles down gentle slabs through open lodgepole and juniper to the northern junction with the Lillian Lake Loop. From this junction our trail heads east and begins a long descent to Madera Creek.

Initially, the trail descends gently, enters a forested gully, and crosses a small creek. Continuing southeast under red fir, lodgepole pine and occasional Jeffrey pine and juniper, our trail gains the crest of a moraine where we get views east through the trees. The trail then becomes steep, completes two sets of switchbacks and passes a junction with the Timber Creek Trail. After some more dusty switchbacks we arrive at a shaded flat alongside peaceful Madera Creek. Proceeding across this flat, we pass a signed junction with the Walton Trail, left, and some good campsites, and then ford wide Madera Creek (wet in early season). The trail climbs steeply up the south bank and then continues on a moderate ascent through lodgepole pine and red fir. Along the ascent you notice a mixture of light and dark rocks on the ground. Many times during the Pleistocene Epoch glaciers originating near Madera Peak flowed over this area, bringing darker, metamorphic rocks from the vicinity of Madera Peak and lighter, granitic rocks from farther east, perhaps around Staniford Lakes.

Forest cover thins and views improve until we reach the southern end of the Lillian Lake Loop. Here, atop a broad ridge, we leave Ansel Adams Wilderness and begin the 2-mile descent southeast to the Fernandez trailhead. This section of trail, which passes two laterals to the Norris Creek trailhead, is described (in reverse) in the first day of Trip 85.

Chiquito Creek to Bridalveil Creek

84

Distance	29.4 miles
Type	Shuttle trip
Best season	Mid or late
Topo maps	**Merced Peak**, Sing Peak, Mariposa Grove

Grade (hiking days/recommended layover days)

Leisurely	4/2
Moderate	4/0
Strenuous	3/0
Trailhead	Chiquito Pass Trailhead (34), Bridalveil Creek (33)

HIGHLIGHTS   This shuttle trip crosses some of the more scenic southern Yosemite Park boundary country. Some of the finest fishing in the Park is found along this route at Chain and Royal Arch lakes, and bonus angling spots can be explored on layover days at Breeze, Spotted, Johnson and Crescent lakes. The gigantic, sweeping effects of glacial action are seen throughout this trip. The resulting cirques, U-shaped valleys, jagged crests, and polished granite are a constant source of awe and delight to the traveler.

DESCRIPTION (Leisurely trip)

1st Hiking Day: Follow Trip 82 to Middle Chain Lake (7.3 miles)
2nd Hiking Day (Middle Chain Lake to Royal Arch Lake, 9 miles): First, retrace your steps to yesterday's junction, and then continue downstream. In ⅓ miles the trail veers north to a junction, where we turn left (west) and parallel the outlet creek from Chain Lakes as it falls to rendezvous with the South Fork Merced. Just

before the South Fork a signed lateral trail leads south ¼ mile to good camping at Soda Springs. Our route fords the South Fork and swings southwest over a lodgepole-covered slope. The depth of the U-shaped, glacially formed slopes gives a good account of the forces that were at work when the ice flow originating in the Clark Range to the north was in its heyday.

After fording Givens Creek the trail passes a southbound trail to Chiquito Pass. Just 60 yards farther we choose a well-used left fork over a little-used right fork and then continue ½ mile to meet the Buck Camp/Merced Pass Trail on a ridgetop. Turning southwest, we descend through red-fir forest and then climb northwest to the meadowy precincts of Buck Camp. At Buck Camp, Yosemite National Park has a summer ranger station, and emergency services may be obtained.

From Buck Camp the trail ascends a tough 750 feet via switchbacks, then drops 350 feet to a junction with the Royal Arch Lake Trail. From this point it is but ¾ mile to Royal Arch Lake (8685'). Large, black, rainbow-arched striations across the eastern wall of polished granite gave this picturesque lake its name. These distinctive markings are the result of water discoloration due to centuries of seepage. They make a magnificent backdrop to the excellent fishing for brook and rainbow (8–14") and anglers may well regard this relatively small lake as the high point of the trip. Numerous good campsites are on the west shore, and this lake makes an excellent base camp for scenic and angling excursions to nearby Buena Vista, Johnson and Crescent lakes. Swimming is good in late season.

3rd and 4th Hiking Days: Reverse the steps of the 2nd and 1st hiking days, Trip 67, 13 miles.

Granite Creek to Rutherford Lake   **85**

Distance	20.7 miles
Type	Semiloop trip
Best season	Mid or late
Topo maps	**Merced Peak**, Timber Knob

Grade (hiking days/recommended layover days)

Leisurely	3/1
Moderate	3/0
Strenuous	2/0
Trailhead	Fernandez Trailhead (36)

HIGHLIGHTS   The lake-filled area east of Gale and Sing peaks provides a choice trip for the angler. Except for a midsummer slack period, these lakes are good producers of brook, rainbow, and even golden trout. Add to this benefit the dramatic peaks that lie to the west, and the 35-mile views to the south, and every hiker will find cause for visiting this country. This trip is the answer for the hiker with a short time for travel who wishes to get into the spectacular South Boundary Country.

DESCRIPTION (Leisurely trip)

1st Hiking Day (Fernandez Trailhead to Vandeburg Lake 4.5 miles): From the west side of the turnaround loop at the end of the road, the signed Fernandez Trail begins a gentle ascent through a forest of white fir, Jeffrey pine and lodgepole pine. In ⅓ mile our route arrives at a signed junction with a lateral to the Norris Creek trailhead. Here we turn right and soon begin a moderate ascent to another signed junction with a trail to the Norris Creek trailhead. From here we gain an open ridgetop, where we meet a signed junction with the Lillian Lake loop. With grand views over our shoulder, we turn west onto the loop and enter Ansel Adams

Wilderness. In a mixed forest of red fir, mountain hemlock, and lodgepole and western white pine, we pass two cow-infested meadows on the left, and then swing north and climb steeply up a rocky ridge. From the ridgetop we descend for a short distance through hemlock forest to ford the outlet of Vandeburg Lake. A little uphill to the west are the well-used campsites on the north side of this attractive lake.

2nd Hiking Day (Vandeburg Lake to Rutherford Lake, 7.5 miles): From the northwest side of Vandeburg Lake our trail ascends west up slabs to a signed junction with a trail to Lady Lake, at the edge of a lodgepole-pine-covered flat. A moderate ¾-mile ascent up this trail would bring one to the shady campsites on the northeast side of Lady Lake.

From the Lady Lake junction the main route continues up more slabs dotted with lodgepole pines. Where the trail tops a low ridge, we can pause to take in the expansive views of the Ritter Range to the northeast. After a short descent to the north we arrive at the first of the trout-filled Staniford Lakes. Then our scenic trail passes above the largest Staniford Lake and boulder-hops Shirley Creek. Continuing north across slabs our trail crosses several seasonal creeks before swinging west to ford the shaded outlet of Lillian Lake.

Instead of proceeding to the well-used campsites on the northeast side of this large lake, our route turns east and descends moderately under lodgepole pine and hemlock for about a mile. Then the grade levels off, we ford the creek from Rainbow and Flat lakes, and after an easy ¼ mile arrive at a junction with the Fernandez Trail. We turn left on it and ascend gently over juniper-and-lodgepole-pine-covered slabs for over a mile to a junction with a trail to Rainbow Lake. (If you want to visit this lovely lake, this trail will take you there in 1½ miles. Follow the trail across the creek and ascend southwest through timber and slabs for ¾ mile. The ducked trail then turns northwest and descends to cross the same creek above Flat Lake. A short ascent leads to the wooded east side of fishless Rainbow Lake, where overnight camping is prohibited.)

From the Rainbow Lake trail junction, the Fernandez Trail heads north and climbs up a shaded ravine onto a flat ridge. For another mile the route is a gentle stroll through open lodgepole-pine forest to a junction with the Post Peak Pass Trail. Here turn left and ford Fernandez Creek. The Fernandez Trail then swings west and ascends moderately under tall red firs for about ½ mile. Then the trail begins a series of switchbacks up the rocky, sun-drenched north canyon wall. This ascent passes through sections of red metavolcanic rock, and views to the south and east are good reasons to pause and rest in the shade of a juniper or a western white pine. Our trail re-enters timber at a small flat where we arrive at a junction with the short trail to Rutherford Lake. This very steep and badly eroded trail ascends ¼ mile to the small dam on the south side of well-used Rutherford Lake (9800'). The shores of this scenic lake have been abused, so camp well away from the water This deep lake contains a number of large golden and brook trout.

3rd Hiking Day: Follow the 3rd hiking day, Trip 83, 8.7 miles.

86   Granite Creek Road to Isberg Lakes

Distance	28.3 miles
Type	Shuttle trip
Best season	Mid or late
Topo maps	**Merced Peak**, Timber Knob, Mt. Lyell
Grade (hiking days/recommended layover days)	
Leisurely	5/1
Moderate	4/1
Strenuous	3/1
Trailhead	Fernandez Trailhead (36), Granite Creek Campground (35)

HIGHLIGHTS   This is a challenging hike, with an altitude gain of over 3000 feet. Scenery varies from the cloisters of dense forests and the intimacy of small meadows to the overwhelming panoramas from two high passes. Fishing is best in early and late season, and ranges from fair to excellent.

DESCRIPTION (Leisurely trip)

1st Hiking Day: Follow Trip 85 to Vandeburg Lake, 4.5 miles.
2nd Hiking Day (Vandeburg Lake to Post Peak Pass Trail, 5.7 miles): Follow the 2nd hiking day, Trip 85, to the junction of the Fernandez Trail and the Rainbow Lake Trail, by a small marsh. From the junction turn right on the Fernandez Trail and climb a short, shaded ravine up to a low ridge. On the ridge the trail makes a northwest traverse through open lodgepole-pine forest, passing a broken dome on the west. After a nearly level mile and then a short, gentle descent we arrive at a junction with the Post Peak Pass Trail

going right. There is a good campsite just north of the junction, by
Fernandez Creek, and more are to be found several hundred yards
down the Post Peak Pass Trail to the east, near the confluence of
Fernandez Creek and the creek from Slab Lakes. Both of these small
creeks contain brook trout.

*3rd Hiking Day (Post Peak Pass Trail to Lower Isberg Lake, 7.8
miles):* This hiking day takes one over two steep passes that have
excellent views. Heading east from the Fernandez Trail, the Post
Peak Pass Trail soon crosses Fernandez Creek on logs. A short
distance beyond we ford the creek from Slab Lakes and pass a
junction with a trail to the lakes. We continue northeast over a low,
wooded ridge past two glacial tarns where one may sometimes see
families of mallards.

Beyond the second tarn the trail descends to ford seasonal Post
Creek (9040') and begins a steep, three-stage ascent to Post Peak
Pass. The first stage takes us up a densely forested hillside to marshy
Isberg Meadow. Beyond this meadow our route leaves timber and
ascends on a washed-out trail along a flower-lined creek. Then the
grade eases and the trail enters the extraordinary "beachball" landscape around Porphyry Lake (10,100'). The dark blotches in this
bedrock are inclusions of quartz diorite in a lighter-colored granite.

The last stage of the climb to Post Peak Pass is a steep ascent over
a rocky, washed-out trail under the western ramparts of Post Peak.
The last several hundred feet of this climb may be snowbound into
summer, but a sign marks obvious Post Peak Pass (10,750'). From
the wind-swept pass, the trail actually climbs a little more as it skirts
a low peak ¼ mile northwest of the pass, where one can have
excellent views. Our trail stays near the ridge as we pass high above
Ward Lakes before descending west into Yosemite Park. A ⅓-mile
descent brings us to a junction with the Isberg Trail, which we turn
onto and then ascend back up to the Park boundary. This rocky ascent
brings us to a point above Isberg Pass, which is a short descent away
over ledges to the north. At the pass (10,520') we again enter Ansel
Adams Wilderness, and then descend towards Upper Isberg Lake.
The trail makes a very long traverse to the northeast, and if there is
a lot of snow when you're there, it may be more efficient to descend
directly east to the north side of the lake. From this lake the trail
crosses the outlet and swings near a viewpoint above McClure Lake,
then veers north and descends to the meadowed north side of Lower
Isberg Lake. Scenic campsites can be found in the trees on the low
moraine on the southeast side of the lake.

*4th Hiking Day (Lower Isberg Lake to Middle Cora Lake, 5.7
miles):* After rejoining the Isberg Trail we head east into forest cover,

cross a small creek and swing south. Soon our lodgepole-pine-shaded trail becomes steep as it winds down to the meadowed fringes of trout-filled Sadler Lake (9345'). Camping is legal only on the south and west sides of this popular lake. Rounding the east side of the lake brings us to the outlet, and then to a junction with the trail to McClure Lake.

From here our trail descends moderately under lodgepole pines, then through a stretch of avalanche-downed trees, before fording East Fork Granite Creek. Descending more gently now, the trail follows the orange bedrock channel for ½ mile before veering away from the creek and passing a junction with the Timber Creek Trail. Our trail continues to descend, crossing several small creeks before it levels off in the cow-infested environs of the East Fork. Then the trail crosses to the east side of the creek (wet in early season), skirts a number of meadows, and swings away from the creek to cross a low bedrock ridge. Over a mile from the ford we pass a junction with a lateral to the Stevenson Trail. From this junction it is an easy ½ mile over a low moraine down to the shaded east shore of middle Cora Lake. Camping is legal only on the southwest side of the lake.

5th Hiking Day (Middle Cora Lake to Granite Creek Campground, 4.6 miles): From the outlet on the southeast side of middle Cora Lake, our trail heads south through lodgepole forest, and in 1¼ miles we ford East Fork Granite Creek for the last time (wet in early season). The trail descends the west bank for ½ mile and then swings west and passes a wilderness boundary sign. Soon we turn south again and the descent steepens as the trail winds down a ravine under red fir, lodgepole pine and Jeffrey pine. The grade eases before the last, dusty descent brings us to a trailhead parking lot on the east side of West Fork Granite Creek. A bridge downstream takes us to the east end of Granite Creek Campground (7040').

Lake Edison to Graveyard Meadows

87

Distance	10.4 miles
Type	Out and back trip
Best season	Mid
Topo maps	Sharktooth Peak, Graveyard Peak
Grade (hiking days/recommended layover days)	
Leisurely	2/0
Moderate	Day
Strenuous	Day
Trailhead	Vermilion Campground (43)

HIGHLIGHTS   The grail at the end of this quest is a pretty, meadowed campsite within the boundaries of John Muir Wilderness. This route travels densely forested country abounding in wildlife, and tops a crest offering superlative views.

DESCRIPTION

1st Hiking Day (Vermilion Campground to Graveyard Meadows, 5.2 miles): To reach the trailhead, proceed beyond the turnoff to the campground and follow the dirt road 0.15 mile to a parking area, turn right, up the hill, and go past the turnoff to the packstation (on the left) to a parking area at a Forest Service sign. Park here under the tall Jeffrey pines. After a stroll of 0.3 mile we reach a signed junction with the trail to Quail Meadows, and we veer right onto it and down to the bridge across Cold Creek. Beyond the bridge, our route reaches a junction, where we take the Goodale Pass Trail, the left fork, and proceed under Jeffrey pines, white firs and junipers. We soon begin a long, dusty ascent under a dense cover of mostly Jeffrey pines. Our route passes a meadow on the lower part of this climb, but the ascent is fairly monotonous until very near the top, where we are rewarded with good views of Lake Edison and the peaks of the Mono Divide. From the crown of the climb it is but a short distance to Cold Creek, which we ford in order to join a jeep road for a short distance before we arrive at the signed boundary of John Muir Wilderness. Graveyard Meadows (8850′) are on the right, and secluded camping can be found at the head of the meadows. Or if one prefers, one can stay at the more-used sites near the ford. Fishing in Cold Creek is poor-to-fair for brook (to 8″).

2nd Hiking Day: Retrace your steps, 5.2 miles.

Looking south over Lake Edison

Lake Edison to Graveyard Lakes 88

Distance	16.8 miles
Type	Out and back trip
Best season	Mid or late
Topo maps	Sharktooth Peak, Graveyard Peak
Grade (hiking days/recommended layover days)	
Leisurely	4/1
Moderate	3/1
Strenuous	2/1
Trailhead	Vermilion Campground (43)

HIGHLIGHTS The California Department of Fish and Game has never been called overly creative, but it named the lakes in the Graveyard Lakes chain well. Beneath tombstone-granited Graveyard Peak lie lakes with DF&G names like Vengeance, Murder, Phantom, Headstone, Spook and Ghost. This country is worth investigating if for no other reason than to satisfy one's curiosity about these names. The truth is that this particular lake basin is one of the loveliest and most regal in the Silver Divide country.

DESCRIPTION (Leisurely trip)

1st Hiking Day: Follow Trip 87 to Graveyard Meadows, 5.2 miles.

2nd Hiking Day (Graveyard Meadows to Lower Graveyard Lake, 3.2 miles): From the south end of Graveyard Meadows, the trail enters the John Muir Wilderness and skirts the north edge of the meadows under a dense cover of lodgepoles and red firs. Birdlovers should keep an eye out for the Brewer blackbird, whitecrowned sparrow, Cassin finch, robin and sparrow hawk that inhabit this mountain field. At the north end of the meadow, the trail begins climbing moderately, and soon we cross Cold Creek on rocks (difficult in early season). This forested, duff trail ascends the narrowing Cold Creek valley, fording the creek in two places at the south end of Upper Graveyard Meadow.

The trail continues its gentle-to-moderate ascent under lodgepoles to a junction with the trail to Graveyard Lakes. We turn left onto it and ford Cold Creek in Upper Graveyard Meadow. Beyond the ford, the trail enters a cover of lodgepole and hemlock and begins a steep, rocky climb to the basin above. The lodgepole pine and mountain hemlock at the top of this 600-foot ascent give way to lush meadows at the eastern fringes of beautiful lower Graveyard Lake (9950′). Good though heavily used campsites may be found in the lodgepole stands where the trail first meets the lake, or along the east side of the lake between this point and the inlet stream.

From any of these places, the camper has marvelous views of Graveyard Peak and the tumbled granite cirque wall that surrounds the entire Graveyard Lakes basin. It is easy to derive the logic behind the name, "Graveyard Peak." Tombstone-makers have for years shown a preference for this particular kind of salt-and-pepper granite. These campsites along the east side of lower Graveyard Lake make an excellent base camp from which to fish and explore the remaining five lakes in the basin. The three small lakes directly above offer pretty and cleaner camping, and they can be reached by following the trail around to the head of the lake and climbing the hill. Fishing is good on lower Graveyard Lake for brook trout (to 13″) and fair-to-good on the upper lakes, due to poor spawning waters.

3rd and 4th Hiking Days: Retrace your steps, 8.4 miles.

Coldwater Campground to **89** Upper Crater Meadow

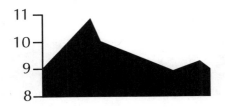

Distance	17.4 miles
Type	Shuttle
Best season	Late
Topo maps	**Devils Postpile,** Bloody Mountain, Crystal Crag

Grade (hiking days/recommended layover days)

Leisurely	3/1
Moderate	3/0
Strenuous	2/0
Trailhead	Coldwater Campground (42), Horseshoe Lake (44)

HIGHLIGHTS Moderate trails lead through wonderfully varied scenery, including a pair of cinder cones, the Red Cones. The Eastern Sierra has many fascinating volcanic features like the Red Cones, though it's been hundreds of years since there's been a volcanic event, other than an occasional tremor, in this area. The trailheads are only a few miles apart, so this is an easy shuttle to set up.

DESCRIPTION (Leisurely trip)

1st Hiking Day (Coldwater Campground to Duck Creek, 6 miles): Head southeast past an information sign, crossing an unmapped streamlet to enter John Muir Wilderness at a junction: left (north) to Mammoth Consolidated Mine, right (southeast) to Duck Pass. Turn right and follow the dusty Duck Pass Trail as it climbs gradually to moderately before beginning a series of lazy switchbacks. At 1 mile you reach an inconspicuously marked junction: left (southeast) to Arrowhead Lake (barely visible below), right (south, ahead) to Duck Pass. Stay on the trail to Duck Pass, climbing through granite outcrops to pass lovely Skelton Lake (9915′; campsites). Although there are campsites throughout this drainage, thoughtful

Arrowhead Lake

hikers will note that the area is overused and will continue over Duck Pass.

Until late season, and after a heavy winter, the trail may be under snow beyond Skelton. If the trail is open, you climb moderately past alpine meadows and presently top a rise overlooking desolate Barney Lake (10,203′; campsites; no fires within 300 feet of the lake). The trail crosses Barney's outlet and traverses its east shore before attacking the steep, winding, rocky, view-rich ascent to Duck Pass. At unmarked Duck Pass (10,797′) you discover a spectacular overlook of huge Duck Lake and its companion to the east, smaller Pika Lake (10,530′; campsites). In this basin, no fires are allowed and no camping is permitted within 300 feet of Duck's outlet.

Just below the pass, a spur trail darts off left toward Duck and Pika, while the main trail stays high above Duck almost to its outlet, called Duck Creek. You stay on the main trail, cross Duck Creek, and soon begin a rocky, switchbacking descent to meet the John Muir/ Pacific Crest Trail. Turn west (right) onto the northbound Muir Trail to descend a little farther to an attractive bench flanking Duck Creek, where there are fair campsites (10,000′) at 6 miles and fine views across Cascade Valley to the Silver Divide.

2nd Hiking Day (Duck Creek to Upper Crater Meadow, 7.7 miles): Late in the year, or in a dry year, there may be no water

between Duck Creek and Deer Creek, almost 6 miles away, so fill
your water bottles at Duck Creek. The northbound John Muir/Pacific
Crest Trail leaves the bench and begins a long, gradual, northwestward
traverse on lightly wooded slopes high above Cascade Valley.
Views south to the Silver Divide are awe-inspiring. The footing
changes from dirt to pumice—volcanic rock so light it floats on
water, though here it simply slips and crunches underfoot.

Approaching Deer Creek, the trail veers away from the valley's
rim, curves over low knolls, and descends a little to ford the well-
forested creek (overused campsites) nearly 5⅔ miles from Duck
Creek. Just beyond is a junction with a spur trail right (east) up Deer
Creek; you stay on the Muir/Pacific Crest Trail (left, west). The
gradually graded trail curves north and soon begins to pass through
one charming meadow and over one pretty stream after another. The
gentle, forested slopes cupping these meadows offer an occasional
campsite.

In flowery Upper Crater Meadow, you reach a junction with a
trail north to Mammoth Pass, a little more than 7.7 miles from Duck
Creek. It's signed as a two-way junction whose right fork goes to
Mammoth Pass and Horseshoe Lake and whose left is the northbound Muir/Pacific Crest Trail to Reds Meadow. But the Crystal
Crag topo shows this as a three-way junction, with the rightmost fork
going to Mammoth Pass, the middle fork being the John Muir Trail,
and the leftmost fork going to the Red Cones and Crater Meadow.
However, the Muir Trail has been rerouted onto the leftmost fork,
and the old middle fork is growing very faint from erosion and
disuse. Look for good campsites on the forested slopes around the
meadow, especially on a rise reached by briefly following the faint
old middle fork. Those taking a layover day here can enjoy a looping
dayhike via the Red Cones and Crater Meadow.

***3rd Hiking Day (Upper Crater Meadow to Horseshoe Lake, 3.7
miles):*** Although you could head directly to Mammoth Pass and
Horseshoe Lake by taking the rightmost fork at the junction in Upper
Crater Meadow, you won't want to miss the Red Cones. So return to
the Muir Trail and descend a sandy ravine northwest along Crater
Creek, fording the creek and passing the less-striking, forested,
southern Red Cone. The Red Cones get their name from the predominantly brick-red color of the volcanic cinders forming them. You
ford Crater Creek again at the base of the northern Red Cone and
reach a junction with another trail right (northeast) to Mammoth
Pass. Near this junction, an obvious use trail takes off up the open,
red-cinder slopes of the striking, northern Red Cone, from whose
cratered summit hikers enjoy wide-ranging views back to the Silver

Divide; of the bare hulk of Mammoth Mountain, an 11,053-foot remnant of a 400,000-year-old volcano that's a major ski area in winter and a busy mountain-bike park in summer; of the Middle Fork San Joaquin River; and of the dark, jagged Ritter Range. This is a classic cinder cone, fit to occupy a spot in Maui's famed Haleakala Crater, except for its sprinkling of conifers. The ascent is optional but highly recommended.

Whether or not you've climbed the northern Red Cone, turn east-northeast onto the trail to Mammoth Pass to continue this trip. Passing more use trails up the cone, the main trail climbs gently along blooming Crater Meadow, fed by a fork of Crater Creek, to a faint junction with the old Muir Trail segment from Upper Crater Meadow. Turn left (west), away from the meadow and creek, and shortly reach another junction: left (northwest) to Reds Meadow, right (north) to Mammoth Pass. Turn right to climb gradually to moderately to a junction by a noisy spring with the trail that was the rightmost fork at the junction in Upper Crater Meadow: right (south) to Upper Crater Meadow, left (ahead, north) to Mammoth Pass and Horseshoe Lake.

Go ahead to cross broad, forested, viewless Mammoth Pass, leaving designated wilderness behind. The gradient is so gradual that you may not notice you've crossed a pass. You presently skirt beautiful McCloud Lake (no camping), tucked picturesquely under the light-colored cliffs of the Mammoth Crest, and reach a junction: left on a different route over Mammoth Pass, right to Horseshoe Lake. Take the right fork ahead to descend to a parking lot by Horseshoe Lake, a popular swimming hole, where your shuttle ride is waiting.

It's believed that the dead trees around this lot died because their roots were smothered by carbon dioxide seeping up in measurable amounts from some underground source; the source is still being debated. The seepage is small enough that it poses no threat to people when they're in the open air.

Coldwater Campground to **90** Purple Lake

Distance	16 miles
Type	Out and back trip
Best season	Late
Topo maps	Bloody Mtn.

Grade (hiking days/recommended layover days)

Leisurely	3/1
Moderate	2/1
Strenuous	2/0
Trailhead	Coldwater Campground (42)

HIGHLIGHTS   The rewards for crossing a mountain pass amount to more than the views that are presented. Most experienced knapsackers know that passes have a way of separating the day hikers from the overnighters. So it is with this trip across the Mammoth Crest. Those seeking the satisfaction of seeing what lies beyond the top of the hill will find this hike a worthwhile choice.

DESCRIPTION (Moderate trip)

1st Hiking Day (Coldwater Canyon to Purple Lake, 8 miles):
Follow Trip 89 over Duck Pass to the junction with the John Muir/ Pacific Crest Trail, but instead of turning right onto the northbound trail, turn left onto the southbound trail. Climb away from Duck Creek and then make a pumice-covered traverse of the southern slopes of Peak 3464T, high above Cascade Valley, enjoying spectacular views of the Silver Divide. The trail eventually curves into the valley holding Purple Lake and descends to a junction: left (north) to campsites along Purple Lake's east shore, right (southeast) to stay on the Muir Trail and cross Purple's outlet. There is no camping allowed within 300 feet of that outlet, so take the left fork along lovely Purple Lake (9928'), where fishing is fair-to-good for rainbow and some golden and brook (8–13"). Purple Lake's partly-timbered, rocky shoreline gives way to meadow at the northeast end of the lake. The rocks above the meadow give this lake its name; they have a rosy tint during the day, but around sunset they turn purple and violet.

2nd Hiking Day: Retrace your steps, 8 miles.

91　Coldwater Campground to McGee Creek

Distance	28 miles
Type	Shuttle
Best season	Late
Topo map	**Devils Postpile, Mt. Abbott,** Bloody Mountain, Graveyard Peak, Convict Lake, Mt. Abbott

Grade (hiking days/recommended layover days)

Leisurely	——
Moderate	4/1
Strenuous	4/0
Trailheads	Coldwater Campground (42), McGee Creek Roadend (45)

HIGHLIGHTS　　Dramatic scenery, sparkling lakes, broad meadows, and rugged Sierra Crest passes lend beauty and adventure to a trip of great contrasts.

DESCRIPTION

1st Hiking Day (Coldwater Campground to Purple Lake, 8 miles): Follow Trip 89 to the junction with the John Muir/Pacific Crest Trail. Turn left onto the southbound Muir Trail and follow the rest of the 1st day of Trip 90 to Purple Lake.

2nd Hiking Day (Purple Lake to Tully Lake, 7.5 miles): Return to the junction with the Muir Trail and turn left (southeast) toward Purple Lake's outlet. Just before the outlet you reach another junction, this one with a trail into Cascade Valley that branches right (southwest). You turn left (ahead, east) to stay on the Muir Trail and cross Purple's outlet to ascend increasingly exposed switchbacks out of this valley. After topping out on a broad saddle, you descend southeast to windy Lake Virginia (10,335′; campsites), cross its inlet, and then climb along its northeast shore.

Now you curve southeast across a lightly forested saddle before descending over 800 feet on switchbacks to Tully Hole, a broad meadow where Fish Creek and a tributary meet before dashing down into Cascade Valley. At well-flowered Tully Hole (9500′) you find good campsites at the northwest edge of the meadow, near the junction of the John Muir Trail with the McGee Pass Trail. Here, Fish Creek is sometimes bowered by willows, but the long, swirling, curved line of its waters is for the most part open and pleasant, with grassy, overhung banks and several deep holes. At the trail junction it's right (southwest) on the Muir Trail, left (ahead, east) on the McGee Pass Trail.

You go left on the McGee Pass Trail, cross Fish Creek on a large, flattened log, and begin ascending along the creek. Beyond Tully Hole, there are no acceptable campsites and two potentially foot-soaking fords before the next campsites, on upper Fish Creek. Just before the lush meadow called Horse Heaven, you pass through a drift fence and splash across the creek. Horse Heaven is pretty to look at but dank and filthy with pack-animal dung, and lacks acceptable campsites. Beyond Horse Heaven, you begin long, dusty, dung-strewn switchbacks up some 500 feet to a bench where you ford the creek again. The climb moderates as you stroll up this charming bench to yet another wet ford, this one just below the pretty meadow where the outlet of Tully Lake joins the headwaters of Fish Creek.

An unmapped use trail branching right traces Tully Lake's outlet back to that lake, while the McGee Pass Trail goes left (east) across the creek. Follow the unmapped use trail about ½ mile to 10-acre Tully Lake (10,400′) and look for good campsites in the trees above the lake, which sustains fair-to-good fishing for golden and brook (to 13″). Tully is just one of many lakes in this area, which is the headwaters of Fish Creek, and you may want to seek a different campsite in this magnificent basin. A layover day here permits exploration of its dozens of lakes and streams and its huge meadows. Anglers will want to try the waters of Red and White Lake, about 1 mile away over the ridge to the east, with fair-to-good fishing for rainbow that often run to 16 inches. Those wishing stream fishing can find smaller rainbow, brook, and some golden along meandering Fish Creek.

3rd Hiking Day (Tully Lake to Big McGee Lake, 5.5 miles): First, return to the McGee Pass Trail, ford Fish Creek, and climb past a charming cascade into the immense, meadow-floored basin at the creek's headwaters. The trail ascends gently as it traverses this lovely basin, crossing seasonal streamlets, to the beginning of the interminable, rocky switchbacks nearly a thousand feet up to McGee Pass. There is little accessible water and no acceptable campsites once you begin the ascent of McGee Pass from the west until the vicinity of Little McGee Lake for water, Big McGee Lake for campsites.

You toil up, up, up to stand on the shattered red rock of McGee Pass (11,909') at last, where views back over the headwaters of Fish Creek and of the Silver Divide are breathtaking—almost worth the climb. Well-named Red Slate Mountain towers to the north. Snow patches may linger all year on the east side of this pass, so you descend carefully and steeply into a narrow canyon filled with the same broken, reddish rock. With the help of a few switchbacks, you head southeast to pass above Little McGee Lake, which lies down in a rocky cup. The trail curves east over a stream, makes an exposed descent toward timberline, and offers welcome glimpses of Big McGee Lake far below as it traverses steep meadows. A trail that once led from here toward Hopkins Pass has now vanished.

Continuing the moderate to steep descent, you traverse the rocky slope north of Big McGee Lake. Where the grade eases above the broad, south-trending peninsula on McGee's north shore, use trails lead to poor, exposed, overused campsites—even on the benches below the lake, acceptable campsites are almost nonexistent. However, anglers will enjoy the fair-to-good fishing for rainbow and brook (to 13") on Big McGee Lake (10,472') and, if time and inclination allow, will want to explore the equally good fishing at Little McGee Lake, or nearby Crocker Lake, or picture-book Golden Lake.

4th Hiking Day (Big McGee Lake to McGee Creek Roadend, 7 miles): Reverse the steps of Trip 95 from Big McGee Lake past "Round Lake" (9957'—the unnamed lakelet labeled "3035T" on the Convict Lake topo; campsites) and down along McGee Creek to the roadend.

Coldwater Campground to **92**
Iva Bell Hot Springs

Distance	28 miles
Type	Shuttle trip
Best season	Mid or late
Topo maps	**Devil's Postpile**, Bloody Mtn., Crystal Crag

Grade (hiking days/recommended layover days)

Leisurely	——
Moderate	4/1
Strenuous	3/1
Trailhead	Coldwater Campground (42), Rainbow Falls Trailhead (40)

HIGHLIGHTS   This trip offers beautiful views along much of the route, good trails, and idyllic cold-water pools. But the high point is one of the handful of wilderness hot springs in the entire High Sierra.

DESCRIPTION (Moderate trip)

1st Hiking Day (Coldwater Canyon to Duck Creek, 6 miles): Follow the 1st hiking day of Trip 89 over Duck Pass to the campsites on Duck Creek.

2nd Hiking Day (Duck Creek to Fish Creek, 5 miles): Retrace your steps to the junction of the John Muir-Pacific Crest Trail with the Duck Pass Trail. Now turn right (south) to stay on the Muir Trail and follow the steps of the latter part of Trip 90 to the junction with the spur trail to campsites at Purple Lake. Instead of turning left to the campsites, go right (southeast) on the Muir Trail. You shortly reach another junction: left (ahead, east) to stay on the Muir Trail, right (southwest) to Cascade Valley and Fish Creek.

Take the right fork to descend, gently at first, parallel to Purple Creek, enjoying fine views of the Silver Divide. The cover is initially lodgepole pine, giving way to Jeffrey pine and juniper near the valley floor. The going gets steeper, and the long switchbacks terminate at last in a large meadow on the floor of Cascade Valley where, in a few more steps, you meet the Cascade Valley Trail: left (southeast) upstream along Fish Creek to meet the Muir Trail again, right (northwest) to Iva Bell Hot Springs.

Turn right and soon reach a junction: right (ahead, northwest) to stay on the Cascade Valley Trail, left (southwest) along Minnow Creek. You go ahead, staying on the Cascade Valley Trail. Descend the dusty path through a beautiful, mixed forest, repeatedly approaching and veering away from Fish Creek, which cascades in smooth sheets over molded boulders into glorious pools. Choose one of the many idyllic campsites between here and Second Crossing. Wood is plentiful.

3rd Hiking Day (Fish Creek to Fox Meadow, 9 miles): The trail crosses Fish Creek at Second Crossing (very difficult in early season), then continues down-canyon. Polished granite walls rise steeply on both sides, and giant Jeffreys and cedars spring from the rock. Turning south, the route steeply ascends the south wall, then breaks out onto a granite saddle with vistas up Cascade Valley. To the south rise the slopes of Sharktooth Ridge, and directly below you can see the intense green foliage marking the outflow of the hot springs. The trail drops steeply through dry manzanita, then levels out abruptly in dense, wet forest, with a ground cover of ferns and wildflowers. Shortly, just beyond Sharktooth Creek, your route meets the Fish Valley Trail (signed). Campsites here are fair.

Immediately north of Sharktooth Creek, an unsigned trail leads uphill (east) about ⅓ mile to Iva Bell Hot Springs. Each streamlet you pass on the way is increasingly warmer. The trail ends in a meadow, at the northwest end of which a hot spring flows directly out of a granite outcrop into a small pool, offering luxury bathing at 100°, with improbable views. A second pool is located a little higher in the meadow. Heavy camping and constant stock use are rapidly destroying this meadow, so we recommend that if you spend the night around here, you camp below it.

Return to the main trail, cross the stream and, at the signed junction, take the right fork to Fish Valley. The level trail follows the stream through large Jeffrey pines and firs to Fox Meadow. Many laterals lead to excellent camping here.

4th Hiking Day (Fox Meadow to Rainbow Falls Trailhead, 8 miles): The outdated topo map shows Island Crossing east of Fox Meadow. Instead, just west of Fox Meadow at a signed junction, turn north (right) over a sturdy bridge at Island Crossing. Get water here: contrary to the topo, the trail does not touch water again for some time. Now the trail switchbacks steeply up the hot, dusty, exposed north slope of Fish Creek canyon. There are expanding views up and down Fish Creek, and eventually into Middle Fork San Joaquin. Then the route levels off through a mixed forest, now including oak, alternating with open meadows. After a welcome pause at Cold Creek, you break out onto exposed ledges of continuously sloping granite. This dramatic section of trail alone is worth the trip. The extensive views include Crater Creek falls. Excellent camping sites are located near the Crater Creek crossing and beyond along the creek. The trail follows Crater Creek, mostly in forest, then ascends on dusty footing through tall trees, passing several sheer granite walls and waterfalls. Forest and water combine to host numerous wildlife: noisy Steller jays and busy chickadees record your progress, and you are likely to see several kinds of small ground animals. The last section of this dusty trail ascends under tall trees to a junction with trails to Rainbow Falls (left, west) and to Devils Postpile, the Rainbow Falls Trailhead, and Reds Meadow Resort (north, right). Rainbow Falls is only ¼ mile away from this junction; its sheer, 101-foot cascade is regarded by many as the most classically beautiful in the Sierra outside of Yosemite. The detour is highly recommended.

For this trip, your shuttle ride will be at the Rainbow Falls Trailhead near Reds Meadow Resort and Pack Station, so take the broad, very dusty right fork. You walk under trees charred by the August 1992 lightning-caused Rainbow Fire as you ascend gradually, crossing Boundary Creek (you're just east of the eastern boundary of Devils Postpile National Monument). Just beyond the creek, you reach a fork: left (north) to Devils Postpile, right (northeast) to your trailhead. Go right, shortly reaching another junction: left (north) to your trailhead, right (northeast) to Reds Meadow Resort. Go left to hop over an unnamed creeklet, step across the intersecting John Muir/Pacific Crest Trail, and reach the dirt parking lot at the trailhead, where your shuttle ride should be waiting. This lot is a short walk or drive from the resort. Also, those interested in another hot-spring treat may want to head for nearby Reds Meadow Campground, where there are hot springs fed into free showers.

93   Lake George to Deer Lakes

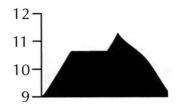

Distance	13 miles
Type	Shuttle trip; part cross-country
Best season	Mid
Topo maps	**Devils Postpile**, Crystal Crag, Bloody Mtn.

Grade (hiking days/recommended layover days)

Leisurely	——
Moderate	2/0
Strenuous	Day
Trailhead	Lake George (41), Coldwater Campground (42)

HIGHLIGHTS   This fine weekend trip crosses both stark alpine and dense forest terrains. The lightly traveled route to Deer Lakes follows the Mammoth Crest, with expansive views to either side, to these lakes of exceptional beauty. Wood is so scarce at these lakes that stoves are a must.

DESCRIPTION (Moderate trip)

1st Hiking Day (Lake George to Deer Lakes, 7 miles): There may be no water, and therefore no acceptable campsites, before you drop into Deer Lakes' basin. The trail leaves the Lake George parking lot (9008′) at its north end. Climbing above the resort cabins there, it switchbacks fairly steeply up through tall mountain hemlocks and lodgepole pines, affording views down to Lake George and eastward to "Red and Gold Mountain." At a signed junction with the trail to Crystal Lake, your route continues toward Mammoth Crest. A long switchback leg ends at a view of Horseshoe Lake almost directly below, and each succeeding north switchback turn offers more open views. From being granite, the rock underfoot abruptly changes to volcanic red cinders; stunted whitebark pines record the prevailing wind direction.

Just past the John Muir Wilderness boundary (signed, but mislocated) the trail descends briefly, and you pass a pair of unsigned trails to the right. Continuing leftward (south), you dip through the remnant of a crater, pass another unsigned trail to the right, and reach the crest. From this point, you can see the Ritter Range to the west, and to the southwest, the Silver Divide and the Middle Fork San Joaquin River canyon, converging with Fish Creek's canyon. Your rocky-sandy route continues south, and the crest broadens into a moonscape of red and white pumice, dotted with rounded clumps of wind-pruned whitebarks. By making brief excursions eastward, you'll get spectacular views of Crystal Crag, Crystal Lake, and the Owens Valley.

The often sandy trail climbs moderately, then steeply, just west of the crestline, with expanding views into Crater Meadow. The trail briefly touches the crest on an eastward-facing knife edge that offers a dizzying view east down a sheer, snow-filled chute to Hammil and Way lakes far below, a view reminiscent of those from the Mt. Whitney Trail eastward from Day and Keeler needles. The terrain here is misleading: Deer Lakes are not in the bowl to the right. The crest curves eastward (left) and so does the trail, and then it descends fairly steeply into Deer Lakes basin. The trail terminates near the middle (northernmost) Deer Lake (10,700'). Find a Spartan campsite near this lake or along the stream connecting it with the lowest Deer Lake. Use stoves here.

2nd Hiking Day (Deer Lakes to Coldwater Campground, 6 miles): The terrain is gentle and rocky, and several indistinct trails head toward the pass that overlooks Duck Lake, directly east of the highest (easternmost) Deer Lake. One trail of use leaves from the east end of the middle Deer Lake. Another, often-indistinct trail, your route, leaves just east of the outlet of the same lake. Take it, and if you lose it, continue in a straight line toward the very obvious low point just east of the highest Deer Lake. When you reach the edge of the talus, walk along its base, almost reaching a small tarn not shown on the topo map. From this point an obvious steep use trail snakes 200 feet up on loose scree and dirt footing to a lovely, wide meadow. The trail crosses this meadow eastward past a lone, very large boulder in a low saddle. Ignore the ducks and the use trail that lead upward to the left (north) face from this boulder, and continue directly ahead toward Duck Lake. Soon the trail descends among whitebark pines. It is occasionally hard to see. If you lose the trail, head straight downhill (avoid contouring leftward) and you will soon intersect the well-maintained Duck Pass Trail. Turn left (north) onto the trail, which leads levelly to Duck Pass, 350 yards ahead. The remainder of your route, nearly all downhill, reverses the first part of the 1st hiking day of Trip 89.

94 McGee Creek to Steelhead Lake

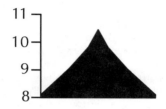

Distance	12 miles
Type	Out and back trip
Best season	Mid or late
Topo maps	**Mt. Abbott**, Convict Lake, Mt. Abbott
Grade (hiking days/recommended layover days)	
Leisurely	2/1
Moderate	2/0
Strenuous	——
Trailhead	McGee Creek Roadend (45)

HIGHLIGHTS   Travelers new to east-escarpment entry to the Sierra will find the ascent to Steelhead Lake fascinating because of the swirling patterns in the highly fractured red metamorphic rocks of the canyon wall. Get an early start: the first few miles, up a narrow, nearly shadeless canyon, can be very hot in the middle of the day.

DESCRIPTION

1st Hiking Day (McGee Creek Roadend to Steelhead Lake, 6 miles): From the parking area (8136') near the restrooms, the sandy, official trail veers right at an information sign and up onto McGee Canyon's northwest slopes. (Ignore an old road that leads into the canyon along the creek; it once led to a now-vanished campground.) The multicolored, contorted rock layers making up the canyon's walls contrast pleasantly with the open, scrub-covered moraine the trail traverses. Ascending gradually to moderately, we enter John Muir Wilderness at a little over ¾ mile; beyond here, the trail begins to curve slowly southward, deeper into McGee Canyon, and begins to cross streams that nourish splendid, though seasonal, flower gardens. Stunted aspens offer occasional shade as we splash through

Buzztail Spring's waters, and we presently glimpse aptly-named Horsetail Falls on the canyon wall to our right.

The gentle ascent continues to a ford of tree-lined McGee Creek (difficult in early season). Then the unshaded trail climbs until it reaches a shelf above a beautiful meadow, through which the stream wanders in sensuous curves. It's not long before the trail fords the creek to the forested west bank on an increasingly untrustworthy log upstream from a stock crossing; without the log, this crossing would be difficult. As the trail curves around a large outcrop, it crosses a marshy area and reaches a sometimes-signed junction where a path intended for stock forks right (south), while hikers take the left (generally southeast) fork over another marshy area, passing some campsites. The trail ascends gradually along the creek, crossing a tributary, to reach another junction: right (southwest) to McGee Pass; left (south) to Grass and Steelhead lakes.

Take the left fork and ford McGee Creek again before beginning a steep, switchbacking, 460-foot climb up the canyon's east wall to yet another junction: left (north-northeast) less than ¼ mile to little Grass Lake (9826'; campsites), right (east-southeast) to Steelhead Lake. Go right to Steelhead; angler's casual trails connect the lakes around here, so be sure to keep a lookout for the main trail, which leads generally southeast to Steelhead. After crossing a lodgepole-dotted flat, we climb to a narrow meadow, cross an unmapped stream, and ascend more switchbacks, one leg of which offers a fine view of sparkling Grass Lake far below and of Red Slate Mountain's outliers to the west.

The trail presently levels out and at an unmarked, unmapped junction, we take the left fork a short distance to Steelhead Lake. Top a rise, pass some tarns, and descend past good campsites to 25-acre Steelhead (10,380').

Views from these campsites take in the granite grandeur of Mt. Stanford and Mt. Crocker to the south and west, and rust-and-buff-colored Mt. Baldwin to the north. Anglers will find the fishing for rainbow and brook excellent (best in early and late season). They will also find the name "Steelhead" Lake a misnomer, though an understandable error. Over the years, catches of rainbow trout from this lake have exhibited pale, faded markings, giving an appearance much like their silver cousins of coastal waters.

2nd Hiking Day: Retrace your steps, 6 miles.

95 McGee Creek to McGee Lake

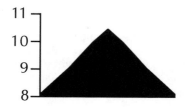

Distance	14 miles
Type	Out and back trip
Best season	Mid or late
Topo maps	**Mt. Abbott**, Convict Lake, Mt. Abbott

Grade (hiking days/recommended layover days)
Leisurely	2/1
Moderate	2/0
Strenuous	——

Trailhead   McGee Creek Roadend (45)

HIGHLIGHTS   In an alpine setting close under the Sierra crest, Big McGee Lake shares a large granite basin with three other fishable lakes. This beautiful spot nestles under the sheer, colorful walls of Red and White Mountain, and close to impressive Mt. Crocker, a setting that helps compensate for the poor camping here.

DESCRIPTION

1st Hiking Day (McGee Creek Roadend to Big McGee Lake, 7 miles): Follow Trip 94 as far as the creekside junction where it's right (southwest) to McGee Pass; left (south) to Grass and Steelhead lakes.

Go right to McGee Pass, continuing south when the stock path that split off earlier comes in on the right to rejoin the main trail. The trail begins a moderate ascent of some 460 feet on numerous, short, rocky, hemlock-shaded switchbacks along granite cliffs, soon rising high enough that Mt. Stanford is visible over the bench holding Trip 94's Grass Lake (the lake itself isn't visible). Near the top you pass through a ruined drift fence, dip through a damp, forested hollow; and top out at a little under 5.5 miles by locally named "Round Lake" (Lake 3035T on the metric Convict Lake topo). There are fair, overused campsites just south of Round Lake (9957′), which is half-hidden from the main trail by the outcrops around it.

Continuing, we veer north past a meadow south of which there's a campsite, and begin climbing switchbacks to a series of meadowed benches that may be dry by late season and which offer surprisingly few campsites—almost none. The grade eases on these benches, which the trail ascends while carefully skirting the meadows and brushing against a tributary just once. Just before the trail strikes west across a talus slope north of Big McGee Lake, follow use trails south onto the chunky peninsula that protrudes south into the lake and look for poor, overused campsites here. It's a steep, loose scramble down to the lakeshore here. There are no acceptable campsites readily accessible from the main trail between Big McGee Lake and the west side of McGee Pass, at the headwaters of Fish Creek.

Anglers will want to enjoy the fair-to-good fishing for rainbow and brook (to 13″) on Big McGee Lake, and, if time and inclination allow, will want to explore the equally good fishing at nearby Little McGee Lake, Crocker Lake, or picture-book Golden Lake.

2nd Hiking Day: Retrace your steps, 7 miles.

Steelhead Lake

96 McGee Creek to Rock Creek

Distance	30.6 miles
Type	Shuttle trip, part cross-country
Best season	Late
Topo maps	**Mt. Abbott**, Convict Lake, Mt. Abbott, Graveyard Peak, Mt. Morgan

Grade (hiking days/recommended layover days)

Leisurely	6/2
Moderate	5/2
Strenuous	3/1
Trailhead	McGee Creek Roadend (45), Mosquito Flat (47)

HIGHLIGHTS   *For experienced knapsackers only,* this rugged route offers excitement and challenge sufficient to satisfy the most jaded appetite. High-country lakes surrounded by rampartlike peaks characterize this colorful route, and the fishing is good-to-excellent.

DESCRIPTION (Moderate trip)

1st and 2nd Hiking Days (Mc Gee Creek Roadend to Tully Lake, 12.5 miles): On the first day of this trip, follow Trips 94 and 95 to Big McGee Lake. On the second day of this trip, reverse the steps of the 3rd hiking day of Trip 91 and go from Big McGee Lake over McGee Pass to Tully Lake.

3rd Hiking Day (Tully Lake to Grinnell Lake, 3.5 miles cross country): From the east shore of Tully Lake our route ascends the grassy swale that lies due east of the lake. At the outlet stream from Red and White Lake our route turns right (southeast) and follows this stream to the lake itself. Fishermen will wish to try these icy, clear, blue waters for large rainbow (to 18"). Although there's no good camping, Red and White Lake offers an excellent vantage point from which to take in the spectacular and aptly named heights of Red and White Mountain. The saddle (11,600′) that this day's route traverses is clearly discernible at the lowest point of the right shoulder of Red and White Mountain, and the easiest route to the saddle takes the traveler around the rocky east shore of the lake. The steepest part of the ascent is over treacherous shale—or snow in early and mid season—and the climber is well-advised to take it slow and easy. Rope should be carried and used, especially if ascending the west side of the pass.

From the top one obtains a well-deserved and exciting view of the surrounding terrain. To the north the immediate, dazzling blue of Red and White Lake sets off the buff browns and ochre reds of the surrounding rock. Beyond this basin the meadowy cirque forming the headwaters of Fish Creek is a large greensward that contrasts sharply with the austere, red-stained eminence of Red Slate Mountain, and the distant skyline offers sawtooth profiles of the Ritter Range, with its readily identifiable Minarets, and the Mammoth Crest. To the south, the barren, rocky shores of the Grinnell chain of lakes occupy the foreground, and, just beyond, the green-sheathed slopes of the Mono Creek watershed drop away, rising in the distance to the Mono Divide.

Like the ascent of this saddle, the descent should be taken with some care. The sudden, shaley drop terminates in a large "rock garden," a jumble of large boulders, just above Little Grinnell Lake. Our rock-hopping route takes us along the east shore of this tiny lake to the long, grassy descent leading to the west side of Grinnell Lake (10,800′). Midway along this side, where the most prominent peninsula infringes on the long lake, our route strikes the marked fisherman's trail that veers southwest down a long swale to tiny Laurel Lake. There are several fair campsites at this junction which offer excellent views due to their situation on a plateau above the lake. Fishermen will find Grinnell Lake fair-to-good fishing for brook and rainbow (8–14″). Alternative good campsites can be found along the meadowy fringes of Laurel Lake (10,300′), about 1 mile southwest. Fishing on this lake is excellent for brook (to 10″).

4th Hiking Day (Grinnell Lake to Fish Camp, 4.5 miles): The fisherman's trail from Grinnell Lake to Laurel Lake descends via a long, scooplike swale to the grassy meadows forming the headwaters of Laurel Creek. The trail, though very faint from Grinnell to Laurel Lake, becomes clearer as it descends gently along Laurel Creek. At this point the creek is still a "jump-across" stream, but a careful approach along the banks will reveal an abundance of brook trout (to 9″), and fly fishermen who favor stream angling will find this tiny watercourse a delight.

The gradual descent along the creek becomes somewhat steeper just above the larger meadows. The pleasant, timber-fringed grassland is divided by the serpentine curves of Laurel Creek. The trail across the meadow is difficult to follow, and the traveler who loses it should cross to the west side of Laurel Creek and look for the trail in the vicinity of the campsites at the south end of the meadow. The dense lodgepole cover at the end of the meadow soon gives way to manzanita thickets and occasional clumps of quaking aspen as the trail reaches the steep, switchbacking descent above Mono Creek. These switchbacks are unmaintained, and are subject to heavy erosion. However, the difficult going is more than compensated for by the excellent views across the Mono Creek watershed into the Second Recess. Particularly impressive are the heights of Mt. Gabb and Mt. Hilgard, which guard the upper end of this side canyon. When our route strikes the Mono Creek Trail, it turns right (west) for a gently descending ½ mile to the campsites at Fish Camp (8500′). Due to heavy use here, the Forest Service encourages you to camp downstream. Fishing is good for brook and rainbow (to 12″) on Mono Creek.

5th Hiking Day (Fish Camp to Mosquito Flat, 10.1 miles): This is a long, strenuous day; an early start is in order. Reverse the steps of the 2nd hiking day of Trip 100 by heading upstream on the Mono Creek Trail, across Mono Pass, down to the lateral to Ruby Lake. From there, reverse the steps of Trip 99 to the trailhead.

Dominating Bear Creek Spire above Little Lakes Valley

Hilton Lakes   **97**

Distance	8.6–10 miles
Type	Out and back
Best season	Mid or late
Topo maps	**Mt. Abbott,** Mt. Morgan, Mt. Abbott
Grade (hiking days/recommended layover days)	
Leisurely	2/1
Moderate	2/0
Strenuous	Day
Trailhead	Hilton Lakes (46)

HIGHLIGHTS   Just north of Rock Creek, lovely Hilton Creek flows from rugged Sierra-crest peaks through a small basin of charming lakes, the Hilton Lakes (or Hilton Creek Lakes). Backpackers will find appealing campsites at Lakes 3 and 4 and fine dayhiking up and down the basin.

DESCRIPTION

1st Hiking Day (Rock Creek Road to Hilton Lake 3 or 4, 4.3–5 miles): The trail immediately begins a gradual-to-moderate climb north-northeast on the ridge separating Rock and Hilton creeks, first through forest, then on exposed slopes that boast an amazing array of flowers in season. A switchback turn affords excellent views over Rock Creek Lake and the peaks south around Little Lakes Valley, and tantalizing glimpses into the basin west of Wheeler Ridge. Now you begin a long traverse and at ⅔ mile cross a stream and enter John Muir Wilderness. Beyond here, a junction shown on the 7½′ topo, with a steep trail down to Pine Grove Campground, no longer exists.

A little past 1.6 miles, the trail curves northwest and presently swings up to a junction at a little over 2 miles where the left fork has been intentionally blocked off. Go right (northwest) and enjoy glimpses of Peaks 11950 and 11962 upslope on your left as you curve through an open, sandy forest of lodgepoles, skirt a large meadow, and then curve generally west. After another mile, the grade increases, and the trail soon tops out on a saddle at 10,380 feet.

Heading west toward Peak 12508, you cross an area covered by the sun-bleached trunks of trees felled by an avalanche in the early 1980s. The re-established trail descends on gradual-to-moderate switchbacks to a trail junction at 4 miles: left (southwest) to Hilton Lakes 3 and 4; right (north) to Hilton Lake 2 and Davis Lake (a.k.a. Hilton Lake 1).

Lake 2 and Davis Lake are heavily used by horse packers, so backpackers should head for higher Lakes 3 and 4. From the junction at 4 miles, go left to cross a seasonal stream, pass a small meadow, and begin a series of unrelenting switchbacks up, leveling out at fabulous views northward over Hilton Lake 2 and Davis Lake, and across Long Valley to Glass Ridge. At the stream connecting Lakes 3 and 2, you'll spy Hilton Lake 3 (10,300') upstream at 4⅓ miles, with a dramatic backdrop of Mts. Huntington and Stanford. Those wishing to stay at this lake can take use trails from here to campsites.

To continue to Hilton Lake 4, stay on the main trail to cross the stream and curve southwest along Hilton Lake 3's northwest shore—contrary to what the topo shows, there's no trail branching left to the next-higher set of lakes. The trail then veers west across a low ridge offering a fine view of the dashing cascades of Hilton Lake 5's outlet. You descend to cross the outlet in a meadow, bob over another ridgelet, and reach Hilton Lake 4 (10,353') at almost 5 miles. The peak on the lake's far side is Mt. Huntington—a breathtaking sight from campsites overlooking the lake.

A layover day at Hilton Lake 3 or 4 offers an opportunity for a dayhike to beautiful but overused Hilton Lake 2 and Davis Lake. Or consider a cross-country scramble to the wild, scenic upper lakes; a good route starts from Lake 3 and approximates that nonexistent "trail" that's shown on the topo.

2nd Hiking Day: Retrace your steps, 4.3–5 miles.

Rock Creek to Gem Lakes 98

Distance	6.6 miles
Type	Out and back *dayhike only*
Best season	Mid or late
Topo maps	**Mt. Abbott**, Mt. Morgan, Mt. Abbott

Grade (hiking days/recommended layover days)

Leisurely	——
Moderate	Day
Strenuous	——
Trailhead	Mosquito Flat (47)

HIGHLIGHTS   Majestic scenery dominates this short, popular trip. Because of its moderate terrain and high country "feel" this route through the Little Lakes Valley is a favorite with hikers. The good fishing for brook and rainbow makes it an excellent choice for anglers, too. The area receives very heavy use and has few acceptable campsites, so we strongly recommend seeing it on a dayhike. Those determined to backpack through the area should see the suggestion in the last paragraph of this trip.

DESCRIPTION

Dayhike (Mosquito Flat to Gem Lakes, 3.3 miles): The magnificent Sierra crest confronts the traveler at the very outset of this trip. From the trailhead at Mosquito Flat (10,200′), the wide, rocky-sandy trail starts southwest toward the imposing skyline dominated by soaring Bear Creek Spire. In a few minutes we enter John Muir Wilderness and then reach a junction at which the Mono Pass Trail is the right fork and our trail, the Morgan Pass Trail, is the left fork. Soon our route tops a low, rocky ridge just west of Mack Lake, and from this ridge one has good views of green-clad Little Lakes Valley. Gazing out, one cannot help but feel a sense of satisfaction that this beautiful valley enjoys protection as part of John Muir Wilderness. Aside from some early, abortive mining ventures, this subalpine valley remains relatively unspoiled.

From the ridgetop viewpoint our trail descends to skirt a marsh that was the west arm of Marsh Lake before it filled in. Anglers may wish to try their luck for the good fishing for brown and brook trout in Marsh Lake and the nearby lagoon areas of Rock Creek. While fishing on the numerous lakes and streams of Little Lakes Valley, one has views into the long glacial trough to the south—a long-time favorite of lensmen. Flanked by Mt. Starr on the right and Mt. Morgan on the left, the valley terminates in the soaring heights of Mts. Mills, Abbot, Dade and Julius Ceasar, and Bear Creek Spire, all over 13,000 feet. Still-active glaciers on the slopes of these great peaks are reminders of the enormous forces that shaped this valley eons ago, and the visitor cannot help but feel contrasting reactions of exhilaration and humility.

From the meadowed fringes of Marsh and Heart lakes, the trail ascends gently past the west side of Box Lake to the east side of aptly named Long Lake. For the angler with a yearning to try different waters, the Hidden Lakes on the bench just to the east offer good fishing for brook and rainbow. However, the Hidden Lakes are surrounded by marshes; getting to and around them may involve more wading than hiking. Beyond Long Lake the trail ascends through a moderately dense forest cover of whitebark pines past a spur trail branching left to Chickenfoot Lake. Then we dip to cross a seasonal stream, climb slightly, and dip again, to the outlet stream of the Gem Lakes. Ahead on the left we see the last switchback on the trail up Morgan Pass, through which the abandoned road that has been our trail once reached the tungsten mines in the Pine Creek drainage.

Just after a rockhop ford of the Gem Lakes outlet, we reach a junction: left (ahead, east) to Morgan Pass and Morgan Lakes, right (south) to the Gem Lakes. Turn right and take this sometimes-faint trail upstream to the lowest of the three main Gem Lakes, under the sheer north wall of peak 11654. Fishing is fair-to-good for brook and rainbow trout to 10. The Treasure Lakes, located in barren cirques above here, are traditional basecamp locations for climbers bound for the high peaks to the west.

Retrace your steps, 3.3 miles.

Backpacking. Those determined to backpack through Little Lakes Valley should consider making their camp beyond Morgan Pass at pretty Lower Morgan Lake, where there are a few fair, lodgepole-shaded campsites. Upper Morgan Lake is rockbound.

Rock Creek to Ruby Lake **99**

Distance	4.6 miles
Type	Out and back *dayhike only*
Best season	Mid or late
Topo maps	**Mt. Abbott**, Mt. Morgan, Mt. Abbott
Grade (hiking days/recommended layover days)	
Leisurely	——
Moderate	Day
Strenuous	——
Trailhead	Mosquito Flat (47)

HIGHLIGHTS From the Little Lakes Valley upward to the heights of the Ruby Lake cirque, the traveler gains an appreciation of glacially formed country. One can almost see the main trunk of the glacier flowing northeast through the valley and being joined by the feeder glacier from the cirque that now holds Ruby Lake. The terminus of this trip, Ruby Lake, lies amidst the barren peaks of the awe-inspiring Sierra Nevada crest. Like neighboring Little Lakes Valley (Trip 98), the Mono Pass Trail and Ruby Lake get so much use that we strongly recommend seeing them as a dayhike.

DESCRIPTION

Dayhike (Mosquito Flat to Ruby Lake, 2.3 miles): First follow Trip 98 to the junction of the Morgan Pass and Mono Pass trails. Here our route branches right (west) and ascends steeply over rocky switchbacks. In the course of this switchbacking ascent, the traveler will see the moderate-to-dense forest cover of whitebark and lodgepole diminish in density as we near timberline. Views during the climb include the glacier-fronted peaks named in Trip 98 and, midway up the ascent, Mt. Morgan. Immediately below to the east, the deep blue of Heart and Box lakes and some of the Hidden Lakes reflects the sky above, and the viewer looking at the panorama of the valley can readily trace the glacial history that left these "puddles" behind.

Near the meadowed edge of the outlet stream from Ruby Lake is a junction, where we turn left. It becomes apparent that a cirque basin is opening up, although one cannot see Ruby Lake, which completely fills the cirque bottom, until one is actually at water's edge (11,121'). This first breathtaking view of the lake and its towering cirque walls makes the climb worth the effort. Sheer granite makes up the upper walls of the cirque, and the crown is topped by a series of spectacular pinnacles, particularly to the west. To the north, also on the crest, a notch indicates Mono Pass, and close scrutiny will reveal the switchbacking trail that ascends the south ridge of Mt. Starr. The lower walls of the cirque are mostly made up of talus and scree that curve outward to the lake's edge, and it is over this jumbled rock that ambitious anglers must scramble to sample the fair fishing for brook, rainbow and brown (to 12").

Retrace your steps, 2.3 miles.

At the outlet of Ruby Lake

Rock Creek to Fish Camp **100**

Distance	20.2 miles
Type	Out and back trip
Best season	Late
Topo maps	**Mt. Abbott**, Mt. Morgan, Mt. Abbott

Grade (hiking days/recommended layover days)

Leisurely	4/1
Moderate	3/1
Strenuous	2/1
Trailhead	Mosquito Flat (47)

HIGHLIGHTS Mono Creek's valley offers access to several lake basins as well as to the famed Mono Recesses, four glacier-sculpted hanging valleys that invite exploration. Hikers may be tempted to abandon their Mono Creek campsites for Spartan sites high in these splendid basins and valleys! A late-season trip has three distinct pluses: First, the luxuriant aspen groves along Mono Creek take on their golden hue about this time. Second, the mid-season fishing slump usually ends as the weather cools off. Last, this popular route sees heavy foot and animal traffic during early and mid season, but this activity tapers off when the leaves begin to turn.

DESCRIPTION (Strenuous trip)

1st Hiking Day (Mosquito Flat to Fish Camp, 10.1 miles): Follow Trip 99 to the junction with the lateral to Ruby Lake. Stay on the Mono Pass Trail to ascend steeply over rocky switchbacks on the south slope of Mt. Starr to Mono Pass (12,000′), a notch in the cirque wall just west of Mt. Starr. On this climb, views constantly improve, and views from the pass are excellent, but those wishing a panoramic outlook on the spectacular Sierra crest should ascend the granite shoulder of Mt. Starr, an easy climb to the east. From this vantage point one has a complete perspective of Pioneer Basin and Mts. Stanford, Huntington, Crocker and Hopkins, and Red and White Mountain to the north. To the south one has an "end-on" view of Mts. Abbot and Dade, Bear Creek Spire, and Mt. Humphreys.

From Mono Pass the trail descends over granite slopes past barren Summit Lake, and then drops more severely as it veers west above Trail Lakes (poor-to-fair fishing for brook). Our route then turns northward and fords Golden Creek. Following the north side of the stream in a moderately dense forest cover, the trail passes the lateral to Pioneer Basin (north) and the lateral to Fourth Recess Lake (south). Anglers may elect to try their luck at the good fishing for brook (8–14″) at Fourth Recess Lake, ½ mile south over a gentle climb.

Our route continues to descend, fording the outlet streams from Pioneer Basin and paralleling the westward course of Mono Creek. As the Mono Creek valley opens up beyond Mono Rock, the trail passes the steep lateral to Third Recess Lake (south), and, about a mile farther, descends past the turnoff to Lower Hopkins Lake and the Hopkins Lake basin (north). Anglers will find the many fine holes that interrupt dashing Mono Creek good fishing for brook, rainbow and occasional golden (to 12″). In late season the groves of quaking aspen that line the stream's banks are an incomparably colorful back drop to an otherwise steady conifer green. Owing to heavy traffic, this segment of trail becomes somewhat dusty where it passes the Grinnell Lake lateral and descends to Fish Camp (8500′). This traditional camping place marks the junction of the Mono Creek Trail with the Second Recess lateral. Due to heavy use here, the Forest Service encourages you to camp downstream.

The lateral trails you've passed as well as the Second Recess lateral here lead to hanging valleys and lake basins you'll want to spend a few days exploring. In fact, you may even prefer to make your camp earlier, farther up Mono Creek and nearer more of these laterals. Enjoy!

2nd Hiking Day: Retrace your steps over Mono Pass to Mosquito Flat, 10.1 miles.

Recommended Reading

Brewer, William H. *Up and Down California*. Berkeley: University of California Press, 1966.

Browning, Peter. *Place Names of the Sierra Nevada*. Berkeley: Wilderness Press, 1991.

Farquhar, Francis. *History of the Sierra Nevada*. Berkeley: University of California Press, 1965.

Darvill, Fred. *Mountaineering Medicine*. Berkeley: Wilderness Press, 1992.

Graydon, Don (ed.). *Mountaineering: The Freedom of the Hills*. Seattle: The Mountaineers, 1992.

Hill, Mary. *Geology of the Sierra Nevada*. Berkeley: University of California Press, 1975.

Ingles, Lloyd G. *Mammals of the Pacific States*. Stanford, CA: Stanford University Press, 1965.

Jardine, Ray. *The PCT Hiker's Handbook*. LaPine, OR: AdventureLore Press, 1992.

King, Clarence. *Mountaineering in the Sierra Nevada*. New York: Penguin, 1989.

Krist, John. *50 Best Hikes in Yosemite and Sequoia/Kings Canyon*. Berkeley: Wilderness Press, 1993.

Latimer, Carole. *Wilderness Cuisine*. Berkeley: Wilderness Press, 1991.

Matthess, François. *The Incomparable Valley*. Berkeley: University of California Press, 1964.

Morey, Kathy. *Hot Showers, Soft Beds, and Dayhikes in the Sierra*. Berkeley: Wilderness Press, 1996.

Muir, John. *My First Summer in the Sierra*. Boston: Houghton Mifflin, 1979.

——— (ed. Fred Gunsky). *South of Yosemite*. Berkeley: Wilderness Press, 1987.

Niehaus, Theodore, and Charles L. Ripper. *A Field Guide to Pacific States Wildflowers*. Boston: Houghton Mifflin, 1976.

Peterson, Victor P. and Victor P. Peterson, Jr. *Native Trees of the Sierra Nevada*. Berkeley: University of California Press, 1975.

Peterson, Roger Tory. *A Field Guide to Western Birds*. Boston: Houghton Mifflin, 1990.

Roper, Steve. *Climber's Guide to the High Sierra*. San Francisco: Sierra Club, 1976.

———. *Sierra High Route*. Seattle: The Mountaineers, 1997.

Russell, Carl P. *100 Years in Yosemite*. Yosemite: Yosemite Association, 1968.

Schaffer, Jeffrey P. *Yosemite National Park*. Berkeley: Wilderness Press, 1992.

———. *Carson-Iceberg Wilderness*. Berkeley: Wilderness Press, 1992.

Schifrin, Ben. *Emigrant Wilderness*. Berkeley: Wilderness Press, 1990.

Storer, Tracy I. and Robert L. Usinger. *Sierra Nevada Natural History*. Berkeley: University of California Press, 1964.

Watts, Tom. *Pacific Coast Tree Finder*. Berkeley: Nature Study Guild, 1973.

Weeden, Norman. *A Sierra Nevada Flora*. Berkeley: Wilderness Press, 1996.

Whitney, Stephen. *A Sierra Club Naturalist's Guide to the Sierra Nevada*. San Francisco: Sierra Club, 1979.

Winnett, Thomas. *The Tahoe-Yosemite Trail*. Berkeley: Wilderness Press, 1987.

Winnett, Thomas, and Melanie Findling. *Backpacking Basics*. Berkeley: Wilderness Press, 1994.

Trip Cross-Reference Table

Trip No.	Hiking Days*	Pace*			Season			Trip Type			
		Leis	Mod	Str	Early	Mid	Late	O&B	Shut	Loop	Semi
1	2	•					•	•			
2	4	•				•		•			
3	6	•				•		•			
4	2	•				•		•			
5	4		•		•						
6	5		•			•				•	
7	2	•	•			•		•			
8	2	•	•			•				•	
9	2	•	•			•		•			
10	3	•				•				•	
11	2		•			•					•
12	2		•			•	•			•	
13	3			•		•				•	
14	4		•			•					•
15	2	•	•			•	•				•
16	4		•			•			•		
17	6		•			•	•		•		
18	2		•		•	•		•			
19	4	•				•	•	•			
20	4	•				•	•	•			
21	7	•				•	•				•
22	2	•				•	•	•			
23	4	•				•	•	•			
24	4	•	•			•	•	•			
25	6		•			•	•			•	
26	5	•				•	•			•	
27	5	•				•	•			•	
28	7	•				•	•			•	
29	2		•			•	•	•			
30	3		•			•	•	•			
31	4		•			•	•				•
32	5		•			•	•				•
33	5		•		•	•				•	
34	2		•			•	•	•			
35	2		•		•	•	•	•			
36	4		•			•	•	•			
37	3			•		•	•			•	
38	3		•			•	•				•
39	6		•			•	•	•			
40	8	•				•	•				•

*Number of hiking days reflects the pace described in the trip's text. You can take most trips at another pace by taking more or fewer days.

Trip No.	Hiking Days*	Pace*			Season			Trip Type			
		Leis	Mod	Str	Early	Mid	Late	O&B	Shut	Loop	Semi
41	2	•			•	•	•	•			
42	4	•	•			•	•		•		
43	2	•	•			•	•		•		
44	2	•			•			•			
45	4	•			•			•			
46	2	•	•			•	•			•	
47	2		•			•	•	•			
48	3		•			•	•		•		
49	2		•	•		•	•				•
50	2	•				•	•	•			
51	2	•	•			•	•	•			
52	2	•				•	•	•			
53	4	•				•	•	•			
54	5		•			•	•		•		
55	4	•				•	•	•			
56	4	•				•	•	•			
57	2	•	•			•	•	•			
58	2		•			•	•	•			
59	2	•	•		•	•	•	•			
60	2	•	•			•	•	•			
61	4		•			•	•				•
62	6		•			•	•				•
63	7		•			•	•				•
64	2	•	•		•	•	•	•			
65	6		•		•		•			•	
66	4	•			•			•			
67	4	•			•	•		•			
68	4		•		•	•			•		
69	4	•			•	•			•		
70	5	•			•	•					•
71	4	•	•		•			•			
72	10		•			•	•			•	
73	7	•				•	•		•		
74	3		•		•	•					•
75	2	•				•	•	•			
76	3	•				•	•				•
77	3	•				•	•				•
78	2	•				•	•			•	
79	2	•	•			•	•	•			
80	3		•			•	•			•	

*Number of hiking days reflects the pace described in the trip's text. You can take most trips at another pace by taking more or fewer days.

Trip No.	Hiking Days*	Pace*			Season			Trip Type			
		Leis	Mod	Str	Early	Mid	Late	O&B	Shut	Loop	Semi
81	2		•			•	•			•	
82	2	•	•			•		•			
83	3		•			•	•			•	
84	4	•	•			•	•			•	
85	3	•	•			•	•				•
86	5	•				•	•			•	
87	2	•				•		•			
88	4	•				•	•	•			
89	3	•					•			•	
90	2		•				•	•			
91	4		•	•			•			•	
92	4		•			•	•			•	
93	2		•			•				•	
94	2	•	•			•	•	•			
95	2	•	•			•	•	•			
96	5		•				•			•	
97	2	•	•			•	•	•			
98	Day		•			•	•	•			
99	Day		•			•	•	•			
100	2			•			•	•			

*Number of hiking days reflects the pace described in the trip's text. You can take most trips at another pace by taking more or fewer days.

Index

Updates for Our Books

Since most of our books are guidebooks, they are all too subject to becoming out of date. Every day, probably, some statement in one of our guidebooks becomes out of date. Therefore "update" is one of the most important words in our dictionary.

Whenever we learn of a change in the world out there that we think our customers really should be informed of, we print that change (or changes) on a loose sheet of paper and put the sheet into each book that we ship. We also notify our mailing list, via *The Ram's Head*, that the update sheet is available for a mere SASE (stamped, self-addressed envelope). We are the only guidebook publisher we know who does that routinely. Of course we don't do it for every change we hear about, and people don't expect us to. If we did, the average book we shipped would have about 15 sheets of paper tucked into it. It's the important changes that we tell our customers about.

How do we learn about changes? Most often from the author, sometimes from another of our authors or staff people, and sometimes from a user of the book. If a customer sends us an updating item that we deem reliable and useful, we send him or her a coupon good for $10 on the purchase of any of our books or maps.

When it comes time to reprint a book containing updates, we do one of two things: 1) change the text on the page(s) affected by the update(s), or 2) print the updating language on a blank page if there is one at the back of the book.

What about new editions? Yes, we publish them when the changes needed for a book require a whole new edition. For example, *Sierra South* is now in its sixth edition, and it has been reprinted with some changes thirteen other times. Usually a new edition involves setting all the type all over again and making a new page layout. For us, though not for the author, it is almost as much work as publishing a new book.